1992

Legal Issues
and Older Adults

Choices and Challenges:
An Older Adult Reference Series
Elizabeth Vierck, Series Editor

Forthcoming

Legal Issues and Older Adults

Linda Josephson Millman

Choices and Challenges: An Older Adult Reference Series
Elizabeth Vierck, Series Editor

ABC-CLIO
Santa Barbara, California
Denver, Colorado
Oxford, England

Library of Congress Cataloging-in-Publication Data

Millman, Linda Josephson, 1960–
    Legal issues and older adults / Linda Josephson Millman.
      p.   cm—(Choices and challenges)
    Includes bibliographical references and index.
    1. Aged—Legal status, laws, etc.—United States. I. Title.
  II. Series.
  KF390.A4M55 1992   346.7301'3—dc20   [347.30613]   92-31475

This publication is designed to provide accurate and authoritative information in regard to the subject matter covered. It is sold with the understanding that the publisher and author are not engaged in rendering legal, accounting, or other professional services. If legal advice or other expert assistance is required, the services of a competent professional should be sought. [From a Declaration of Principles jointly adopted by a committee of the American Bar Association and a committee of publishers]

ISBN 0-87436-594-5

99 98 97 96 95 94 93 92   10 9 8 7 6 5 4 3 2 1 (hc)

ABC-CLIO, Inc.
130 Cremona Drive, P.O. Box 1911
Santa Barbara, California 93116-1911

This book is printed on acid-free paper ⊖.
Manufactured in the United States of America

Contents

Preface

At present, demographers estimate that approximately 12 percent of Americans are 65 or older. This number will continue to rise well into the next century as the baby boom generation ages. Along with this growth, seniors can expect to see an explosion in products and services intended to satisfy the needs of seniors. One of the services seniors may need most, and yet one that they are least likely to turn to, is legal services.

Many seniors face the same legal issues as other Americans—landlord-tenant problems, consumer fraud, divorce. Other issues, such as pensions, Social Security, Medicare, wills and probate, guardianship, and grandparents' visitation rights, are unique to seniors. In addition, the American Bar Association's Commission on Legal Problems of the Elderly indicates that many seniors do not recognize that some of their problems are actually legal issues.

Legal Issues and Older Adults is an attempt to identify some common legal issues and provide some basic background to seniors and their advocates, to allow them to intelligently resolve them either with the assistance of qualified professionals or on their own.

This book is divided into two sections. The first section consists of eight chapters, each chapter addressing a discrete issue: legal issues, personal autonomy, income security, health care, housing, consumerism, family law, and estate planning. The second section mirrors the organization of the first, but is a list of organizational, print, and other media to which the reader can turn for further inquiry.

As the reader will soon realize, none of the topics is entirely self-contained. Chapter 2, which describes options for maintaining personal autonomy such as durable powers of attorney, living trusts, and living wills, is inextricably entwined with considerations underlying Chapter 8, which addresses estate planning. Chapter 4's discussion of health care facilities is connected to Chapter 5's outlining of housing options.

Unfortunately, many Americans take the same dim view of the legal profession that Henry V did in Shakespeare's famous play ("First, let's kill all the lawyers"). *Legal Issues and Older Adults* seeks to identify areas where an informed layperson can fend for him or herself. Chapter 8 focuses particularly on other sources of legal assistance and information. It also contains some tips on how to find a lawyer, how lawyers and law firms operate, and how best to work with a lawyer.

Legal Issues and Older Adults will not answer all of your questions on all of the issues. As Part Two indicates, entire books have been written on each of the issues covered in this volume. *Legal Issues and Older Adults* is an annotated road map for finding the answers. I hope it will give you a good idea of the big picture and provide a useful shortcut to further resources.

Acknowledgments

No resource book is written without the helping hands and minds of scores of individuals. I would like to thank the many librarians, organization staff members, government employees, and professionals who answered my questions and spurred me onward. Special thanks to Sallie Birket Chafer, who provided valuable assistance in gathering resources for Part Two, and to my editors, Elizabeth Vierck and Laurie Brock, for their insight and patience with this project.

Finally, thanks to my parents, Gerald and Edith Josephson, who always told me I could do something like this, and to my husband, Bert, who was the first of us to believe it.

How To Use This Book

Each book in the Choices and Challenges series provides a convenient, easy-access reference tool on a specific topic of interest to older adults and those involved with them, including caregivers, spouses, adult children, and gerontology professionals. The books are designed for ease of use, with a generous typeface, ample use of headings and subheadings, and a detailed index.

Each book consists of two parts, which may be used together or independently:

A narrative section providing an informative and comprehensive overview of the topic, written for a lay audience. The narrative can be read straight through or consulted on an as-needed basis by using the headings and subheadings and/or the index.

An annotated resource section that includes a directory of relevant organizations; recommended books, pamphlets, and articles; and software and videos. Where appropriate, the resource section may include additional information relevant to the topic. This section can be used in conjunction with or separately from the narrative to locate sources of additional information, assistance, or support.

A glossary defines important terms and concepts, and the index provides additional access to the material. For easy reference, entries in the resource section are indexed by both topic and title or name.

PART ONE

Legal Issues
and Older Adults

Chapter 1

Legal Services

Basics

- According to the American Bar Association, there are over 800,000 lawyers in the United States.

- Only a lawyer can practice law. This means that there are certain jobs that only a lawyer can do.

- Lawyers, like doctors, have different specialties, and in many cases, a specialist can do the job more efficiently than a generalist.

- One of the best resources for finding a good lawyer is a referral from a friend or business associate. Local and state bar associations, area agencies on aging, or senior centers may also make referrals.

- The Legal Services Corporation is a national resource for advocates for low-income individuals. Funding is also provided under the Older Americans Act for legal services for seniors. All state and local bar associations encourage pro bono representation of individuals who cannot afford a lawyer.

Introduction

Every page in this book is aimed at giving seniors a general knowledge of their rights in certain settings. There is only so far that a layperson can go on his or her own, however. At some point it becomes advisable—and even necessary—to seek the counsel of a legal advisor.

The lawyer's domain generally involves proceedings in state or federal court. In other areas the advice of persons familiar with the law can often fill the need. These may include non-lawyer volunteers and paralegals who, though not lawyers, have received some training in legal research and reasoning or who are intimately familiar with a government program such as Medicare or Social Security.

When You Need Legal Services

It is a lawyer's curse to think of all issues as in some way legal issues. Most relationships between institutions or governments and individuals involve legal rights and responsibilities. As a rule of thumb, if a senior's expectations are not met, he or she should seek the counsel of a legal advisor. The decision maker may not be wrong, but the senior will have more comfort with the outcome if he or she understands the basis for the decision.

The questions a senior might ask him or herself are:

- Is the matter a complex legal issue or one that is likely to be taken to court, or is a large amount of money, property, or time involved? If so, involving a lawyer sooner rather than later makes sense.

- Is there a form or self-help book available that can be used? If so, the senior may be able to handle matters on his or her own to a point.

The following circumstances suggest the need for a lawyer's involvement:

- Denial of public benefits such as Social Security, Supplemental Security Income, Medicaid, Medicare, food stamps, or other income assistance

- An unclear or unfavorable decision concerning an individual's rights under an employer's retirement or health benefit plan

- Making a will and general estate planning

- Settling the affairs for a friend or loved one after he or she has died

- Buying or selling real estate

- Landlord/tenant problems

- Any situation where the senior feels he or she has been unfairly treated based on age, sex, religion, race or national origin, or disability

- Where a senior feels the need to authorize third parties to act on his or her behalf in financial or personal decision making

- Where a third party has initiated conservatorship, guardianship, or commitment proceedings

Who Can Give Legal Advice

Lawyers

Strictly speaking, only a lawyer can give legal advice. This does not mean that other people don't or can't be of assistance with legal issues. However, it is uniquely the job of the lawyer to advise individuals as to the legal aspects of their affairs and to use the legal system to exercise their clients' rights. The lawyer may accomplish this goal through drafting proper documents, negotiation or litigation.

In order to practice law in a given state a lawyer must be licensed by the state. Once a lawyer passes a test, he or she may be "admitted to the bar." Almost all lawyers have been to law school in order to prepare them to practice law. All states now require that persons who wish to practice law attend law school.

Lawyers, like doctors, have different specialties. Some specialize in estate planning, for example, to the exclusion of all else. Others engage in only criminal law. Many lawyers are generalists, advising clients on a broad range of issues. A senior who is seeking a lawyer's advice should find out whether the lawyer is a specialist or a generalist and choose counsel accordingly.

In larger law firms, lawyers often carry the titles of "partner" and "associate." A partner is generally a person who
owns a part of the business. Associates, on the other hand,
are employees of the firm. Even where a senior considers the
partner to be "his lawyer," the partner will often delegate work
to his or her associate(s) to hold down legal fees. An associate
may know as much, or more, than the partner about the law in
a given area.

Paralegals

Increasingly lawyers have begun to use the services of paralegals.
Generally speaking, a paralegal is an individual who has received
some special training in legal research and writing that allows
him or her to perform many of the functions of a lawyer. For
example, a paralegal can research legal issues or draft legal documents. His or her work must be supervised by a lawyer, however. Many community legal assistance programs make use of
paralegals for much of their client counseling.

Where To Find Legal Services

There are many paths to finding good legal services. Perhaps the
best resources are referrals from friends or business associates.
Alternatively, the local bar association or area agency on aging
may be able to make a referral. Some state and local bar associations also have commissions or committees of lawyers specializ-
ing in legal issues for seniors.

Two national organizations publish listings of attorneys who
specialize in legal issues concerning seniors: the Commission on
Legal Problems of the Elderly of the American Bar Association,
located in Washington, D.C.; and the National Academy of Elder
Lawyers, located in Tucson, Arizona.

Whatever the source of the referral, a senior should inquire as
to the lawyer's specialty, if any, and experience. Many lawyers
will meet for an initial consultation for free. Others charge for
this meeting. When the senior meets with the lawyer he should
inquire as to the lawyer's education and experience in handling
the type of matter the senior is concerned about. For example, a

lawyer with an extensive estate planning background may not be the appropriate person to handle a Medicare appeal.

Since the mid-1980s lawyers have been allowed to advertise more aggressively to attract clients. These advertisements sometimes overstate the results a client can expect and understate the cost of the legal services. A personal referral is best.

Affording Legal Services

Seniors should not assume that they cannot afford legal representation. Many sources, both public and private, try to meet the needs of lower-income individuals, including seniors. Local senior centers and area agencies on aging generally maintain current information on these programs and their availability in a given locality.

The Older Americans Act (OAA), enacted in 1965, provides some funding for states to assist seniors aged 60 and older in securing adequate legal counsel in noncriminal matters. As with all OAA programs, the services are not allocated based on financial need, but are available to all seniors. A phone call to the local area agency on aging will yield a list of programs available; however, limited funding means limited availability.

The Legal Services Corporation, a quasi-public agency, also provides assistance on a broad range of topics to seniors whose income does not exceed 125 percent of federal poverty guidelines. Its main mission is to provide funding for local legal assistance projects, rather than provide services directly.

Seniors are accepted as clients based on initial interviews that determine whether they satisfy the eligibility criteria and whether the case is of a type that the Legal Services Corporation can handle. According to a study in 1985, most cases taken on for senior clients concern public benefit programs such as Social Security and Medicare.

Another resource available to seniors is local legal aid societies and offices. Legal aid offices are federally funded to provide help to low-income people of all ages. Some receive OAA funding and provide help without income and asset restrictions. Others employ some kind of income and assets limitation. Offices are listed in the telephone book under "Legal Aid" or "Legal

Services Office." Make sure that services are provided free; some private attorneys will use the same name for clinics that operate under more traditional fee schedules.

Law schools often sponsor clinics in which law students assist individuals with various kinds of civil (and sometimes criminal) matters at little or no cost. These clinics are usually listed under "legal clinics" in the yellow pages, but again, beware of private clinics that misleadingly use the same title. If there is no such listing, seniors might try calling the office of the dean of the law school.

If these resources are not available, the local bar association may make a referral to a lawyer who will take a senior's case on a pro bono basis. The American Bar Association and state bar associations nationwide have committed their members to providing legal services to those in need for little or no cost, depending upon ability to pay. Many state bar associations have established committees to address the legal problems of seniors.

Finally, a senior may be able to negotiate an affordable fee or payment schedule up front with a law firm or lawyer.

How To Select Legal Services

As with all things, the cheapest legal advice is not always best, and those who can afford to do so may benefit from shopping around. If at all possible, the senior should make a careful study of the available options and not be in a rush to engage a lawyer.

A senior should interview the lawyers who have been recommended to him or her. Generally the lawyer will not charge for this meeting, but some do. The interview should clarify the following issues:

- The lawyer's previous experience in handling the area of law about which you are seeking advice

- The lawyer's fee structure (including his or her charges, as well as other costs such as copying, typing, or telephone expenses)

- Who else in the lawyer's office will be working with him or her (an associate or paralegal)

- His or her general approach or philosophy in cases such as yours

- Any court or filing costs associated with the legal proceeding

- How long it will take for the lawyer to complete the work

Where a matter is likely to become complicated, and requires special expertise, it is advisable to look for a lawyer who specializes in that area.

The lawyer should be someone in whom a senior has complete confidence. Most of all a good lawyer will be able to explain even more complex issues in a way that makes them understandable to the senior.

Communicating with Legal Professionals

Legal advice is expensive. The best way to guard against unnecessary charges is to become an effective consumer of legal advice. Generally speaking, this means doing as much advance preparation as possible. Before attending any conference with a lawyer, a senior should:

- Find out what information and documents the lawyer will need and gather them together.

- List the questions he or she wants to ask the lawyer, and check them off as they are addressed.

- Find out if there are any books or articles that he or she can read in order to better understand what is happening.

- Do as much legwork for the lawyer as possible. For example, if the lawyer needs a certified copy of a marriage certificate, a senior could write to the town clerk himself or herself. Generally speaking, if the lawyer or his or her paralegal has to do it, the senior will be charged for that service.

- Work with the lawyer to minimize fees and ask what particular things he or she might do toward this end.

Billing

There is no single answer to the question "How do lawyers charge for their services?" Often it depends upon the custom in the area where the lawyer practices, or on the type of law. In general, there are three major trends: hourly fees, contingency fees, and flat fees.

Whatever the lawyer's billing practice, it is important to find out what's included and what's not. A recent trend among law firms is to allocate a portion of the firm's overhead to each client through billing separately for things like photocopying, mail, long distance phone calls, word processing, and secretarial help. Where litigation is involved, court fees are generally not included in the lawyer's estimate of his fee.

Hourly Fees

When a lawyer bills on an hourly basis, the client's bill will reflect the amount of time that the lawyer spent doing the work he or she was asked to do. The time billed will include conversations and telephone calls with the senior and others, including other attorneys, staff, court personnel, government agencies, and so on. It will also include time spent researching, preparing legal documents, and even correspondence.

With hourly fee schedules, it is especially important for a senior to organize his or her thoughts and information before meeting with the lawyer—or even calling the lawyer on the phone—to maximize efficiency and keep costs down. Some lawyers do not like to give estimates when they bill on an hourly basis. Nevertheless, a senior should insist on a written estimate.

Contingency Fees

In a contingency fee arrangement, a lawyer agrees to take on legal work for a percentage of the amount collected by the client or awarded by the court. The lawyer gets nothing if the case is lost, and the only cost to the client is court fees. The percentage may be fixed, or may change depending upon the point at which the case is settled. This type of arrangement is common in personal injury suits or where a large amount of money is at stake.

Before agreeing to a contingency fee arrangement, a senior should make sure he or she understands how the lawyer's percentage will be calculated. Some lawyers calculate the fee after all costs have been deducted from the award made by the court. Others do just the opposite, resulting in less of the money going to the client.

Flat Fees

In a flat fee arrangement, the lawyer specifies an exact amount that will be charged to a client. These types of fees are more common in will-drafting and real estate transactions, for example. Just as in the contingency fee arrangement, it is important that a senior understand what the lawyer is agreeing to do for the flat fee. He or she may not include services that seem to the senior to be part of the overall project. The fee may not include complications that arise.

A Final Word about Fees

In some cases, legal fees are subject to the approval of a court or a state or federal agency. For example, fees charged by lawyers assisting seniors in Social Security retirement benefit appeals are limited to not more than 25 percent of the recovered amount, and may be adjusted below that amount according to the discretion of the administrative law judge (see Chapter 3). Some states require court approval of legal fees associated with guardianship or probate proceedings.

Evaluating Legal Services

In the final analysis, the only person who can truly evaluate legal services is the person who has received them. A senior should expect a lawyer above all to be responsive to his or her concerns. This does not mean that the lawyer will always achieve the result that his or her client seeks. But if he or she fails to do so through some negligence or malfeasance, the senior does have recourse.

The first recourse is to discuss his or her dissatisfaction with the lawyer. A second recourse is to the firm with which the lawyer practices. In most firms, there is an individual designated as the managing partner who oversees the business operations. He or she may be able to act as an intermediary.

If the senior's complaint is not resolved satisfactorily, the next step is to file a complaint (sometimes called a grievance) with the local bar association. Generally, this will result in an investigation of the lawyer's conduct by the bar association's grievance review committee. The committee may assess a penalty against the lawyer up to and including removing his or her license to practice law, if it finds that the lawyer violated his or her obligations to the client.

Finally, it is possible to sue a lawyer for malpractice. In order to prevail in such a case, a senior must show that the attorney violated a duty to him or her, and that as a result the senior suffered monetary damages. These suits can be extremely time-consuming and difficult to win. They invariably involve significant legal fees. Before proceeding with such a case it is wise to pursue action through the bar association grievance procedures.

Chapter 2

Personal Autonomy

Basics

- A living will serves a dual purpose: it indicates the health care preferences of an individual in the case of a terminal illness, and it protects health care providers and family members from the difficulties and liabilities of making such decisions.

- The power of attorney allows an individual to act on behalf of another in a legal capacity. Durable powers of attorney may be used to enable an individual to make medical care decisions on behalf of an incapacitated individual.

- In certain limited circumstances, the government is empowered to step in where an individual has failed to make provision for unforeseen incapacity. A court may appoint a guardian or conservator for an individual to protect that individual's person or property. If an individual is a danger to himself or herself, or to the community, a court may commit an individual to an institution for care.

- Based on an investigation conducted by a team of reporters, a 1987 Associated Press special report estimated that 300,000 to 400,000 seniors were under protective guardianships. In the majority of cases, their own children acted as guardians.

Introduction

When we reach the age of majority, the law provides us with greater personal freedom than we were allowed as children. As adults we are able to do pretty much what we choose—within the parameters of the law. In the eyes of the law we have achieved legal capacity. This means not only freedom, but also responsibility. Together these two concepts add up to personal autonomy.

Nobody likes to think that they may sometime not be able to make their own decisions. In 1983 Nancy Cruzan, age 26, was involved in a serious car accident. She suffered irreversible brain damage that left her in a persistent vegetative state—unaware of anything—with no prospect of recovery. Friends and family argued that Ms. Cruzan would want to be allowed to die with dignity, and that she had said so on several occasions although she had never formalized this wish in a living will. It took nearly eight years, and a decision by the Supreme Court of the United States, to enable Ms. Cruzan's parents, acting as her guardians, to order doctors to remove a feeding tube that kept her body alive. She died 12 days later.

The simple fact is that all of us may require assistance, if only in special situations, in making important decisions. Whatever the circumstances, it is important to understand the ramifications of these legal mechanisms to determine whether any of them can be useful in a senior's circumstance.

There are three basic ways a senior might cope with incapacity. A senior can:

1. Make no provision whatsoever.

2. Leave clear and complete directions about a decision he or she has already made about specific circumstances.

3. Delegate decision-making responsibilities to another person, for example, a spouse, close relative, or friend.

Advance planning can give the senior a voice in decisions made on his or her behalf, even if he or she is unable to participate in the actual decision itself. Living wills, for example, are designed to inform medical personnel and family about the health care an individual wishes to receive when he or she is seriously or terminally ill. Powers of attorney allow a senior to designate an individual to make decisions on his or her behalf, including decisions concerning health care. A new federal law requires hospitals to inform patients of their rights under state law to make such delegations of authority. A senior can use a trust to turn over management of his or her financial affairs to a trusted individual.

In certain limited circumstances, the government is empowered to step in where an individual has failed to plan for unforeseen circumstances. It may limit or deny a senior's autonomy involuntarily by appointing individuals as legal guardians who may take over the senior's personal or financial decisions. This may happen in cases where a court finds a senior incompetent to exercise his or her rights. In extreme cases, the court may even commit an individual to an institution.

The discussion that follows outlines five common issues in personal autonomy: living wills, powers of attorney, *inter vivos* ("living") trusts, guardianship, and civil commitment. In this area, state law controls. It is important before taking the steps outlined in this chapter that seniors consult with someone who is familiar with the laws of the particular state.

Living Wills

Living wills are a natural by-product of the advance of medical science in the last several decades. More and more people may be kept alive despite serious (and formerly fatal) medical conditions. Some have argued that the process of dying and not "life" in a meaningful qualitative sense has been prolonged. This concern has led to the passage of "natural death act" legislation in all but a few states. A natural death act permits a competent individual to choose to forgo medical treatment even if that choice would lead to the death of the individual.

A living will is designed to accomplish two goals:

1. To indicate the health care preferences of an
   individual in the case of a terminal illness.

2. To protect health care providers and family members from the difficulties and liabilities of making such decisions.

Most commonly the individual creating the living will is interested in limiting the steps that will be taken to prolong life where there is no real hope of recovery. There have been cases where health care providers have been sued—or even been brought up on criminal charges—for withdrawing medical treatment.

Living wills (also called declarations or directives) are creatures of a state's natural death act. In order to be valid they must carefully follow the requirements of that law in terms of content and form, just as conventional wills must do (see Chapter 8, page 133). These requirements differ among states and, unlike a conventional will, a living will valid in one state is not necessarily honored by another. Accordingly, seniors who relocate from one state to another, or who have two residences, should be sure that their living will complies with both states' laws, or alternatively, have a valid document in each state. Still, even if the form is not observed and the living will is not valid, it may provide persuasive evidence of an incapacitated individual's wishes.

Content

A living will generally provides that in the case of an incurable or irreversible condition that will lead to death, the individual wants any treatment that prolongs the process of dying to be withdrawn or withheld. The living will takes effect only when the individual is no longer able to make decisions. While the individual is competent, he or she may continue to make decisions as to his or her treatment. In fact, he or she may revoke the living will at any time.

Formalities

Most states provide statutory forms to create a living will, although, with few exceptions (California, Idaho, and Oregon), individualized documents may be used as long as they contain the information required under state law. These forms may be obtained by writing to Choice in Dying/Society for the Right to Die, an organization in New York that monitors these issues (see Resources list for address, page 174).

Two witnesses must be present when the living will is signed. As in the case of conventional wills, the witnesses are present so that they can testify (if necessary) that the willmaker had the requisite mental capacity to make the living will and that he or she was not coerced into doing so. To avoid possible conflicts of interest, at least one (and sometimes both) witnesses should be disinterested persons. This means relatives or possible heirs to the estate should not act as witnesses. A few states require a designated state or nursing home official to witness when a nursing home resident signs a living will. Notarization of the living will is required in some states. Some states require that the document be registered or filed with a government office. Finally, three states (California, Oklahoma, and Hawaii) require that an individual must be diagnosed with a terminal condition before he or she executes a valid living will.

What To Do with a Living Will

There is no one best place to keep a living will. Signed copies should be given to one's primary care physician. It is advisable to provide copies to one's spouse or significant other, children, or close friends who may be able to ensure that the living will is honored. One alternative is the Living Will Registry operated by an organization called Choice in Dying. For a one-time fee of $35, a copy of an individual's living will is maintained in the Registry. The individual receives a notification card to carry in the wallet stating where the living will may be obtained.

Revocation of a Living Will

Most statutes provide that a living will may be revoked in any manner—in writing, orally, or by symbolic destruction of the document, such as tearing the document in half or otherwise mutilating it. Revocation is effective when it is communicated to the attending physician.

Problems with Living Wills

The seriousness of the circumstances surrounding the exercise of living wills raises particular problems in ensuring that they will be honored. The chief problem is definitional. As noted above, living wills generally become effective when a patient has a terminal illness. Just when and if a condition is considered to be terminal may differ under law and in the judgment of the attending physician. In order to increase the likelihood that the terms of a living will will be honored, an individual should take time to find a primary care physician whose philosophy closely approximates one's own.

Not all medical interventions involve life-or-death decisions. Yet even a curable illness or injury may render a senior unable to participate in decisions concerning treatment options. Doctors traditionally turn to family members to make decisions in these situations. A senior may wish to designate an individual to make these choices for him or her. In this circumstance, a durable power of attorney (see below) might be a better option.

Finally, a living will only addresses medical decision making. Other issues—such as seeing that a senior's bills get paid—remain unaddressed.

Other Voluntary Delegations of Authority

Powers of Attorney

Despite the word "attorney," a power of attorney simply creates what is known in the law as an agency. This means that the senior assigning his or her power of attorney (often called the principal) is giving another individual the power to act as his or her agent (sometimes called attorney in fact) with third parties. The agent need not be a lawyer.

The most common type of power of attorney ends automatically if the principal becomes incompetent while it is still in force. This is not true of the so-called durable power of attorney discussed below. All powers of attorney end when the principal dies.

CONTENT

The power of attorney is a relatively simple document. The senior granting the power of attorney defines its limits, so it is very flexible. In a power of attorney, a senior delegates the authority to act on his or her behalf to one or more individuals. It is advisable to designate successors to the first-named agent in case that individual is unable to act in a given circumstance. The power may be general or specifically limited to certain trans-actions or time periods. For example, the agent may only have authority to use money from the senior's bank account to pay the household bills. The senior's other assets may be beyond the agent's control.

Documents creating the power of attorney may be drafted by the senior granting the power or by the individual being ap-pointed as agent. Forms also may be available from third parties such as banks or other financial institutions. Usually these third-party documents are valid only with respect to assets in the institution's custody. For example, a bank power of attorney form would only allow the agent to access the senior's accounts within that bank. In some states, forms are created under a state law and must be used in all cases.

Whatever the source, it is advisable to involve an attorney before granting the power. The simplicity of creating a power of attorney should not lead a senior to underestimate its signifi-cance. Third parties (such as banks) may act on the agent's instructions without fear of liability to the senior who granted the power. For example, an unscrupulous agent could empty the principal's bank account and use the funds for his or her own benefit. The bank would be absolved from any responsibility. Perhaps the most important decision is the choice of the person to act as agent. It should be someone the senior knows and trusts.

To minimize risks, it is also important that the document confer only as much authority as is necessary. It should specifi-cally state the instances in which the agent may act for the senior.

DURABLE POWERS OF ATTORNEY

A "durable" power of attorney differs from a standard power of attorney in that it survives a change in the principal's competency.

For example, with an ordinary power of attorney, if the senior who created it passed into a coma, the authority created by the power of attorney would terminate automatically. This would not happen with a durable power of attorney. Because of this special feature, durable powers of attorney are commonly used to ensure that health care decisions are made for the senior by the person he or she designates. These types of durable powers of attorney are often called durable medical powers of attorney to make clear their special purpose. Nineteen states explicitly provide that durable powers of attorney can be used in this manner.

A durable power of attorney may be effective currently (while the senior is competent), or may "spring" into effect at some stated event such as when the senior is unconscious with a life-threatening illness. The latter, not surprisingly, is called a springing durable power of attorney. Like the standard power of attorney, the durable power of attorney may be as broad or narrow as the principal wishes.

Durable powers of attorney have all of the same advantages of standard powers of attorney. Where there is a risk that a senior may become incompetent, durable powers of attorney have the obvious additional advantage that the person designated as agent will be able to continue to act on behalf of the senior. In the context of making important health care decisions, durable powers of attorney may be more helpful than living wills in that they may provide not only direction as to the individual's wishes, but an advocate for those wishes as well.

FORMALITIES

In order to execute a valid power of attorney, the principal must be legally competent. This generally means that he or she must understand the action and its significance. There must be a written document. State laws generally require that a power of attorney be witnessed. Some require notarization.

Because a durable power of attorney gives the agent relatively broader authority unsupervised by the principal, some state laws impose certain additional formalities for these documents. Some states restrict the types of decisions that an agent can make even if the durable power of attorney is in place.

REVOCATION

The power of attorney is revocable at all times. Revocation is accomplished by notifying the agent as well as any third parties with whom the agent was empowered to represent the principal.

PROBLEMS WITH POWERS OF ATTORNEY

There are two key problems in using powers of attorney. The first is that third parties may not choose to honor them. While court cases have established a broad protection for third parties in dealing with the agent, as mentioned above, there is no requirement that the third party accept the agent's authority. For example, a bank may not allow an agent to withdraw funds for fear the power of attorney is not valid or has been revoked.

The second risk is that the principal may make a poor choice of agents. An agent is not subject to court supervision (as would be a guardian, for example). A senior would be well-advised to review statements of accounts to which he or she has given the agent access. In the case of durable powers of attorney, supervision by the senior him or herself may be a practical impossibility if the senior is incapacitated or incompetent.

The disadvantages of durable powers of attorney, however, may be somewhat magnified by the indefinite duration of such powers. If the principal has become incapacitated he or she may be unable to rectify the failure of a given institution to recognize the agent. Conversely, if the agent abuses his or her authority, the principal will be an unknowing victim. To address this problem some durable powers will request that guardianship or conservatorship proceedings be instituted upon incapacity and will nominate a guardian.

Inter vivos (Living) Trusts

One option open to those for whom management of an individual's financial affairs is the goal is an *inter vivos* (or "living") trust. A trust is an agreement between a "grantor," the senior contributing the assets, and the "trustee" who becomes the legal owner of the assets. A trust only addresses issues of property and income management, and is not a tool for making other decisions such as health care.

The trustee is required by the terms of a trust document to manage and use the trust fund for specific purposes. These purposes might begin with the support of the senior. A trust may provide that the senior him or herself will serve as trustee until some stated event, such as incapacity, at which point a successor trustee will take over.

The trust is established by a document that identifies the trust assets, the person for whom the trust is established (the "beneficiary"), the trustee, and the terms that the trustee must observe in managing and spending the trust fund. The trust may be revocable or irrevocable from the outset. If it is revocable, the person establishing the trust may terminate it at will. A trust may provide that it will become irrevocable upon a determination that the grantor is incompetent. State law determines the formalities of establishing the trust.

Trustees do not suffer the same lack of recognition from banks and other third parties that affects agents under powers of attorney. Further, they can retain greater control for the senior since he or she can dictate the manner in which the trustee exercises his or her powers. Finally, a living trust can avoid the expense and delay of probate upon the death of the grantor by providing a successor beneficiary, such as the senior's grandchild or close friend (see Chapter 8, page 141).

The principal disadvantages of a trust are the expense and complexity of such arrangements. The individual establishing the trust should certainly work with an attorney to establish a valid trust and to ensure that there are proper safeguards for the trust assets. Form documents are not appropriate since each person's assets and objectives will be different. As in the case in the choice of agents, the choice of trustees is the key to ensuring that the senior's interests will be served.

Involuntary Mechanisms

Where an individual is incapacitated and he or she fails to provide advance directives as to his or her wishes in a particular circumstance, the government steps in to create mechanisms for substituting a decision maker. This also occurs where advance directives are not honored. The most common avenue is the appointment of a guardian or conservator. In extreme cases, it may involve the involuntary commitment of an individual to an institution. Heavy procedural safeguards seek to ensure that the individual's liberty is protected as much as possible.

Guardianship and Conservatorship

Many people associate the term "guardian" with the adoption of children. However, where seniors who have not designated an agent or trustee are determined to lack the capacity to make their own decisions, state courts are empowered to designate guardians to act on their behalf. Not all guardianships are entirely involuntary, of course. A senior may choose an individual to serve as guardian in advance of the need to appoint a guardian.

Guardianship proceedings are begun when it appears that an individual is unable to handle his or her own affairs. A senior isn't incompetent simply because he or she makes unusual or even irrational decisions. There must be a pattern of behavior or decisions that indicate that the senior lacks the capacity to understand important facts, to comprehend the risks and benefits of different courses of action, to identify his or her own values, and to make responsible decisions. There is no one test that will determine whether a senior meets these standards.

Once a guardian is appointed for a senior, however, the senior becomes that person's "ward." As a ward, the senior may completely lose the power to make decisions concerning his or her personal affairs and/or property. This is why there are procedural safeguards to seek to ensure that the senior's civil liberties are not constrained unnecessarily. A ward may lose the right to vote, to enter into contracts, to consent (or withhold consent) for medical treatment, or to make basic decisions about his or her personal life.

A guardianship can be limited to specific areas (for example, financial transactions) or it can be complete. Complete or "plenary" guardianships are generally preferred by courts since they provide the broadest protection for the senior, although the trend in some jurisdictions is toward granting guardians more specific powers. They also ensure that if the senior's condition deteriorates it will not be necessary for the guardian to petition the court for broader powers. The advantage of a limited guardianship is that it preserves some of the senior's independence if only in certain defined areas. A limited guardianship with respect to the property only is sometimes called a conservatorship. Some jurisdictions use the terms guardian and conservator interchangeably.

PROCESS OF APPOINTING A GUARDIAN

The law presumes that an individual is competent until it is proven otherwise. Although the process by which guardianship is instituted varies from jurisdiction to jurisdiction, there are five common stages: petition, notice, interview and investigation, hearing, and appeal or restoration.

Petition

Most states have standard forms that may be filled out by any "interested person." An interested person may be a relative or an institution that has custody of the senior such as a nursing home. Some states have public guardianships instituted by the government. In some states, the senior him or herself may request that a guardian be appointed. It is not required that the person filing the petition serve as guardian, although he or she may do so. Some states have laws that establish a preference as to who should serve as guardian.

The petition states that the senior is unable to care for him or herself or his or her property and requests that a guardian be appointed. The person making the petition needs to provide details regarding the disability to establish that the condition is serious enough to require a guardian to be appointed under state law. The petition typically includes names and addresses of the senior's legal representatives (if any), family, close friends and neighbors; a schedule of the income and assets of the senior; and the name(s) and address(es) of the individual(s) consenting to act as guardian. Some courts require a physician's statement concerning the senior's condition to be attached.

The petition must be filed with the proper court in the state where the senior resides or has real or personal property. Since court proceedings will be involved, it is advisable, when seeking to institute a guardianship, to have the assistance of an attorney.

Notice

Once a petition is filed, the court or the person making the petition notifies the senior and all persons required by law to receive notice. It is advisable that the senior who is being proposed for guardianship get an attorney to ensure that proper procedures are followed. If he or she cannot afford an attorney, the court will appoint one. A physician is appointed by the court to evaluate the senior's medical or psychological condition. Many states also appoint an individual known as a guardian *ad litem* (meaning, generally, for the purposes of the litigation) for the senior. This individual is assigned by the court to assist in the investigation and hearing phases of the proceedings.

Investigation

Three things happen during the investigation phase of the proceedings. First, the senior who is proposed for guardianship is interviewed and the guardianship proceedings are explained in full. The ramifications of guardianship, including the loss of autonomy (personal or property), should be discussed carefully. The interviewer (either the guardian *ad litem* or the senior's attorney) will also seek information concerning the senior's condition, living arrangements, finances, and so on. He or she will also try to find out what result the senior would like from the court proceedings. The second stage of investigation includes interviews with the senior's doctors, family, friends, and social workers to ascertain his or her needs. Third, the senior will most likely be examined by a court-appointed physician or psychologist as appropriate. The senior's attorney can be present at these evaluations, at the senior's request.

Hearing

Most guardianship hearings are informal and brief, though generally they are held in a courtroom. Most often there is no jury; a judge considers the evidence. Both parties may present witnesses, and cross-examine each other's witnesses. State laws require that the evidence be "clear and convincing" that the senior is incompetent to manage his or her affairs. Courts typically rely quite heavily on the doctor's statement in making their determinations.

The powers of the guardian are determined at this time, and may be limited if the senior's attorney is successful at arguing that a limited guardianship will adequately protect the senior. In some jurisdictions, the trend is moving away from plenary grants of authority over the ward and toward more limited guardianships. The guardian receives an "order of appointment," which sets forth the terms of the guardianship.

Appeal or Restoration

The senior's attorney may appeal the court's decision if there are sufficient grounds to do so. Some states will forestall the guardianship until appeals are complete, or, alternatively, may order an interim temporary guardianship.

A senior who is made a ward in guardianship proceedings may be restored to legal capacity in all but four states. Proceedings may be instituted by the senior personally or by an "interested person." These are generally not successful since the burden is on the senior to prove competency and his or her access to the financial or legal resources to do so may be restricted. If complete authority over personal and financial decisions has been given to a guardian, it will be difficult to demonstrate the senior's ability. Practically speaking, once a senior has been made a ward, he or she remains so for life.

Advantages and Disadvantages

Appointment of a guardian obviously has serious implications for a senior in terms of his or her personal autonomy. Since these arrangements are more or less permanent depending on the reason for the senior's incapacity, the commencement of guardianship proceedings should not be taken lightly.

Court supervision of the guardianship process protects seniors in a way that powers of attorney do not. Unfortunately, this protection may prove to be only theoretical. Most states require annual or periodic accountings of assets under the control of a guardian. Where courts lack the staff or other resources to supervise the guardian, mismanagement or dishonesty can diminish the benefits of guardianship and put a senior at risk.

Commitment

In serious cases of incapacity due to a mental disease or illness, it may become necessary to commit an individual to the care of an institution. This can occur where an individual is found by a court to be dangerous to him or herself, to others, or property. In some states, an individual may be committed if he or she is unable to care for his or her own basic needs.

The extraordinary deprivation of personal liberty involved in commitment—from the confinement to forced treatment or medication—has led states to require courts to consider every option before ordering commitment. Generally a court will institute a guardianship if at all possible, or order outpatient treatment, rather than commit an individual to an institution. Community mental health resources, unfortunately, are often lacking.

STANDARDS FOR CIVIL COMMITMENT

The standards for civil commitment vary by state. Usually, a two-part test applies. First, a determination must be made that the individual is indeed mentally ill, not merely suffering from a "mental disorder." A mental illness is defined as a major emotional or thought disorder that seriously impedes one or more basic life functions. Second, it must also be shown that as a result of such mental illness or disability, a danger exists to the individual him or herself, other persons, or (in some jurisdictions) property.

The second element of dangerousness is difficult to prove. Danger to self can involve suicidal tendencies or an inability to provide for basic needs. Generally an individual is considered to present a danger to others if there are threats of violence or a recent overt act. Precedents set forth in case law determine what satisfies this part of the test. It will differ depending upon the jurisdiction.

PROCESS

The process of civil commitment is virtually identical to that of instituting a guardianship. A petition is filed by an interested party or by the state. A hearing is scheduled as quickly as possible, and notice is given to the individual proposed for commitment, as well as other interested parties.

It is critical that a senior who receives such a notice take it very seriously and contact an attorney. If the individual has already been confined this may be difficult. Most jurisdictions have determined that the potential deprivation of liberty is so serious that it warrants a right to counsel. This means that in these jurisdictions an attorney will be appointed if the senior cannot afford one. Unfortunately, these advocates often receive little notice of the case and so are given little time to prepare the senior's response.

During the investigation phase a psychologist or psychiatrist will examine the senior to determine whether a mental illness or disease exists. The senior's counsel should be interviewing medical personnel, neighbors, friends, and family to determine the senior's needs and whether they can be satisfied by steps short of commitment. Many cases that begin as civil commitment cases are diverted at this point into alternative arrangements such as guardianship, and never go to the next stage.

The next stage is a formal hearing. Hearings are usually held in a courtroom, and usually with only a judge present. Some jurisdictions provide jury trials. At the hearing, the petitioner (who is asking the court to commit this individual) puts forth its case. The senior, through his or her attorney, responds by cross-examining the petitioner's expert witness(es) and by calling his or her own witness(es). Generally, alternatives to confinement will be discussed at this stage. The burden is on the petitioner and the state to prove that the individual meets the two-part test for commitment by "clear and convincing evidence."

An individual who is committed has a right to appeal. Confinement to a facility is usually determined for a set period. The patient's condition is reviewed periodically during confinement.

Chapter 3

Income Security

Basics

- Both federal and most state laws prohibit discrimination against persons based on age. A federal agency called the Equal Employment Opportunity Commission is charged with investigating age discrimination claims.

- Private pension plans constitute only a contract between an employer and its employees to provide some sort of retirement benefit. A federal law called the Employee Retirement Income Security Act (ERISA) regulates such plans, imposing minimum requirements, reporting, and disclosure rules.

- Social Security benefits, which make up a significant portion of seniors' household income, are provided based upon the earnings record of a worker in covered employment.

- Federal income support programs such as SSI, food stamps, and Low Income Energy Assistance make up an important part of the social insurance safety net for seniors, although they are typically underutilized by eligible seniors.

- The federal tax law contains special provisions for those 65 and older, including a higher standard deduction, and special tax treatment for gains from the sale of a principal residence and Social Security benefits.

Introduction

A common metaphor for retirement security is a three-legged stool. The first leg is Social Security. The second leg is pension income. The third leg is personal savings. Increasingly Americans are adding legs to this stool. Many are continuing to work into their "retirement" years. Others rely on additional income supplements from federal, state, and local governments. This chapter surveys the broad range of income sources available to seniors and some of the legal rights associated with those sources. Other chapters, most particularly Chapter 4 concerning securing adequate health care, should also be consulted in this context.

Age Discrimination in Employment

The first resource many people think of is earned income. This is why federal and state laws that prohibit discrimination on the basis of age are so important to seniors. Although most of the discussion here will focus on the federal law, individuals who feel that they have been the victims of discrimination should seek to exercise their rights under the state law as well.

Information about state proceedings can usually be found by calling the state agency titled "equal employment" or "human rights." State laws may be more comprehensive, prohibiting a broader range of activities and covering small employers.

The federal law known as the Age Discrimination in Employment Act (ADEA) was passed in 1967. With certain limited exceptions it prohibits employers, employment agencies, and unions from discriminating against individuals over 40 on account of their age. Federal, state, and local employers are also covered under ADEA. Employers of fewer than 20 employees and labor organizations with fewer than 25 members are exempt from ADEA as are employment agencies that do not serve any covered employers.

For the sake of simplicity the discussion below will refer to "employer" as the party accused of discriminating, but the reader should bear in mind that unions and employment agencies are also subject to ADEA rules.

Nearly all aspects of employment are covered by ADEA. It is illegal to consider age in decisions concerning referrals for employment, advertising for employment, and hiring. An employer may not discriminate against a covered employee in terms of advancement and training, compensation and benefits, or termination. Mandatory retirement is prohibited except for a select group of executives and high policymaking employees aged 65 and over, and tenured employees of higher education institutions aged 70 and over.

ADEA contains an exception for situations where age is a bona fide occupational qualification, where the decision is based on reasonable factors other than age, or is in observance of the terms of a bona fide seniority system or employee benefit plan. ADEA also excepts cases of discharge or discipline of an individual for good cause.

The Older Workers Benefits Protection Act is the most recent amendment to ADEA. It reversed a Supreme Court interpretation of ADEA that would have allowed employers to provide unequal benefits to employees under employee benefit plans based on their age. It is now clear that employers must provide older workers with the same benefits as their younger colleagues, or at least with benefits of equal cost.

ADEA, and most state laws, afford the aggrieved individual two avenues to vindicate his or her rights: filing a charge with the Equal Employment Opportunity Commission (EEOC), or pursuing a private lawsuit in state or federal court. In order to sue, however, an individual alleging violations of ADEA must first file a charge with the EEOC. The EEOC is the federal agency responsible for processing age discrimination claims. It can accomplish this mission either by investigating claims itself or by contracting with agencies in the various state governments with similar jurisdiction to process such claims.

Individuals are required to submit a signed written document under oath providing the name and address of the person or organization alleged to have committed the discriminatory act or practice as well as details of the violation.

In states where the state law or constitution prohibits age discrimination, the individual may, and in some cases must, also file a complaint with the responsible state agency. In fact, in states with their own antidiscrimination laws the EEOC defers to the state agency to conduct its own investigation first. These are called "deferral states."

It is very important that a senior seeking to file an age discrimination charge do so promptly. Federal law requires that charges be brought before the EEOC within 180 days after the unlawful act. In a deferral state this limitation is extended until the earlier of 300 days after the unlawful act, or 30 days after the individual receives notice that the state has terminated its proceedings. This extension is only available if the individual has filed with the state agency on time. Usually the state agency will file with the EEOC on behalf of the person making the complaint. However, because this is not necessarily the case and to ensure against bureaucratic error, the individual making the complaint (called the charging party) or his advocate, a lawyer or other legal representative, should make sure that the filing has been sent.

The EEOC (or a contracting state agency) investigates the discrimination charge. Sometimes a conference is scheduled where the individual who filed the complaint and the employer are brought together by the EEOC to try to work out the problem. If no agreement is reached at such a conference (or no conference occurs) the EEOC can investigate further, refer the case for legal action, or close the case. The EEOC is under no obligation to determine whether the employer violated ADEA. A senior may pursue the matter in federal or state court. If the EEOC files suit its action preempts any suit brought by the senior.

Sixty days after filing a charge with the EEOC or the relevant state agency the individual may file a lawsuit, even if the EEOC or state agency has not concluded its investigation. Suit may be brought in either federal or state court. The suit must be brought within two years of the unlawful act. This statute of limitations may be extended to three years if the violation is "willful." While the EEOC attempts to gain a resolution these limitations are suspended for up to one year. In effect, this extends the deadline.

In general, to prove a case of age discrimination, a senior must demonstrate to the court that age was a determining factor in the employer's action. The senior must demonstrate three things: that he or she is a member of the protected class (i. e., over age 40), that he or she was adversely affected by action taken by the person or organization (defendant), and that age was a consideration in that action. This is called establishing a *prima facie* case. In other words, based on this evidence alone, a court would have to conclude that a violation of the law occurred.

If the senior succeeds in establishing a *prima facie* case, then the employer must demonstrate some legitimate nondiscriminatory reason for its action. For example, an employer may seek to demonstrate that an employee was fired not because of her age, but because she was not doing the job properly. A case involving seemingly neutral practices that affect one group more harshly than another often results in an additional burden on the employer to justify the practice in terms of job-relatedness or business necessity.

If the employer shows a legitimate nondiscriminatory business reason for its actions, the senior must demonstrate that the legitimate reasons offered were not the real reasons, but merely a pretext. If the employer's action affected older employees more than younger, the senior will try to demonstrate that a less-discriminatory alternative was available to the employer.

When a senior is successful, ADEA authorizes both legal and equitable relief. Legal relief means money damages. Equitable relief involves ordering the employer to do or refrain from doing something. Equitable remedies such as reinstatement, in the case of an unlawful firing, or promotion where it has been denied, are generally the preferred remedy unless there are unusual intervening circumstances. Commonly, back pay, unpaid wages, lost commissions, lost welfare, and pension benefits are awarded for the period prior to reinstatement. If reinstatement is not practical, the court may award future lost earnings.

In certain cases, a court may impose an additional fine, called punitive damages, to punish a defendant. Punitive damages are not usually awarded in cases brought under ADEA. Courts do sometimes make exceptions, however, where the court finds that the violations were "willful." In such cases where the employer knew about or showed reckless disregard for violations of ADEA, "liquidated damages" of double the amount of actual damages (meaning lost wages, for one thing) are awarded. Finally, a court may order the employer to pay the prevailing senior's attorneys' fees and court costs.

Private Pensions

Private pension plans constitute a contract between an employer and its employees to provide some sort of retirement benefit. The amount of the benefits as well as the terms under which the benefit is provided are determined by the contract or plan document.

Because special tax status is provided for these funds, and to ensure that employers live up to the contract they've made with employees, the federal government has imposed certain minimum requirements. These minimum requirements govern the design of those plans, their funding, and finally the information that employers must make available to participants. These rules are so comprehensive that they preempt most state laws that previously applied.

Types of Pension Plans

There are basically two types of plans: defined benefit and defined contribution plans. In a defined benefit plan, the sponsor agrees to provide a specified benefit at retirement. Usually these benefits are provided in a stream of payments over a period of time, perhaps as long as the life of the participant or even continuing after his death to a beneficiary. The employer makes contributions to the plan fund over many years to pay for the projected benefit. The amount that needs to be contributed is determined by a complex series of calculations performed by an actuary.

A defined contribution plan, by contrast, does not guarantee a particular benefit at retirement. The employer's contribution is determined by a formula set forth in the plan, usually some percentage of the participant's compensation. Alternatively, the plan may only require discretionary contributions. This type of plan is called a profit-sharing plan, although an employer need not have profits to make a contribution. The payout received by a participant depends upon the value of his account at retirement.

Some plans allow the employee to make contributions. These are commonly called thrift or savings plans. An employer may or may not make contributions to such plans. One example of a savings plan is a so-called 401(k) or Cash and Deferred Arrangement. In this type of plan the employee can defer pretax dollars into the plan. Thrift plans generally allow the employee to make after-tax contributions only.

Plans may also be characterized as either single employer or multiemployer plans. A single employer plan is one maintained by one employer for the benefit of its own employees. Multiemployer plans are collectively bargained between employers and a union. Although many rules that apply to multiemployer plans are the same, there are some significant differences as noted below.

Federal Law Governs Plans

The federal law called the Employee Retirement Income Security Act (ERISA) sets forth the minimum requirements that all private plans must meet in order to be "qualified." A plan may provide more generous terms, but it must meet at least the minimum requirements. If a plan is qualified, the employer's contributions to the pension on behalf of employees are not taxable to the employees when they are made. Only payments from the plan are taxable. The IRS is responsible for overseeing compliance with these requirements.

QUALIFICATION RULES

ERISA puts limits on certain features common to all plans. For example, employers may not generally require an employee to work longer than five years before becoming entitled to the benefit set forth in the plan. This is called vesting. There are important exceptions to the rule. Plans that provide for gradual vesting schedules may take up to seven years to vest participants completely. Multiemployer plans may vest participants after ten years.

ERISA also regulates the way in which employers credit an employee with service to the employer. Service with an employer in turn enables the employee to accrue a benefit. ERISA also limits the amount of contributions that can be made for an employee's benefit in a given year and the amount that can be paid out. Plans may not provide benefits that discriminate in favor of certain highly paid employees and officers.

The plan sets forth the time at which participants may retire and collect benefits. Some plans allow participants to elect to retire early, and some may provide for disability retirement. In any case, federal law requires that a participant must begin receiving pension benefits by 1 April following the calendar year in which a participant attains age 70.5, even if he or she is still employed at that time.

The forms of payment, such as monthly payments, or lump sum distributions, are also set forth in the plan. The employer is not under any obligation to provide any particular form of payment. The only exception is that a qualified plan must generally provide survivor benefits in the form of an annuity for married participants. This coverage is mandatory unless the participant and spouse both sign formal documents waiving the survivor benefits.

ERISA and the federal tax law also regulate how individuals who receive benefits from retirement plans are taxed. Generally, distributions from a qualified plan are simply taxed as income as they are paid out of the retirement fund. If a plan provides for a lump sum distribution, that is, one single payment representing the individual's entire interest in the plan, special tax rules provide that the individual may be able to "roll-over" the whole payment—or just a part of it—to an Individual Retirement Account (IRA). Alternatively, some participants can qualify for special income averaging or capital gains taxation of these amounts.

All of this is accomplished through a maze of rules, regulations, and excise taxes. A plan must be "qualified" in order to retain tax benefits for the employer and participants in the plan.

Certain forms of mismanagement may threaten the tax-favored status of the retirement plan itself. For example, if the plan does not respect limitations on the amount of money an employer can contribute to a plan, the entire plan can be disqualified. Typically these types of defects are discovered by an IRS audit. An IRS audit can be triggered by a taxpayer complaint or an irregularity on IRS filings, or it may be entirely random. If a plan is disqualified, technically all participants are considered to receive money to which they are entitled under the terms of the plan as of the date of its disqualification, even if they haven't actually received it. As a practical matter, the IRS usually works with the plan sponsor to cure the problem and assess some lesser penalty.

REPORTING AND DISCLOSURE RULES

The U.S. Department of Labor (DOL) has jurisdiction over the portion of ERISA that regulates fiduciary rules and protects participants' rights. Sponsors of plans are required to report certain information, principally concerning the financial status of the plan, on an annual basis on IRS Form 5500. A summary of the information in that report should also be provided to plan participants within two months after the report is filed. This document is called a summary annual report or "SAR."

In addition to this report, when an employer establishes a qualified pension plan, the law requires that employees receive a written description of that plan. This document is called a summary plan description (SPD). If the plan is substantially changed the employer must update the SPD by providing employees with a summary of the changes. These documents are also required to be filed with the DOL.

Finally, a participant can request from the employer at least once every year a statement of the value of his or her benefits under the plan. The benefits statement must indicate the extent to which the participant is vested in his or her benefits, as well as other information about the basis of the calculations. Some employers provide these statements automatically each year.

The fiduciary rules under ERISA are designed to ensure that money placed into an ERISA-qualified plan is managed in a prudent manner. The law requires that all investment decisions regarding the plan be made exclusively to benefit the plan's participants. The so-called exclusive benefit rule generally prohibits plan fiduciaries from using the plan's assets to benefit themselves or other persons and entities associated with the employer. This rule often applies even if the transaction would benefit the plan.

A third government agency, the Pension Benefit Guaranty Corporation (PBGC), was created to ensure the payment of benefits to participants from defined benefit plans if a plan would be unable to meet its benefit obligations. Defined contribution plans, such as profit-sharing plans, are not eligible for PBGC insurance coverage. In recent years the financial difficulties experienced in the steel industry, for example, led to problems with defined benefit plans established for their employees. Employers pay premiums to the PBGC for "insurance" against this contingency. Federal law sets forth the amount of each participant's benefit that is insured. For most lower- and middle-income individuals, most if not all of their defined benefit is insured.

PARTICIPANT RIGHTS

Claims for Benefits

ERISA requires that qualified plans have procedures for making claims for benefits. These procedures are usually found in the summary plan description. Ordinarily once a participant makes a claim for benefits, the plan administrator can take up to 90 days to process the claim. If a plan provides notice, however, it can take an additional 90 days. The plan administrator's decision is sent in writing to the participant. A participant has the right to appeal that decision to the administrator and may submit additional materials to show the administrator why the decision should be changed. Such an appeal must be made within 60 days of when the participant receives notice of the initial decision.

It is important that the participant ask for this reconsideration on time, because tardiness may foreclose other avenues of appeal, such as a lawsuit. The plan administrator must generally respond to the request to review a decision within 60 days but may request an additional 60 days if it provides notice. A few plans provide for a hearing at this stage, but most simply make decisions on the documents submitted by the participant and its own records. Once again, the administrator's decision must be in writing. It must set forth specific reasons for denying the claim.

If the participant's claim is denied on this second appeal, or if the claim goes unanswered within the time limits, a participant may file a lawsuit in federal court. The court will review the decision of the plan administrator. If the plan gives the administrator the discretion to interpret the plan, the court will generally only review the administrator's decision to see if it was reasonable under the applicable federal law and the terms of the plan. In effect, the plan administrator is given the benefit of the doubt.

Occasionally a court will review the whole matter *de novo*. This means that no deference will be given to the plan administrator's interpretation. Generally this only occurs when the plan administrator is not given explicit authority under the plan to interpret its terms or when the court finds that the plan administrator has a conflict of interest (for example, if the administrator is employed by the plan sponsor).

PLAN ADMINISTRATION

As discussed above, ERISA sets forth standards of conduct for individuals who manage private pension plans. If a participant suspects mismanagement, there are two courses of action. The first is to contact the enforcement office of the Pension and Welfare Benefits Administration in the federal Department of Labor. This organization is required to investigate alleged misconduct and to enforce the terms of ERISA. In certain cases it may bring a lawsuit against the fiduciaries in federal court.

The second avenue open to a participant is to bring a private suit in federal court for breach of fiduciary duty. This is certainly the more expensive alternative. Under ERISA a successful plaintiff can only hope to win back for the plan what it should have received had the fiduciary properly performed its duty. There are no punitive damages available under ERISA and it is fairly settled that attorneys' fees are not awarded even to successful plaintiffs.

Nonqualified Pension Plans

Certain employers choose to maintain retirement plans for some or all of their employees that do not meet all of ERISA's requirements. These are called nonqualified plans and they are often designed to supplement benefits provided in an ERISA qualified plan. Usually these plans are only made available to upper-level management and executives.

With few exceptions, nonqualified plans are not subject to ERISA disclosure rules. Most are not funded in order to avoid immediate income tax consequences to the participants in the plan.

Because ERISA minimum requirements do not apply it is difficult to generalize as to the terms of such plans. An individual seeking to enforce such a plan must look to the terms of the agreement itself.

Individual Retirement Accounts (IRAs)

Another popular tax-favored retirement savings vehicle is the Individual Retirement Account (IRA). IRAs are accounts maintained by banks and other similar financial institutions to which an individual may contribute on a tax-favored basis provided he or she (and his or her spouse, depending upon the couple's income) is not already covered by a qualified retirement plan. IRAs can also be used to accept a lump sum distribution from a qualified plan and protect it from becoming taxable at that time. Money contributed to an IRA earns income tax-free until it is paid out to the account owner or a beneficiary.

Strictly speaking, IRAs are not qualified retirement plans; however, many of the same tax rules governing payments from qualified retirement plans apply to IRAs as well. For example, an individual must begin withdrawing funds from an IRA by 1 April following the calendar year in which he or she attains age 70.5. If money is withdrawn from an IRA prior to age 55 it is generally subject to an excise tax in addition to regular income taxes.

Social Security

The Social Security program was created in 1935 in response to the problem of widespread poverty among older Americans. It provides income benefits in three circumstances: disability, retirement, and death. The program is administered by the Social Security Administration, whose principal offices are located outside of Baltimore, Maryland. There are field offices throughout the country. Many consider the benefits provided by Social Security to form the base of retirement income security. In 1987, the Social Security Administration issued checks for $183.6 billion to more than 34 million retired workers, dependents, and survivors. The Consumer Expenditure Survey of 1986–1987 indicates that among seniors aged 62 to 74, Social Security accounted for nearly half of household income.

Participation in the Social Security system is mandatory for employees in nearly all sectors of employment, including government employment. Benefits are provided only based upon the earnings record of a worker in covered employment. Three categories of workers are covered: salaried or wage-earning, agricultural, and self-employed workers. In order to be "fully insured" a worker must have worked a specified number of calendar quarters, which for retirement and survivor benefits means at least 40. It does not matter how many employers the worker had during this period.

Presently, at age 62, a fully insured worker is entitled to a retirement benefit from Social Security. If the worker waits until age 65 he would be entitled to a larger benefit. Choosing to receive benefits at age 62 results in permanently reduced benefits because the benefits will be paid over an additional three years. Conversely, choosing to delay receipt of benefits increases the monthly benefit. Postponements past age 70, however, do not result in an increase in benefits. In future years the Social Security retirement age is scheduled to rise.

Other individuals who are dependent upon the worker in the eyes of the Social Security Administration may also claim a benefit when the worker retires. These include: the worker's spouse aged 62 or older; a worker's wife of any age who is taking care of a child entitled to benefits; the unmarried child, adopted child, stepchild, grandchild, or step-grandchild who is dependent upon the worker for support and who has not attained age 18 (19 if he is a full-time student, 22 if he is under a disability). The divorced wife of the worker who has attained age 62, has not remarried, and who was married to the worker for ten years or more is entitled to begin receiving Social Security benefits when the worker attains age 62, even if he does not retire at that time.

Survivor benefits are payable to the widow or widower of a fully insured worker beginning at age 60, or even earlier if the survivor is caring for children or is disabled. This benefit is available even if the couple divorced, provided the marriage lasted at least ten years. Dependent children are also entitled to benefits. Survivor benefits are available to the parent of a deceased worker if the parent depended upon the worker for one-half of his or her support. The Social Security Act provides an additional lump sum death benefit of $255 to assist in burial expenses.

The amount of retirement and survivor's benefits is based upon the insured worker's "primary insurance amount," that in turn is based upon the earnings on which the worker paid Social Security taxes over his career. The Social Security Administration bases its calculations on the W-2 forms submitted each year by employers. Through a complex series of calculations it arrives at a figure called the averaged indexed monthly earnings. The "primary insurance amount" (PIA) is determined by a formula that places more weight on the first dollars earned.

The PIA is the base from which all benefits are figured. The worker's benefit at the standard Social Security retirement age (presently 65) is 100 percent of the PIA. If the worker elects to receive benefits beginning at age 62, his benefits are reduced but will not result in less than 20 percent of the PIA. A spouse is entitled to 50 percent of the PIA. A widow, widower or surviving divorced wife is entitled to 100 percent of the worker's PIA at age 65, but less if he or she elects to begin benefits sooner. Workers and surviving spouses may delay receipt of benefits and increase the amount they receive monthly.

Other than early or delayed receipt of benefits, the factor that most often affects the amount of benefits received is income earned by the recipients. Present recipients of retirement and survivor benefits are permitted to earn up to $10,200 a year if they are age 65 or older, $7,440 if they are under age 65 in 1992. These limits are expected to rise precipitously over the next several years. For every dollar earned in excess of that amount, the recipient loses 33$\frac{1}{3}$ cents in benefits if he or she is over age 65, and 50 cents in benefits if under age 65. This rule does not apply to recipients age 70 and over. If the worker on whose record benefits are based is the individual who works, the benefits of all his dependents, including his spouse, are reduced. However, if one of the dependents works, then only that dependent's benefits are reduced. It is the responsibility of the recipient to inform the Social Security Administration of any earned income.

Receipt of Benefits

Although a fully insured worker is eligible for benefits, in order to obtain them, he must file an application with the Social Security Administration. This may be accomplished by a visit to a local district office or by mail. Eligible individuals should file just before or after retirement, because if the application is filed late the recipient will only be able to receive back payments of the year prior to the date of application.

The district office will require certain information and documentation from an individual making a claim. In all cases it is helpful to have a Social Security card or some other record of the applicant's correct number. An individual seeking retirement benefits should also be prepared to produce proof of age such as a birth certificate or religious record of birth, and a copy of his W-2 or self-employment tax return to show his income from the immediately preceding year. An individual claiming spousal benefits, whether retirement or survivor benefits, should also be prepared to produce a marriage certificate or religious record of marriage, and a death certificate, if applicable. Any other dependent should be prepared to supply proof of his relationship to the insured worker. In most cases the Social Security Administration will require original documents or copies certified by the issuing agency.

The burden is on the claimant to prove his entitlement to benefits. If application for benefits is denied, or if the Social Security Administration takes some other action that adversely affects a recipient or applicant, that individual may appeal the decision. There are three levels of appeal within the Social Security Administration itself. The first step is a request for reconsideration.

An applicant or recipient has 60 days from the date of a letter of denial or other written notice from the Social Security Administration to file a request for reconsideration. At this stage the claimant may submit additional documents and evidence to bolster his claim. Taking all this information into account, the Social Security Administration will reconsider and then mail a letter to the claimant explaining its decision.

If the reconsideration is unfavorable, the claimant can request a hearing before an administrative law judge. This is not a court judge, but an employee of the Social Security Administration. A request for such a hearing must be made within 60 days of the date of the decision of the reconsideration. The claimant or his representative should review the claimant's file at the Social Security Administration to determine the evidence that the administrative law judge will consider.

Although the hearings are supposed to be less formal than a regular court, it is prudent to get advice from a lawyer or someone familiar with such hearings at this stage. Federal law provides that an attorney assisting a claimant in securing benefits may not charge legal fees of more than 25 percent of any retroactive benefits awarded. In fact, less may be owed if the client and attorney have agreed on a smaller fee. The Social Security Administration must approve any attorneys' fees charged.

The Social Security Administration will send a notice of the hearing indicating the issues the administrative law judge will decide. The claimant may bring evidence to the hearing. One of the responsibilities of the administrative law judge is to rule on the admissibility of this evidence. If the claimant has legal representation, he may file a legal brief that advocates the claimant's position by referring to other cases (known as precedent) that favor the claimant. If a brief is not filed before the hearing most administrative law judges will accept briefs at and after the hearing.

If the administrative law judge rules against the claimant, one last appeal may be made within the Social Security Administration to the Appeals Council. The claimant has 60 days after the judge's decision to request this review. The council does not hold another hearing, but reviews the case on the record compiled during the previous proceedings.

If the Appeals Council upholds the decision, the claimant may file a petition with the local federal district court for review of the Social Security Administration's determination. A claimant who has not consulted a lawyer or legal services office before this stage should do so. The petition to the district court must be filed within 60 days of denial of the claimant's claim by the Appeals Council.

One fact that the denied claimant should keep in mind is that the district court will not make an independent determination on the case. Its review is limited to the "substantial evidence" standard. This means that if the findings of the Social Security Administration are supported by substantial evidence, they will not be disturbed by the district court.

One final appeal may be made to the Court of Appeals. Although a disappointed claimant may wish to take his claim "all the way to the Supreme Court," that court has the discretion to decline to review the case.

Special Issues in Social Security

DISABILITY

In addition to retirement and death, Social Security benefits are also paid in cases of the total and complete disability of a fully insured worker. In order to be fully insured, the worker must have work credits in 20 of the last 40 quarters preceding his illness. The disability must be so severe as to prevent the individual from engaging in any substantial, gainful employment for at least 12 months. There is a five-month waiting period before benefits would begin. Benefits are discontinued when or if the beneficiary's condition improves sufficiently to allow him to return to employment. When the individual becomes eligible for retirement benefits his entitlement to disability benefits ceases.

Disability claims, whether at the initial determination or upon review, often result in controversy with the Social Security Administration. The appeals process is the same as noted above. Determinations of disability are made according to Social Security Administration regulations that set forth standards for measuring the "level of severity" of the physical or mental disability. The Social Security Administration assigns a physician and a disability examiner in the state where the applicant lives to investigate the claim. It does not rely strictly upon the opinion of the claimant's doctor.

In order to make a claim, an individual must have a report signed by a licensed physician detailing the disability and the treatment prescribed, as well as copies of medical records, other medical evidence, and reports of clinical findings. To speed the process along it helps to work with a physician who specializes in measuring physical and mental impairments in the way that the Social Security Administration does. Often a state, county, or local medical society can make recommendations.

REPRESENTATIVE PAYEES

If a recipient of benefits can no longer handle his affairs, a relative, friend, or institution can request that payments be made directly to individuals or institutions who will handle the recipient's financial affairs. In recent years the Social Security Administration has begun to monitor these situations more closely in order to prevent abuse. The recipient has the right to terminate payments to a representative payee at any time.

OVERPAYMENT

Occasionally the Social Security Administration discovers that it has overpaid benefits to a recipient. This can be due to administrative error or because a recipient failed to notify the Social Security Administration promptly about a change in circumstances that affected his or her benefits. Chief among these is a failure to report income in excess of the earned income limits. The Social Security Administration has the authority to recoup these overpayments by docking future payments to the recipient.

In certain limited circumstances, the Social Security Administration will waive the overpayment. The benefit recipient must demonstrate that he or she was without fault in causing the overpayment and that repayment will cause the recipient a hardship.

The Social Security Administration looks at all of the circumstances giving rise to the overpayment in determining fault. These include the intelligence, education, and physical and mental condition of the recipient. If the recipient did not make incorrect statements, and did not provide information or accept payment that he or she knew was incorrect, the blame is not placed on the recipient.

Hardship can be established in several ways. If recovery of overpayment would deprive the recipient of ordinary and necessary living expenses such as food, clothing, and rent or of doctors' fees, hospital expenses, or support expenses for which the recipient is responsible, hardship may be found. Finally, hardship may also be established if the recipient relinquished a valuable right or changed jobs because he or she relied on the payment. For example, if other public assistance the senior may have received was reduced or forgone due to the overpayment, this may weigh against repayment.

Income Supplements

Income supplements are an important component of the public safety net for seniors. This chapter focuses on federal income support programs that apply particularly to seniors. Additional federal, state and local programs may also benefit seniors if they meet eligibility criteria. These include Aid to Families with Dependent Children (AFDC), as well as state or local general assistance and welfare programs.

With the exception of Supplemental Security Income, the programs described in this chapter provide assistance with specified expenses. Most are "means"-tested, meaning that they are available to individuals meeting income and asset restrictions. Most, but not all, are entitlement programs, meaning that they cannot be denied to any individual who satisfies the eligibility criteria. Supplements for medical care and housing are not discussed in this chapter, but are described in Chapters 4 and 5, respectively.

Supplemental Security Income (SSI)

SSI is a part of the Social Security Act that provides monthly cash income to U.S. citizens and permanent resident aliens who are: over 65 years of age, blind, or disabled and who meet strict income and asset limitations. Unlike Social Security benefits, no work history is necessary to receive SSI payments. Applicants are required to secure all other benefits to which they may be entitled such as private and public pensions and Social Security benefits.

The goal of the program is to provide a "floor" of income to enable individuals to meet their basic needs for food, clothing, and shelter. Although SSI is principally financed by the federal government, the states are encouraged to (and the majority do) contribute additional amounts to supplement the federal benefit. In 1992 the maximum federal SSI benefit was $422 per month for an individual, $633 for a couple. Individuals living in the household of another and receiving support and maintenance in that household receive two-thirds of these amounts. A $30 monthly payment is made to SSI recipients who are confined to a Medicaid institution on a long-term basis. Benefits vary a great deal from individual to individual, and even from month to month, depending upon the recipient's other income sources.

INCOME AND RESOURCE LIMITATIONS

The resource limitations are $2,000 for a single individual and $3,000 for a couple. Almost any property that could be converted to cash to provide income is countable. Property owned jointly as well as property owned by a spouse is generally considered to be available to the applicant as a resource. Certain properties are exempt. These include:

1. The applicant's home

2. Household goods and personal property up to $2,000 in value

3. An automobile valued up to $4,500, or of any value if used in connection with obtaining medical treatment, employment, to transport a handicapped individual, or to perform necessary daily activities (shopping, for example)

4. Life insurance with a face value of up to $1,500

5. A burial plot

6. A burial fund of up to $1,500

The limitation on income in 1992 was $929 per month for an individual and $1,351 per month for a couple. Income includes virtually all income, earned and unearned. However, the first $65 of earned income is disregarded, as is an additional $20 of unearned income. Certain other assistance such as state welfare payments and food stamps is also disregarded. Again, the income of one spouse is deemed to be available to both.

Once eligibility is established, the amount of the monthly payment is determined by subtracting from the maximum award the individual's countable income, including income derived from countable resources. Once payments begin, the burden is on the benefit recipient to report changes in household resources or income.

ADMINISTRATION OF SSI

SSI is administered at the state level either by the state social services agency or by the Social Security Administration by contract from the state. The process of filing for benefits is the same as for Social Security benefits except that the applicant must be prepared to demonstrate that he or she also meets the resource and income limitations. This means, for example, providing copies of insurance policies, bank books, notes, stocks, bonds, wage statements, and other income records. The appeals rights and procedures are also the same as for Social Security benefits.

Food Stamp Act

The Food Stamp Act is the chief federal program providing nutrition assistance to low-income households. Eligible households are provided with coupons with a stated cash value. These food stamp coupons can be redeemed to purchase most foods in regular grocery stores. Alcoholic beverages, tobacco products, and hot food that is ready to eat may not be purchased with food stamps. However, food stamps may be used to purchase prepared meals by those 60 or older who are housebound, physically handicapped, or unable to prepare their own meals. Additionally, food stamps may be used to purchase meals at senior centers or other facilities.

ELIGIBILITY

An individual must be a U.S. citizen or an alien lawfully in the United States to be eligible for food stamps. Just as in the case of SSI, resource and income limitations determine eligibility for food stamps. These limitations are applied, and food stamp allotments are provided, on a "household" rather than individual basis. An individual or couple living with others may qualify as a separate household, but only if they regularly buy and prepare food separately.

In order to be eligible to participate, household resources cannot exceed $3,000 in a household of two or more, one of whom is 60 years of age or over. Countable resources are generally the same as under the SSI program. Only limited exclusions apply, including, most significantly, the home and automobile of the applicant.

The net includable income of households with an elder member may not exceed the federal poverty level. Both earned and unearned income is counted, with certain limited exclusions. Most significant among these exclusions are general and private assistance payments made directly to a third party providing services to the household. Net income is determined by deducting from the total countable income of the household a flat 20 percent, as well as medical expenses that exceed $35, shelter expenses in excess of 50 percent of the household income (up to the full amount paid for rent), and the standard deduction.

Once eligibility is determined, the household is awarded a food stamp allotment for a defined certification period. Food stamps will only continue if the household is recertified at the end of the certification period. The award is based on the size of the household and is determined according to a schedule published annually by the Department of Agriculture.

ADMINISTRATION

Though the program is directed by the federal Department of Agriculture, it is administered by state agencies under federal mandates. Practices may differ slightly from state to state, so it is a good idea to contact the local social services agency to determine their particular procedures.

Applications for food stamps can be obtained by visiting the state agency offices or by telephoning the agency. Individuals who are eligible or applying for SSI benefits may apply at the Social Security Office. Federal regulations require that the applicant appear for a personal interview with the agency to establish eligibility. This requirement may be waived on a case-by-case basis where the applicant is unable to come to the offices because he or she is aged 65 or disabled. The purpose of the interview is twofold. The first is to provide information about the program to the applicant. The second is to review the documentary evidence of the income and resources of the household. An applicant can speed the process by bringing documents such as Social Security cards, rent receipts, utility and medical bills, proof of income for all household members, and bank books or other papers that indicate the value of includable assets.

If the application is denied, or if the applicant believes that the award is insufficient, the applicant can request a hearing. This request must be made within 90 days of the determination as to entitlement. Conversely, if the state agency determines that there has been an overissuance of food stamps, it is empowered to seek reimbursement. If the overissuance is not due to fraud, and does not exceed $35, a claim will not be made against the household. Federal regulations permit the agency to seek reimbursement in the form of a lump sum, or in installments. The agency may not deny, terminate, or reduce food stamp benefits in order to recoup overissuances.

Programs under Title III of the Older Americans Act

The Older Americans Act (OAA) has been amended 11 times since it was originally passed in 1965, most recently in 1987 when it was reauthorized through 1991. A reauthorization was pending as this book goes to press. It is the OAA that has provided the infrastructure of state and area agencies on aging, constituting an important resource for older Americans. Title III of the OAA supports a broad range of social services, including senior centers, congregate and home-delivered nutrition programs, and legal services. These services can be provided through the state agency itself, or by a private contractor.

Allocations of OAA funds are made to the states in proportion to the percentage of individuals aged 60 and over relative to other states. The states must submit plans to the Administration on Aging designating the manner in which funds will be spent. The states have considerable flexibility in the use of these funds, subject to the requirement that they continue "access" (transportation, outreach, information and referral), "in-home" (homemaker, home health aide, visiting, telephone assurance, and chore maintenance), and legal services.

Congregate nutrition sites funded by the OAA must provide at least one hot or other appropriate meal per day for five or more days per week that provides one-third of the daily recommended dietary allowance. Home-delivered meals must similarly be provided at least once a day for at least five days per week. Title III authorizes the U.S. Department of Agriculture to provide surplus commodities to these programs, or in lieu of such commodities, cash.

All persons 60 years of age and their spouses of any age are eligible to take part in OAA nutrition programs. There is no income maximum. Federal law provides that state agencies administering programs funded by the OAA may request contributions from participants. However, services cannot be denied simply because contribution is not made.

Energy and Weatherization Assistance

LOW-INCOME ENERGY ASSISTANCE PROGRAM

A variety of state and private nonprofit programs provide energy assistance to low-income individuals. The most significant federal government program is the Low-Income Energy Assistance Program (LIEAP). Through this program funds are made available to states to provide assistance in paying energy costs, emergency repair or maintenance of heating equipment, as well as weatherization assistance.

LIEAP funds are available to both owners and renters. Recipients of veterans' pensions, food stamps, AFDC and SSI payments are automatically eligible for assistance under this program. In addition, any household with a total income of less than 150 percent of the state poverty level or 60 percent of the median state income is eligible.

Unlike many programs, LIEAP is not an entitlement program, so funds are available to eligible individuals on a first-come, first-served basis. It is therefore important to apply early for benefits. Generally this program is operated out of the state social services agency.

RURAL HOME IMPROVEMENT LOANS

Rural elderly may also qualify for grants or loans from the Farmers Home Administration (FmHA) under section 504 of the Housing Act of 1949. This program provides loans and grants to assist very low-income households in eliminating safety hazards in otherwise habitable dwellings. Loans are available at a 1 percent per year rate. Grants of up to $5,000 are available to individuals aged 62 and older who do not have sufficient income to repay a loan.

To be eligible, the individual must own and occupy the home that is to be repaired. If a grant is secured, the owner will be required to sign an agreement stating that the property will not be sold for three years following the grant. If the property is sold, the grantee will be required to reimburse the government the full amount of the grant. Applications are available at FmHA offices.

Taxes

Federal Taxes

Along with other Americans, seniors are required to file federal tax returns and to pay income taxes if their income exceeds certain minimal levels. Not all income is taxable, however. Veterans' benefits, certain public assistance payments, benefits received from private health insurance, Medicare and Medicaid, and interest on municipal bonds are all excluded from income.

Revisions to the tax code in 1986 streamlined the tax rates and eliminated many deductions. There remain, in addition to those provisions that benefit all lower-income individuals, provisions designed to provide some relief to seniors regardless of their income. Probably the most significant of these is the exclusion from taxable income of a portion of Social Security benefits.

TAX TREATMENT OF SOCIAL SECURITY BENEFITS

The federal tax code provides that Social Security payments are only taxable if the total income of the taxpayer exceeds certain base amounts. Even then a maximum of one-half of the benefit is subject to taxation. The base amounts are $25,000 for an individual, and $32,000 for a couple filing jointly. If a married couple files taxes separately, there is no base amount, resulting in taxation of the couple's Social Security benefit. In order to determine whether the base amount has been exceeded, the income of the taxpayer, both taxable and tax exempt, plus one-half of the Social Security benefit are added together. If this sum exceeds the relevant base amount, then either one-half of the taxpayer's Social Security benefits or the amount in excess of the taxpayer's base amount, whichever is less, is subject to tax.

For example, Mr. and Mrs. A have income from a pension and tax-exempt bonds of $25,000. Their Social Security benefit comes to $12,000. Since their income plus one-half of their Social Security benefit ($6,000) equals $31,000, their entire Social Security benefit is not taxed. The next year, their income is $100,000 due to the sale of some real estate. Mr. and Mrs. A's income plus one-half of their Social Security benefit adds up to $106,000; therefore one-half of their Social Security benefit ($6,000) would be subject to tax. The remainder would be tax-free.

CREDIT FOR THE ELDERLY AND DISABLED

A senior age 65 or older, or a younger senior if he or she retired due to a permanent and total disability, may qualify for a tax credit under federal tax law called the credit for the elderly and permanently and totally disabled. The law provides a credit equal to 15 percent of an individual's disability income or so-called "initial amount." The "initial amount" each year is $5,000 for a single individual, $5,000 for married individuals filing a joint return ($3,750 each if they file separately) or $7,500 if both spouses qualify for the credit. This "initial amount" is reduced by tax-free Social Security, Railroad Retirement, or veterans' benefits, or other nontaxed pension or annuity income.

The law is structured to apply only to low- and middle-income seniors. Accordingly, the "initial amount" is also reduced dollar-for-dollar above certain income levels. Seniors with incomes above $17,500 (for a single person) or $25,000 (for a married couple) will not qualify for this benefit.

INCREASED STANDARD DEDUCTION

Seniors receive a higher standard deduction from federal taxes. This means that seniors who do not itemize deductions automatically exclude a larger portion of their income from taxation than younger taxpayers. In 1992, taxpayers who were 65 or older or legally blind could claim an additional $700 for an elderly married individual or surviving spouse, and $900 for a single person or one who is a head-of-household. These amounts are adjusted for inflation each year. A taxpayer who is both blind and 65 could claim two additional deductions. This additional amount applies if the individual is 65 (or blind) on the last day of the year.

EXEMPTION OF CAPITAL GAIN ON THE SALE OF A RESIDENCE

Ordinarily, the full gain realized by a taxpayer on the sale of a home is includable in income unless the individual buys another house within two years prior to the sale of the home, or two years following the sale of the home. The tax law thus allows a homeowner to postpone taxation of gains on the sale of his or her home. Recognizing that a senior might not wish to buy a larger home, or might not wish to buy a home at all, the federal tax law provides that the first $125,000 made on the sale of a personal residence for taxpayers aged 55 and over is not taxed. Any gain above the $125,000 limit is taxed at ordinary income rates. To take advantage of this exemption, individuals must have owned and used the property as principal residence for three of the five years preceding the sale. If either the taxpayer or the taxpayer's spouse previously used this exemption then they are both ineligible to take advantage of this provision a second time.

State Taxes

In addition to federal taxes, income may be subject to taxation at the state and local level. Those jurisdictions that tax income often incorporate exclusions similar to those under federal law. For example, the majority exempt Social Security payments, as well as federal and state public pensions, from taxation. Some even exempt private pension income from taxation. The vast majority provide a personal exemption, tax credit, or an additional standard deduction to seniors.

Many states also provide preferences for seniors in property taxes. These include homestead exemptions or credits that reduce the rate of taxation on the owner's primary residence. Deferral programs available in approximately one-third of the states allow certain taxpayers, usually including the elderly, to postpone payment of property taxes until death or the sale of their property. The amount of unpaid taxes plus interest is secured by a lien on the property. These types of programs obviously affect the value of any legacy to an heir. Finally, many states provide rebates of property taxes to certain lower-income people, including seniors, based on their income. This type of provision is sometimes called a "circuit breaker" (in reference to the overload on the senior's resources due to taxes).

Chapter 4

Issues of Securing Adequate Health Care

Basics

- Medicare, Medicaid, employer-sponsored group insurance plans, individual insurance contracts and new products such as long-term care insurance are sources of funding for health care.

- The Agency for Health Care Policy and Research estimates that more than one-half of all women and one-third of all men turning age 65 in 1991 will spend time in a nursing home before they die, and that the situation will affect seven out of every ten married couples in that age group.

- Twenty-five percent of those who enter a nursing home will stay at least one year, at a cost of $30,000 to $40,000 a year.

Introduction

In 1989 health care costs consumed 11.3 percent of the U.S. gross national product. A large portion of these costs is borne by seniors, their employers, and Medicare. In the spring of 1991, Buck Consultants, Inc., a national employee benefits consulting firm, found that medical insurance for an individual retiring before Medicare eligibility can cost as much as $8,000 per year. With prices for health care rising, at twice the rate of other items, securing and affording quality care will continue to be an issue for seniors into the twenty-first century.

This chapter examines the private and public mechanisms that assist seniors in purchasing health care. For a more complete discussion of these issues, see *Paying for Health Care after Age 65* in ABC-CLIO's Choices and Challenges series.

Of course, Medicare is the centerpiece of health care funding for seniors, but most are unaware that Medicare pays only about 40 percent of their health care costs. Medicaid is becoming increasingly important as a secondary source of aid because of the serious gaps in Medicare coverage, particularly in cases involving long-term care. As in the discussions of government programs in Chapter 3, this chapter will treat the substantive provisions of Medicare and Medicaid coverage briefly before a discussion of the procedural aspects of securing benefits.

Affording Health Care

The centerpiece of health care financing for seniors is Medicare, a public insurance program available to seniors beginning at age 65, or earlier in certain circumstances. Unfortunately, Medicare alone leaves up to 60 percent of the average senior's health care bills uncovered. Medicaid picks up some of this for seniors who meet its strict income qualifications.

For seniors who extend their working lives past the traditional retirement age, health benefits provided by employers continue to be most important. Federal and state age discrimination laws guarantee equal benefits or an equal expenditure on behalf of seniors for benefits (see Chapter 3), and certain continuation benefits under those policies. Some employers provide their retirees with health benefits. However, recent changes in the accounting treatment of such benefits have led employers to cut back in this area. Other private options include individual insurance, long-term care insurance, and so-called Medigap policies.

Medicare

Medicare is a two-part program of the federal government to assist seniors and some disabled individuals in meeting the costs of health care. It was created in 1965 as Title XVIII of the Social Security Act and has been amended several times since enactment.

Although Medicare is a federal program, it is actually operated by private companies through contracts with the government. Companies that administer Part A are called "intermediaries." Those that administer Part B are called "carriers." They are bound by the terms of regulations issued by the Health Care Financing Administration (HCFA), a government agency that sets overall policy. HCFA publishes *The Medicare Handbook* each year, describing the benefits provided by Medicare.

The two components of Medicare are Parts A and B, which provide separate but complementary coverage. Essentially, Part A covers hospitalization and Part B pays for doctor's visits. The coverage they provide is by no means complete. The most notable gap is in long-term care. It is generally estimated that only 2 percent of all long-term care costs are covered by Medicare. With few exceptions, neither Part A or B covers eyeglasses, hearing aids, prescription drugs, dentures, or preventive health care.

In order to be covered by Medicare, all costs must be incurred on a physician's orders. Even then, charges under Part A for hospitalization or admissions to a skilled nursing facility are subject to further review by a utilization review committee or peer review organization. Charges that are not covered by Medicare are the responsibility of the senior who received the services. This obligation must be met through Medicaid, private insurance, or other resources.

ELIGIBILITY

Medicare is available to seniors aged 65 or older who are eligible for Social Security or Railroad Retirement benefits. Special rules allow disabled workers, disabled widows, disabled widowers, disabled children, and people with end-stage renal disease to qualify for Medicare benefits even if they have not attained age 65. A senior who is not eligible for Medicare may still enroll in the program but will be required to pay a premium for Part A coverage ($192 per month in 1992). Some states will assist low-income individuals who wish to buy in to Medicare in this way.

Although a senior is eligible to have Part B coverage at the same time as he or she is eligible for Part A, coverage is not automatic. A senior must enroll and promise to pay the required premium for Part B coverage ($31.80 in 1992). If a senior does not elect to purchase Part B coverage at the same time he or she first becomes covered by Part A, he or she may enroll during an open enrollment period, although a higher premium will be charged. Open enrollments occur each year from 1 January through 31 March.

PART A: HOSPITAL INSURANCE (HI)

Medicare Part A helps a senior pay for inpatient hospital and care in a skilled nursing facility. A senior is automatically covered by Part A upon attaining age 65 if he or she applies for Social Security or Railroad Retirement benefits. Part A benefits are provided without premium to eligible seniors (except, as noted above, those seniors who are not eligible for Medicare based upon their work histories or that of their spouses). Like private insurance, there are deductibles and copayment amounts that apply to this coverage. There are also benefit caps.

For each "benefit period" or "spell of illness," Medicare Part A paid the following in 1992:

1. If the senior was hospitalized

   Days 1 through 60   All hospital expenses after the first $652 in "covered charges"

   Days 61 through 90   All but $163 of "covered charges" per day

   Days 91 through 150   All but $326 of "covered charges" per day

2. If, following at least a 3-day hospitalization, the senior requires daily treatment in a skilled nursing facility (and he or she is admitted within 30 days of discharge from the hospital)

   Days 1 through 20   All of the expenses

   Days 21 through 100   All but $81.50 per day

A "benefit period" begins each time a Medicare beneficiary enters a hospital and ends when he or she has been out of the hospital or a skilled nursing facility for 60 days or more. If a senior's hospitalization lasts longer than 90 days in any benefit period, Part A will cover expenses, except for $326 per day, for an additional 60 days. This is the so-called lifetime reserve. Once these 60 days are "used up," hospitalizations that last longer than 90 days are simply not covered. There is no lifetime reserve for expenses incurred at a skilled nursing facility.

"Covered charges" include medically necessary services such as a semi-private room, meals, nursing, lab tests, X-rays and other radiological services, medical supplies, rehabilitation, and the like. They do not include extras such as a private room or nurse, televisions, and telephones. Covered charges also do not include those for services that a Medicare peer review organization deems not medically necessary. This is the subject of many appeals (see page 62).

Other services that are covered by Part A include home health care, hospice care, and inpatient psychiatric care.

PART B: SUPPLEMENTARY MEDICAL INSURANCE (SMI)

Part B pays most of the cost of a doctor's services. This includes the doctor's fees for inpatient and outpatient care, and services such as:

1. Medical services and supplies (for example, ambulance transportation, artificial limbs, or home dialysis equipment).

2. Rental or purchase of medical equipment.

3. Outpatient services (for example, lab tests, X-rays, or radiation therapy).

4. Home health services.

After paying a $100 deductible, Medicare Part B will pay 80 percent of the "reasonable" cost for most services. Certain benefits, such as home health care and second surgical opinions, are paid at 100 percent of the reasonable cost. The reasonable cost is also called the "approved amount," and it constitutes a figure determined by Medicare based on the prevailing rates in the geographical area during the preceding year. If a particular doctor charges more than the approved amount, the senior has to make up the difference in addition to the 20 percent that Medicare requires the senior to pay.

Certain doctors advertise that they accept "assignment" from Medicare. This means that they agree to charge seniors only the "approved amount." Some states, such as Connecticut, Rhode Island, and Massachusetts, require that doctors who are licensed in that state accept assignment in certain instances.

Beginning in 1992, the reimbursement provisions under Part B will change. A new schedule of approved fees is being developed under which Medicare will reimburse doctors according to the time and effort put into a procedure. Once this schedule is in place, doctors will be limited in the amount that they can charge a Medicare beneficiary over that schedule. In 1992, doctors will not be permitted to charge more than 125 percent of Medicare's approved fee to Medicare patients. By 1995, that percentage will drop to 115 percent.

MEDICARE APPEALS

Sometimes a senior incurs a health care cost with the expectation that it will be paid by Medicare Part A or B only to have the claim denied. Unfortunately, this can sometimes occur even when a senior's doctor has recommended a course of treatment. It is important for Medicare beneficiaries to become familiar with the appeal system when claims are denied.

Parts A and B have separate appeals systems, so the first question that must be answered is whether the claim was made for Part A or Part B benefits.

Appeals under Part A

There are four steps in the appeal process under Part A:

1. The request for reconsideration.

2. The administrative hearing.

3. A Social Security Appeals Council review.

4. Appeal to a federal district court.

Each step must be taken in turn. It is extremely important to meet the deadlines at each stage of appeal.

Request for Reconsideration

After a provider files a request for payment with the agency that administers Part A, that agency determines whether the particular items and services are covered by Part A and makes payment. Both the senior and the health care provider receive a notice of "initial determination."

If a portion of the charges is disallowed, the senior may file a request for reconsideration. This request may be filed at a local Social Security office or with a Medicare intermediary. It must be filed within 60 days after the receipt of the notice of benefits. This 60-day period may only be extended if "good cause" is shown for delay.

Upon receipt of the request for reconsideration, the Medicare intermediary reviews the evidence and its previous findings. It then issues a written decision concerning its reconsideration. If the amount in dispute (combining all claims) is less than $100, no further appeals are allowed.

Administrative Hearing

A request for an administrative hearing must be made within 60 days after a reconsideration finding that denies $100 or more of a beneficiary's claim. A form is supplied by the Health Care Financing Administration (HCFA) for this purpose. It may be filed with the senior's local Social Security office or with the Medicare intermediary. An administrative law judge will set a hearing date.

At the hearing the beneficiary may bring in a legal representative—a lawyer or some other person who is familiar with Medicare. The administrative law judge is an employee of the Social Security Administration who interprets the Medicare law and regulations. He or she will determine what issues are to be resolved in the hearing and will give a written decision based on the evidence submitted by the beneficiary and the Medicare intermediary.

Social Security Appeals Council

A beneficiary who is unsuccessful at the administrative hearing level may request review by Social Security Appeals Council, located near Washington, D.C. Such a request must be made within 60 days following the receipt of the decision of the administrative law judge. The council has the authority to deny or dismiss such a request, however. Typically, when such review is granted, the council simply reviews the written record. It may issue a decision itself or refer the beneficiary's claim back to the administrative law judge.

Federal District Court

Claims where $1,000 or more of benefits are in dispute may be appealed to a U.S. district court within 60 days of a Social Security Appeals Council decision. The federal district court's review will generally be limited. The judge will give deference to the decisions of the administrative law judge and the council. It will only determine whether their decisions were supported by substantial evidence and predicated on legal standards of the Medicare law.

Part B: Review Request

Appeals under Part B follow a three-step process. As in Part A, each step must be taken in turn:

1. A request for review by the carrier.

2. A hearing before an administrative law judge.

3. Appeal to a federal district court.

Review

A Medicare beneficiary must request a review of a Medicare carrier decision in writing within six months following the date of the explanation of benefits. A form for this purpose is available from the carrier or the senior's local Social Security office. The carrier merely reviews the documents it has received.

Hearing

If the amount in dispute is $100 or more, the Medicare beneficiary may request a hearing before an administrative law judge. In order to reach the $100 threshold, the beneficiary may combine disputed claims over the six months preceding the request for the hearing. The hearing will usually be held at the local

Social Security office; however, if the beneficiary is homebound, it may be held at the beneficiary's residence. The hearing is designed to be informal, though a beneficiary may bring in a legal representative if he or she chooses. The beneficiary and carrier each may present witnesses.

Appeal to Federal Court

If the Medicare beneficiary still disagrees with the determination of the administrative law judge, he or she may file an appeal with a federal district court, but only if the amount in dispute exceeds $1,000. As in the case of appeals under Part A, the federal court will only overturn a determination of the administrative law judge in very limited circumstances.

Medicaid

Many people confuse Medicare and Medicaid, though they are two completely different programs. The most important difference is that Medicaid is a need-based program. In order to be eligible for benefits a senior must be categorically needy (meaning that he or she meets low-income eligibility requirements), medically needy, or both.

Medicaid is operated by the states with federal financial assistance. The federal law that established Medicaid was Title XIX of the Social Security Act. The states have considerable discretion in how they administer the program for their own citizens, so it is important for a senior who thinks he or she may qualify for benefits to check with the local income assistance office.

ELIGIBILITY

Depending upon the state, a senior who is 65 or older, blind, or disabled, or the parent of a minor child can be covered under Medicaid as either categorically or medically needy. The latter category is not available in all states.

Categorically Needy

The categorically needy are generally those individuals who are receiving or would be eligible to receive Supplemental Security

Income (SSI), SSI and a state supplement, or Aid to Families with Dependent Children (AFDC). Certain other persons with extremely low incomes and assets may also qualify depending upon the state's criteria. Individual states may elect to impose a stricter eligibility standard, provided individuals are able to "spend down" to the more restrictive assets or income level. Such states must also allow individuals to become eligible under the medically needy standard.

Like SSI, certain assets are excluded from consideration. These include a senior's home, car, personal and household items, and (subject to certain limits) property essential for self-support, a small amount of life insurance, and a burial fund. All other assets are considered "countable resources."

The income and resources of a married couple are considered to be available to each to pay medical expenses. However, where one partner in a couple requires care in a nursing home, federal law provides that the spouse who still lives in the community may retain a portion of the couple's income. In 1991, the amount is equal to 150 percent of the federal poverty level. The community spouse may keep more income if it is in his or her own name. In no event may this exempt income exceed $1,500 (adjusted for inflation) monthly.

The community spouse is entitled to a share of the couple's countable resources equal to the greater of: (1) between $12,624 and $63,120 in 1991 (adjusted each year for inflation), as determined by state law; (2) one-half of the couple's countable resources if that half does not exceed $63,120; or (3) a higher limit established by a fair hearing or court order. The remainder of the countable resources is considered to be available to pay for the care of the spouse in the nursing home.

Medically Needy

The medically needy are those individuals who have incurred disproportionately high medical expenses, but who do not qualify for cash assistance because their income or assets are too high. Many states establish a "protected income level" to address this problem. If, as a result of medical expenses, the individual's income would drop below this level, the individual is considered to be medically needy and eligible for Medicaid benefits.

BENEFITS UNDER MEDICAID

As in determinations of eligibility, the states have a certain lati-
tude regarding which benefits they offer under their Medicaid
programs. They may restrict availability of benefits as well as the
amount of benefits. As a result, although all states must reimburse certain mandatory services, there is great variety in the
levels of coverage provided from state to state. Some of these
benefits duplicate the coverage provided under Medicare. Others, most notably, benefits for long-term care, provide additional
protection. The mandatory coverages include:

- Physicians' services
- Inpatient hospital services
- Outpatient services (including rural health clinics)
- Skilled nursing facility services
- Laboratory and X-ray services
- Family planning services
- Early and periodic screening, diagnosis, and treatment of
  physical and mental defects for children
- Home health care for those not eligible for placement in a
  skilled nursing facility

A state may also allow certain optional services to be covered. These include dental care, prescription drugs, intermediate
care services, private-duty nursing, and eyeglasses, among other
things. Medicaid may also pay the premium for Medicare coverage for eligible seniors.

SPECIAL ISSUE: "SPENDING DOWN" ASSETS

The availability of benefits for unskilled nursing and custodial
care, commonly called long-term care, makes eligibility for Medicaid benefits important for seniors of low or moderate income. In
order to meet the strict income and asset restrictions that determine Medicaid eligibility, many seniors engage in strategic transfers (gifts or below-market sales) of assets to family members and

close friends. The Medicaid administration does not look kindly on these types of transfers. If a senior sells an asset below its fair market value during the 30-month period prior to the earlier of: (1) the date he or she begins receiving care in a nursing home, or home- or community-based services, or (2) the date he or she applies for Medicaid, then Medicaid assumes that the sale was made solely for the purpose of securing coverage. As a result, the individual will be ineligible for Medicaid coverage for up to 30 months, depending upon the value of the asset transferred.

Certain transfers are exempt from this provision. They include transfers of:

1. Noncountable resources, such as an automobile.

2. A home, but only if it is transferred to the senior's spouse or a minor, blind, or disabled child; or to a sibling with an equity interest in the home and who has resided there for one year prior to the senior's admission to a nursing home; or to a son or daughter who has resided in the home for two years immediately prior to admission to the nursing home, and who has provided care to the senior that allowed him or her to remain in the home until that time.

3. Countable resources to or from the senior's spouse, or to a third party for the sole benefit of the spouse.

4. Countable resources to a blind or disabled child.

5. Assets to the senior's spouse in the community for his or her support as required by a court order.

6. Assets made with the intention that they would be sold for fair market value or other valuable consideration.

7. Assets made exclusively for another reason than to qualify for Medicaid.

Veterans' Benefits

The Department of Veterans Affairs maintains a large network of medical and health care services for veterans of all conflicts. Veterans who were honorably discharged are required to sign a statement that they are unable to pay for comparable care in a private facility in order to receive benefits. Services are provided to veterans aged 65 and older with no certification of financial need.

Services are generally provided in Department of Veterans Affairs facilities, hospitals, nursing homes, and domiciliaries (special homes for veterans). The Department of Veterans Affairs also contracts with some state-operated facilities to provide care for eligible veterans.

Unfortunately, as veterans of World War II approach retirement, they are taxing the resources of the Department of Veterans Affairs. The department has therefore established a priority of veterans who are eligible for benefits. The priority is as follows:

1. Veterans needing hospitalization due to an injury or disease incurred or aggravated in the line of duty.

2. Veterans who were discharged or retired because of disabilities incurred in the line of duty (who have or are receiving compensation for such injuries), who need treatment for another condition not connected with that disability.

3. Other veterans, including those 65 and older, suffering from conditions not connected with their service.

Because of the large number of veterans seeking treatment, some may be unable to secure benefits quickly or easily. Information on programs available to veterans is available from the Office of Geriatrics and Extended Care at the Department of Veterans Affairs, or from a local veteran's affairs office.

Private Insurance

GROUP AND INDIVIDUAL INSURANCE POLICIES

Seniors who remain in the work force retain rights to continued private health insurance coverage as offered by their employers under the provisions of the Age Discrimination in Employment Act. In fact, the employer's plan is "primary" with respect to

Medicare. This means that the employer's plan pays first, and Medicare pays eligible expenses that are not covered by the employer's plan. The reverse is true for coverage provided to retirees of a company.

The typical private group insurance plan is an indemnity plan, although an employer may (and in some cases, is required to) offer the option of participation in an HMO. An indemnity plan reimburses employees for the cost of covered health care pursuant to a schedule. The schedule may set a reimbursement by procedure, or it may specify what percentage of the physician's fee (or a "reasonable and customary" fee for the procedure performed) will be reimbursed.

While in former times it was fairly common for full-time employees' health care costs to be fully covered, employers now favor plan designs that shift some of the costs of such coverage to plan participants. These designs include deductibles, coinsurance, and co-premium payments, as well as annual and lifetime caps on covered expenses. Some plans incorporate PPOs, precertification for hospitalization, and case management features as well.

The same terms found in group policies are generally present in individual insurance contracts that a senior might be able to secure on his or her own. Even with the same or even less-attractive benefit features, however, an individual policy will cost more than membership in a group policy. This is because the insurance company is unable to spread its risk across a large group.

Retiree Health Benefits—A Special Case

Employers once rewarded their long-service employees with the additional benefit of "lifetime" health benefits at retirement. The recent escalation in cost of health care, coupled with a change in the accounting treatment of these benefits, has led employers to rethink their earlier promises. The federal courts have handed down many important decisions in this area, and it is sure to be a subject of continued litigation as businesses attempt to control costs by cutting benefits.

Initially the courts were reticent to allow employers to change the terms of a retiree's benefits. Borrowing a concept from the pension area, employees argued that the benefits had vested once the employee retired and that the employer could not thereafter change or terminate them. Where unions had secured retiree health benefits, the unions argued that employees had given up wages and other benefits in collective bargaining agreements to get retiree health coverage. This argument continues to prove strong in the courts.

The vested benefit argument has largely been rejected by federal appeals courts. The courts have found that the federal law that governs employee benefits (called ERISA—see Chapter 3) only provides vesting for pension benefits. Cases in this area now focus on the documents describing the benefits. If the employer reserved the right to change or discontinue the benefits in the official plan documents, then it is generally free to do so even if the retiree has been told differently in meetings or informal written documents such as letters or brochures. The question for the court is "What did the employer promise?"

COBRA Continuation Coverage

When an employee or the employee's eligible dependents (spouse and dependent children) would otherwise lose coverage under an employer's plan due to certain events, they are eligible to continue their coverage for a limited period of time. This provision is called COBRA continuation coverage, named after the Consolidated Omnibus Budget Reconciliation Act of 1985, a federal law mandating that employers provide limited continued coverage in the case of specific events.

The federal law applies to all employers of 20 or more employees. It is designed to give employees and their immediate family members who lose coverage due to a "qualifying event" a period to find alternate coverage through a successor employer or another source. Qualifying events include, in the case of the employee:

- Termination of employment (except in cases of gross misconduct)
- A reduction in hours

In the case of a spouse or eligible dependent, in addition to the events noted above, qualifying events include:

- The death of the employee
- Divorce or legal separation of the employee and his or her spouse
- The employee's becoming entitled to Medicare

In the case of a dependent child, the loss of dependent status constitutes the qualifying event.

Retirees who are receiving health benefits due to their previous employment may be entitled to COBRA coverage if their coverage is terminated due to the employer's filing for bankruptcy under federal law.

Employees who elect COBRA continuation coverage may continue to participate in the employer's group plan for up to 18 months after they would otherwise lose coverage, longer if they were determined to have been disabled at the time of the qualifying event. Eligible spouses and dependents may elect the same 18 months of continued coverage, or as much as 36 months, if their loss of coverage was due to a qualifying event other than the employee's termination or reduction in hours.

These maximum continuation periods may be cut short if the qualifying individual secures coverage elsewhere (through a subsequent employer, for example), provided that coverage does not have any preexisting limitations or exclusions that apply to him or her. More significantly for seniors, rights to remain in the employer's plan under COBRA terminate when the senior becomes covered under Medicare. Certain other events, such as if the employer ceases to provide health benefits, can also end coverage.

COBRA continuation coverage is not free. Individuals who take advantage of it must pay the full cost of the coverage, plus a small administrative fee. This is more than just the portion of the premium that the employee was required to pay while an active employee. Generally this cost is less than that of an individual policy, however. If the premium is not paid on time, the individual loses his or her right to continue coverage.

One reason that it might make sense to continue coverage is if the employee or an eligible dependent is receiving treatment for an illness or injury at the time coverage would otherwise end. Such a condition might be subject to a preexisting condition exclusion or limitation in a subsequent health plan, which specifies that such conditions will not be covered for an initial period, usually six months or one year.

Employers are required to provide notices to all employees and their spouses of their rights under COBRA when they are hired. Many may have received explanations in 1986 when the law took effect. Notices are also required when the employee or his or her dependent loses coverage due to one of the events described above. This notice gives important information about when the affected individuals must let the employer know that they wish to purchase COBRA coverage, when the premium payments are due, and how much the coverage will cost. The right to purchase coverage is individual. For example, an employee's spouse might elect coverage even if the employee does not.

Coverage under the employer's plan must be provided on the same terms as that for active employees. If the employer changes insurance companies, the COBRA beneficiary makes the change along with the active employees.

Conversion Privilege

A conversion privilege is the right to convert from a group health insurance policy to an individual policy with the same basic features. A state's insurance law may require insurance companies doing business in its jurisdiction to provide this option in all group health insurance contracts. As mentioned above, these are generally more expensive than group policies.

Medigap Policies

"Medigap" insurance refers to policies that are specifically designed to cover health care expenses not covered by Medicare. They are marketed and operated by private insurance companies, not federal or state governments. A policy that claims to be "approved" by the state insurance commission merely meets minimum requirements under the law. It is not endorsed by the commission.

All Medigap policies are not created equal, but they are required by federal law to meet certain minimum standards. Such policies are also subject to regulation by state insurance commissions. In 1990 the National Association of Insurance

Commissioners (NAIC) recommended standards that were incorporated into federal law and became effective in mid-1992.

MINIMUM FEDERAL STANDARDS

Under federal law, insurance companies may only call a policy "Medigap" if it is one of ten standard types designated by the letters A through J by the NAIC. The cost of such policies will vary depending upon the features of coverage, as well as a variety of factors such as the region of the country in which the senior lives, his or her age, and the underwriting policies of the particular insurer.

All ten standard policies pay Medicare Part A coinsurance, all additional charges for up to a full year of hospitalization, and the coinsurance for Part B medical and outpatient services. All but the bare-bones plans pay Medicare's coinsurance for skilled nursing care. From that point, the plans diverge; some pay Part A or B deductibles, others pay for certain types of preventive medical care, prescription drugs up to an annual cap, excess charges under Part B, and home care after a hospital stay.

Other consumer protections are also built into federal law:

1. Medigap agents are required to inform consumers that they may be eligible for Medicaid and are prohibited from selling duplicate coverages.

2. No insurance company may deny coverage to seniors who apply within the six months following their enrollment in Medicare Part B, although a company may impose waiting periods for coverage of certain medical conditions.

3. Medigap policies must be guaranteed renewable, although the insurance company may raise its rates.

4. If a senior is moving from one policy to another and the coverages are essentially the same, the replacement policy must waive any waiting periods.

5. Insurance companies must pay out at least 65 cents of every premium dollar they collect.

The law endeavors to protect consumers by allowing them to cancel policies within 10 days of the time the policy is purchased through an agent, and within 30 days when it is purchased by mail. It also penalizes insurance companies and agents for deceptive sales practices. Agents are required to provide disclosure materials to would-be purchasers. One describes the coverage being purchased. The other, called a "Notice to Applicant Regarding Replacement Insurance," must be provided to an individual replacing one policy with another. This document must be signed by the policy purchaser.

Criminal penalties apply for failing to comply with the federal law regulating Medigap policies. Therefore, seniors who encounter illegal policies or marketing tactics should contact the local U.S. Attorney's office.

POLICIES DIFFER

Even with the new federal law, there are obviously still considerable differences among Medigap policies. Seniors should read carefully the policy contracts and question the agent about the terms of individual policies. Within the limits of the law, the terms of the policy will control what benefits are paid.

Policies are marketed on a group or an individual basis. Group policies are usually less expensive.

Whether a senior has a group or individual policy, it is important to answer all medical questions completely and accurately. A senior should not do business with an agent who advises him or her to misrepresent facts on the application. Information that is incomplete or false can lead to claims being denied or to a termination of the policy altogether.

Disputes that arise under such policies should be brought to the consumer affairs office at the state insurance commission. Generally, staff from this office will investigate complaints and seek a resolution with the insurance company.

Long-Term Care Insurance

Long-term care insurance is an emerging product for insurance companies. In contrast to more traditional health insurance, long-term care insurance is not eligible for special tax benefits to employers as "health insurance." This has slowed its growth, as has a general confusion among insurers as to the appropriate cost of such insurance. Some larger employers have begun to offer group long-term care insurance to their employees in concert with reductions in retiree medical plans.

A long-term care insurance policy is designed to assist the insured senior in meeting the costs of long-term custodial, unskilled, or home health care. Because of the chaotic state of the insurance market, it is difficult to generalize about terms. A careful reading of the terms of the contract is extremely important.

Typically, the coverage provision (sometimes called a gatekeeper provision) is triggered by a certification by the senior's physician that he or she is disabled, a period of hospitalization or confinement to a skilled nursing facility, or by the inability of a senior to perform everyday tasks such as bathing, dressing, eating and so on. Coverage depends upon the policy provisions.

Once coverage begins, these policies typically provide a benefit based on a flat dollar amount per day of covered expenses. Some policies include inflation protection; many do not. Expenses covered by long-term care policies are not uniform, either. Some policies pay both unskilled nursing home and home care expenses, but many do not cover home care.

Seniors who are considering such policies will doubtless be asked questions concerning their health histories. Insurance companies may seek to weed out high-risk clients or merely to identify the risk they are taking on. Generally seniors with bad health histories (chronic heart disease or Alzheimer's disease, for example) will find it more difficult to secure coverage or will only be offered coverage at higher premium rates. Notwithstanding, it is imperative that they answer health questions truthfully since failure to do so can result in a denial of claims at a later date.

In reviewing and comparing policies, seniors should pay close attention to the points noted above, and to the following:

- Premium rates and whether and by what amount they may increase from year to year
- Any "vesting" in benefits after a period of premium payments
- Any waiting period for benefits

- A waiver of premium payments while confined in a nursing home

- Any exclusions of particular illnesses (such as Alzheimer's disease) or of preexisting conditions

- Whether the insured can purchase additional coverage at a later date and on what terms

- Whether the policy is renewable unconditionally

- The financial health of the insurance company

A senior who has a problem in securing promised benefits under a long-term care policy should contact the insurance commissioner in his or her state. Such policies are required to be approved by the commissioner before they can be offered for sale.

Finally, if a senior qualifies for Medicaid (or, with estate planning or financial counseling, could qualify), purchase of long-term care insurance may not be cost effective. Medicaid pays for long-term care. However, long-term care insurance benefits can provide a senior with more options concerning facilities and services.

Chapter 5

Issues in Housing

Basics

- The landlord-tenant relationship is regulated by state and local governments.

- For many Americans home ownership is a symbol of security. In later years it also usually represents the individual's single largest asset.

- A 1989 American Association of Retired Persons survey of 1,500 seniors found that 86 percent wished to remain in their homes as long as possible.

- Home equity conversions allow the owner to tap into the equity locked up in the value of that asset while remaining in the home.

- In 1987, $13.2 billion was spent by the federal government on various kinds of housing assistance.

- Through Section 202 of the Housing Act of 1937 the federal Housing and Urban Development department (HUD) provides direct loans to nonprofit sponsors to help them create new housing for the elderly or disabled with low incomes.

- The Section 8 program, also part of the Housing Act, provides direct payments to landlords of eligible individuals.

- Under the housing voucher program, local offices of the Public Housing Administration (PHA) issue a voucher to lower-income people equal to the difference between 30 percent of a family's adjusted income and the local "fair market rent" for households of that size.

Introduction

Securing adequate shelter has long been one of the most important goals of human beings. This simple fact does not change once one attains older ages, but the issues surrounding it often do. Individuals whose responsibilities have included providing housing for children now have different needs. Those receiving or anticipating fixed incomes must ensure their ability to maintain acceptable housing arrangements for the rest of their lives.

The choices are daunting. They range from remaining in one's present home, to moving into a smaller place as either an owner or a tenant, to relocating to a retirement or life care community setting that is tailored toward the needs of older adults. Those needing financial assistance face the further obstacle of inadequate funding. Although more than 40 percent of households receiving housing assistance are senior households, nearly one-half of eligible seniors receive no assistance due to inadequate funds.

This chapter will examine four issues in housing. First, it will provide a brief overview of the relationship between landlords and tenants. Next, it will examine home equity conversions. Third, it will consider condominiums and cooperatives as alternative forms of ownership. The final section will review the various housing assistance programs available to older adults.

Landlords and Tenants

The Lease

Although there are federal laws and programs regulating housing (most notably, the Fair Housing Act of 1968), there is no comprehensive federal law regulating the relationship between landlords and tenants. The landlord-tenant relationship is regulated by state and local governments, and so it varies from one town or city to another. Provisions in certain jurisdictions may be more favorable to a tenant or landlord, so it is a good idea to contact your local housing authority or a legal advisor for the specifics. Nevertheless, there are certain strains that run through most of these laws.

The terms of any rental housing relationship are generally governed by a lease, which is simply a contract between the landlord and tenant that identifies the duties and responsibilities of each. The landlord generally agrees to furnish the tenant with sole possession of the leased property in a livable condition for the period of time covered by the lease in exchange for payment of rent and a reciprocal promise by the tenant to do, or refrain from doing, certain things with that property. For example, many leases will require that the tenant maintain the property. Others may prohibit the tenant from operating a business out of the rental property.

At a minimum, the lease should specify the parties involved in the lease, the length of the lease, and the amount and due dates of rental payments. Needless to say, the lease should also specifically identify the property that is the subject of the agreement. It commonly includes other terms defining the landlord's obligations (usually briefly) and the tenant's responsibilities (at great length). Commonly included are provisions describing termination of the lease, late charges, and restrictions on use of the property such as subletting, pets, and even guests.

Customarily a lease is in writing, although it need not be in most places if the term is less than one year. If a lease is not in writing, however, the terms of the lease are susceptible to misunderstanding and/or frequent changes. Where possible, it is best to have a written lease.

The terms in the lease govern the rental relationship unless a particular provision is prohibited by law. Many local laws concern the safety and "habitability" of the leased property. Landlords are required to maintain the dwelling in a livable condition. For example, an apartment lacking working plumbing generally is not considered habitable. On the other hand, a dripping faucet would not render a dwelling uninhabitable. Other terms pertain to the contractual rights between the landlord and the tenant. For example, in some cities, rent control laws limit increases in rent.

A lease is an important legal document, and it should be read carefully and fully understood before it is signed. Breaking a lease may result in serious financial repercussions including eviction or loss of a portion of the security deposit. Although the prospective tenant may be presented with a preprinted form that seems unchangeable, many terms are negotiable. Whatever terms are changed should be clearly noted on the lease *before* the document is signed.

Disputes

Even with the best lease, disputes often arise between landlords and their tenants. Most often they concern maintenance of the leased property, a change in the terms, or the termination of the lease. While it is not necessary, it may be prudent to consult an attorney or legal advisor concerning the applicable law. Local housing commissions or small claims courts are sometimes available when the parties cannot resolve their differences between themselves. Other resources may be available in certain jurisdictions including government- or court-sponsored mediation or conciliation programs.

The tenant's first weapon in a dispute is the rent payments, and in certain circumstances it is permissible for a tenant to withhold rent. For example, if the leased property is not livable because of lack of heat, a tenant can sometimes withhold rent or deduct a portion of the rent. However, because the failure to pay rent could result in the eviction of the tenant for failure to comply with the lease, a tenant would be well-advised to consult an attorney or other legal advisor before taking such action.

Life Care Communities

A life care community is a housing option that is being marketed to middle- and upper-income seniors. At its best it is a retirement community with a continuing care component. It offers residents the flexibility between private residential living and necessary assistance with daily living and health care.

Each senior enters into a contract with the facility owner (typically a charitable organization). This contract provides that the individual will have a right to reside in the life care community for a stated period. Usually the resident may remain in his or her designated unit for life, unless his or her health dictates a need to move to a supervised or care setting. Residents do not own their dwellings (a townhouse or apartment), but have a contractual right to reside in it. They have a further right to call upon other graduated care facilities within the community—from mere custodial, often up to and including skilled nursing care.

Seniors who join a life care community typically pay an entry fee plus a continuing monthly fee. The entry, or "founder's," fee may be based upon the age and health of the applicant. The monthly fee (also called an accommodation fee) is generally designed to cover increases in operating costs due to inflation. In some states, the life care community sponsor is entitled to require residents to transfer title to all their assets to the community. This practice has been banned in some states. At a resident's death, any property that is transferred remains the property of the community.

The contract that residents sign governs their relationship with the life care community sponsor. For example, typically residents assign the right to receive Medicare reimbursements to the life care community operator. If a resident leaves a life care community, the operator is usually entitled to damages. This means that the senior may not get a full refund of the entry fee. The life care community operator may be entitled to deduct a prorated or fixed amount from the entry fee. It is very important to read carefully all of the terms of the contract, and it may help to have legal counsel in order to ensure that the terms in the contract comply with the law.

These types of facilities are heavily regulated by state laws designed to ensure their solvency and residents' rights. A state may limit monthly fees (or increases in them) and require minimum financial reserves and periodic financial reports before issuing an operating license.

Home Equity Conversions

For many Americans home ownership is a symbol of security. In later years it also represents the individual's single largest asset. Home equity conversions allow the owner to tap into the equity locked up in the value of that asset while ensuring to some degree that he or she will continue to live in the home. The arrangements come in many different shapes and sizes, but they all come down to three basic types: loan, sale, and deferral programs. The availability of such arrangements is governed by state law and the condition of the real estate market.

Loans

Home equity conversion loan programs are also known as "reverse mortgages" or rising-debt loans. In a conventional mortgage, the mortgagee (the person taking out the mortgage) borrows a sum of money up front, putting up the property being purchased as collateral. The same is true in the reverse mortgage. The twist is that the bank or lending institution agrees to make payments to the homeowner over a period of time, rather than all at one time. At some future date (usually when the house is sold) the lender is entitled to repayment of the loan, plus interest.

These loans are categorized by their payout provisions. Term reverse mortgages provide income for a specified period of time. The repayment date is likewise fixed. The mortgagee must repay the loan from other assets or sell the home. If the receipts from the sale of the property exceed the amount to be repaid, the mortgagee usually retains the excess.

A so-called split-term reverse mortgage also provides a fixed payment schedule. In contrast to a simple term reverse mortgage, however, repayment of the loan occurs when the borrower moves from the property, at its sale, or upon the death of the mortgagee. Thus, in addition to income, the mortgagee has the further security of rights to continue to live in his or her home. The mortgagee, or his estate, is generally entitled to all proceeds from the sale of the property in excess of the loan amount. This is not the case where such a loan contains a "shared appreciation" clause. Such a provision provides that the lender is entitled to all or a portion of the appreciation in the market value of the property from the time the loan is made.

Another version of the home equity loan is a line of credit. The lender agrees to loan up to a stated sum, but the borrower determines the time at which the payments are made. This is the most flexible option. It allows the borrower to take the loan (and incur interest) at the time and in the amounts that it is needed.

A reverse annuity mortgage (RAM) is yet another variation on the home equity conversion theme. The proceeds of the loan are advanced up front to purchase an annuity contract from an insurance company. This annuity contract provides regular income to the mortgagee. Like the split term loan, repayment is delayed to some stated event such as the relocation or death of the borrower, or the sale of the property.

The terms of any home equity conversion loan are determined by the promissory note that the borrower and the lending institution sign. It will state important terms, such as:

- Loan origination fees and other "front-end" charges

- The interest rate that will be charged and how it will be calculated

- The payment schedule and whether the borrower may take any larger payments

- The amount of each payment and any scheduled cost-of-living adjustments

- The repayment date or events

It is very important to carefully read all of the documents that the lending institution provides, *especially* documents that the borrower is asked to sign. The lending institution will be entitled at some point to force a sale of the property subject to the mortgage to repay the loan.

AVAILABILITY

A measure of the success of home equity loans is the fact that the Federal Housing Authority (FHA) moved to extend its program in the spring of 1991. As a result of this action, it is projected that more lenders will make this sort of loan. Home equity conversion loans are unfortunately not widely available. Only a few banks, savings and loans, state housing finance agencies, and mortgage companies offer them. Applicants must own their home (shares in a cooperative are not eligible) and must meet age minimums (generally 62 or over). Some plans also have income limitations.

ADVANTAGES AND DISADVANTAGES OF HOME EQUITY CONVERSION LOANS

The principal advantage of home equity conversion loans is that they give homeowners a chance to use the equity built up in their homes without selling the home. Payments that the borrower receives are not taxable and do not affect Social Security or Medicare benefits. Supplemental Security Income (SSI) payments may not be affected if the borrower spends the entire home equity conversion payment within the month it is received. The same is true for Medicaid eligibility in most states.

The principal advantage, however, is also a disadvantage. All home equity conversion loans use up some or all of the equity in the borrower's home. This means that less is left for the borrower to pass on to heirs. If the loan is the type that comes due while the borrower is still living in the home, he or she may be forced to sell the home and move.

Sales

Home equity conversion sales transactions differ from loan transactions in that the homeowner actually sells his or her home. As part of the sale, however, the buyer makes guarantees to the seller about continuing income and residency during the seller's lifetime.

The sale/leaseback transaction is by far the most common home equity conversion sale plan. In it, the homeowner sells his or her home to an investor who in turn gives the homeowner a lease for a specified period of time or life. The purchase price is discounted to reflect the fact that the new owner may not occupy the property or sell it out from under the former owner (now tenant) during that time. The new owner assumes all of the responsibilities of ownership—payment of taxes, insurance, and maintenance—and all of the tax benefits of owning a property for investment.

The purchase price is paid in such a way as to guarantee income to the seller for an agreed-upon period or for the rest of the seller's life. The buyer may be obliged to purchase an annuity for the seller. Alternatively, the seller may "finance" all or part of the sale, that is to say, the seller may loan the buyer the money to buy the home. The buyer then makes monthly payments directly to the seller after deducting the seller's rent. These payments, like any other loan payment are in part principal, and in part interest income. It all depends on the deal negotiated between the parties.

Sale/leaseback transactions are extremely complicated. They must be structured carefully to meet federal tax laws and to ensure that the homeowner is assured of his or her future occupancy rights. Depending upon the structure of the arrangement, a number of legal documents may be required including:

- A sale/leaseback agreement

- Secured promissory note

- Deed of trust

- Lease

- Memorandum of lease and deed of trust detailing the buyer's ongoing obligations to the seller

ADVANTAGES AND DISADVANTAGES OF SALE/LEASEBACKS

The advantages of a sale/leaseback can be quite substantial for the seller, particularly to a homeowner who does not want to borrow against his or her home. Properly structured, the transaction can ensure that the seller will be able to continue to live in his or her home for life. Any future increases in maintaining the home or decreases in the value of the home pose no risk to the seller. A sale/leaseback transaction can allow the seller to take advantage of the one-time exclusion on $125,000 of capital gains from the sale of the residence. (See Chapter 3, page 55.)

The disadvantage of a sale/leaseback transaction consists in its complexity. If the legal documents are insufficient, they may jeopardize the seller's eligibility for tax benefits such as property tax relief or the exclusion of Social Security benefits from taxation, or eligibility for public benefits such as SSI or Medicaid. In addition, the seller is now a tenant, with all of the potential inconveniences of that status.

Life Estates

Another home equity conversion sale is the life estate option. In this transaction the only thing that the homeowner actually sells *is* the right to ownership of the property after his or her death. Ownership remains with the homeowner for life. This is called a "life estate," and the seller buys a "remainder interest." Sales of this kind are not eligible for the same tax advantages as a straightforward sale of the property. Accordingly, these types of transactions are most often entered into with nonprofit organizations such as hospitals and universities.

ADVANTAGES AND DISADVANTAGES OF LIFE ESTATES

The major advantage of this type of transaction is that the homeowner retains ownership of the property along with whatever tax benefits and security that offers. The disadvantages are several. First, the income from the sale of the remainder interest is generally not high. Second, the homeowner generally remains responsible for taxes and maintenance but does not benefit from any future appreciation in the property.

Deferral Arrangements

The benefits of home equity conversion deferral arrangements are limited in both amount and purpose. In exchange for a lien on the property, the lender makes a loan for a specific purpose— necessary repairs, weatherization, or renovations to the borrower's home. The lender is a nonprofit or public agency. Notes generally bear little or no interest and repayment is not required until the death of the borrower or sale of the property.

Another type of deferral arrangement is property tax deferral, available in about one-third of the states. These are discussed in Chapter 3.

Condominiums and Cooperatives

Rather than operate large rental facilities, real estate developers in recent years have increasingly experimented with different forms of ownership: condominiums and cooperatives. Many factors should be considered in purchasing a home in such a development—and not all of them are legal.

Condominiums

Often people are attracted to condominiums because someone else will do the yard work. But much more is involved when one lives in a condominium. The term refers to a development where the individual has purchased his or her individual dwelling, as well as an undivided interest in all of the common area. Depending upon the facility the common area may consist of anything from the hallways and exterior walls and roof of the buildings to parking lots, pools, and recreation areas. Although the earliest condominiums were commonly apartments or townhouses, more recently other types of residential units have joined the condo market in some areas.

A condominium owner is subject to the terms of the condominium declaration establishing the condominium and the condominium bylaws. These documents together are the "constitution" of the condominium development. They create a "government" for the condominium consisting of a board of directors. They set forth basic rules about management of the condominium association and use of the common areas. These documents also generally restrict the condominium owner's actions even with respect to his or her own unit. For example, some condominiums restrict occupants—or even long-term guests—below certain ages. When an individual purchases a unit, he or she must also agree to abide by these restrictions.

A board of directors is usually elected by unit owners to oversee the common areas. They may perform management functions themselves or contract with a professional management company. In either case, any maintenance, improvements, or services performed in the common areas are funded by common charges or fees paid by the unit owners. Payment of the common charges is one of the obligations that a condominium purchaser assumes in buying a unit.

TO BUY OR NOT TO BUY

Anyone considering purchasing a condominium should read several documents carefully:

- The condominium declaration
- The bylaws
- Any rules or regulations issued by the board of directors (in an established development)

If the development is several years old, a prospective buyer might also review the financial records to see whether and how much common charges have risen in recent years, or whether any special assessments have been made. It is advisable to check annual statements of the association to determine what reserves have been established for long-term maintenance such as septic systems, and rehabilitation of units. As in any purchase of real estate, it is advisable to secure legal advice to review the documents and guide the buyer through the transaction.

CONVERSIONS

Of course, condominiums are not for everyone, and occasionally a facility that was previously operated as a rental property will be "converted" to condominiums by the landlord. Such conversions can be disruptive to longtime tenants.

A tenant faced with a proposal to convert to condominiums should first look at the lease to determine if it contains any provisions concerning conversions. The lease may give the tenant a "right of first refusal" with respect to the unit he or she occupies. This means that they must be given the opportunity to purchase it before the landlord offers it for sale to anyone else. Sometimes the purchase price offered to insiders is less than the price that will be asked of new purchasers. Needless to say, the tenant must carefully consider the same documents as noted above, as well as the financial projections.

The tenant should also study state and local statutes concerning condominium conversions. Several cities and states provide protective statutes that control the manner in which a landlord converts rental property. These statutes are designed to curb displacement of long-term and older tenants. At a minimum they may provide additional rights regarding the notice of conversion and the time period in which the tenant must purchase or relocate.

For example, in New Jersey a tenant has the following rights:

1. To be the exclusive potential buyer of the property for 90 days.

2. To receive three years' notice of eviction because of the conversion.

3. To request that the landlord find him or her comparable housing.

4. To petition a state court for one-year stays of the eviction (up to a maximum of five).

In addition, the New Jersey law provides that certain tenants aged 62 or older may not be evicted at all due to a condominium conversion.

Cooperatives

Cooperatives are yet another form of alternative home ownership. In a cooperative an individual does not own any real property, but a share (or shares) of the stock of a corporation that owns the property. That share of stock entitles the owner to occupy one of the units (customarily apartments).

The cooperative corporation must be established under state law, and empowered to own real estate. Like the condominium association, the corporation establishes bylaws and a board of directors to govern the cooperative. Individuals buying shares in the cooperative sign an occupancy agreement in which they agree to pay a one-time membership fee plus monthly charges.

One of the major differences among cooperatives is the manner in which equity is built up and allocated to individual members. In market equity cooperatives, a departing member is entitled to sell his share in the cooperative at whatever price it will fetch on the market. In a limited equity cooperative, by contrast, the member's asking price is determined by reference to the original purchase price plus a predetermined portion of equity appreciation. In a fixed equity cooperative, the member's share must be sold at the member's purchase price. The latter two types of cooperatives are designed to preserve membership in the cooperative for middle- and lower-income individuals.

Housing Assistance Programs

Housing assistance programs operated by local, state, and federal governments take many forms. As discussed in Chapter 3, some states provide assistance by reducing the older person's property taxes, or by subsidizing weatherization improvements or energy use. Other programs are designed to make rental housing more affordable whether by encouraging developers to create affordable housing through low-interest loans or by providing direct rent subsidies.

At the federal level these programs are administered principally by the department of Housing and Urban Development (HUD). The Farmers Home Administration (FmHA) operates programs that in many ways parallel those administered by HUD. HUD accomplishes its task by contracting with local public housing authorities (PHAs). The PHAs in turn perform most of the day-to-day operations.

There are two major housing assistance programs for the elderly or disabled that are operated by HUD through the local PHAs: Section 202 housing and Section 8 rental assistance.

Section 202 Housing

Through Section 202 of the Housing Act of 1937, HUD provides direct loans to nonprofit sponsors to aid them in creating new housing for lower-income persons who are elderly or disabled. In theory the developer is able to offer the housing at more affordable rents. Because the program no longer provides subsidized interest rates, benefits tend to flow to moderate- rather than lower-income elderly. Rent charged at facilities funded under Section 202 may not exceed 30 percent of the resident's annual income. Unfortunately, low funding levels have led to long waiting lists for such units.

Section 8 Rental Subsidies and the Housing Voucher Program

The Section 8 program provides direct payments to landlords of eligible individuals, effectively lowering the rent they must pay out of their own resources. It provides assistance for existing housing as well as new construction or substantial or moderate rehabilitation.

Participants in the program pay rent equal to the greater of:

- 30 percent of their monthly adjusted income

- 10 percent of their gross income minus deductions

- If they receive public assistance, the housing allowance under that program

The program is administered locally by PHAs.

Almost all income is taken into account in determining whether the applicant meets the income restrictions. However, there are exclusions:

- Income from household members under age 18

- Foster care payments

- Lump sum additions to assets such as inheritances, or insurance payments (see below for assets exceeding $5,000)

- Medical insurance reimbursements

- Income of a live-in aide

- Scholarships

- Military hazardous duty pay

- Certain government benefits specifically excluded by federal statute

- Temporary, nonrecurring, or sporadic income (as in the case of gifts)

Assets of less than $5,000 are disregarded. If assets exceed $5,000, then 10 percent of the value of the assets is added to the countable income.

Adjusted income is determined by subtracting certain allowances from the gross income. In the case of older applicants, the relevant exclusions are:

- $480 for each dependent

- $400 for a family in which a member is over age 62 or disabled

- Any medical expenses totalling over 3 percent of the household's gross income as determined above

- If there is a disabled member in the household, any "handicapped assistance expenses" that total more than 3 percent of the household's gross income plus all medical expenses or combined medical and "handicapped assistance expenses" that exceed the 3 percent

- Child care expenses, or in the case of families assisted by Indian housing authorities, the greater of child care expenses or excessive travel expenses up to $25 per week

Compliance with the income limitations is recertified annually.

Under the existing housing program, once the household completes an application and is approved, the PHA issues a certificate of family participation. The individual then has 60 days to find an open unit eligible for Section 8 payments. An additional 60-day extension may be granted if the household is unable to find an acceptable unit.

In order to qualify, the rent for the unit generally must not exceed the fair market rent determined by the PHA. Fair market rent includes utilities except for telephone. The property and lease between the participant and the landlord must also be approved by the PHA.

HOUSING VOUCHER PROGRAM

A permutation of the Section 8 program is the so-called housing voucher program. This program was a Reagan administration initiative designed to "privatize" housing assistance. Once the applicant satisfies income restrictions the PHA issues a voucher to him or her equal to the difference between 30 percent of the participant's adjusted income and the local "fair market rent" for households of that size. As under the Section 8 program, the participant has 60 days to find suitable housing (plus a 60-day extension if the senior is unable to find an acceptable unit).

However, unlike Section 8, the individual is then free to select whatever housing he or she can find. If the housing is below the "fair market rent" the individual might pay less than 30 percent of his or her income. Conversely, if the rent is higher, the individual would pay a proportionately larger share.

For example, consider an older couple with an adjusted income of $400 per month. If the fair market rent is considered to be $500, the housing assistance award will be the standard amount ($500) minus 30 percent of their adjusted income ($120), or $380.

APPEALS OF ADVERSE DETERMINATIONS

Families receiving Section 8 assistance or housing vouchers are required to supply information, as required by the PHA, while receiving benefits under the program. In addition, they must allow inspections of the rental property. They may not sublease the unit or use it for any purpose other than as a residence. Participants must advise the PHA if they receive any redundant housing assistance. Failure to comply with these and other terms as imposed by the PHA, or perpetration of a fraud to obtain or retain assistance, can result in denial or termination of assistance.

Denial of assistance or of placement on a waiting list, or termination of assistance, generally creates a right to request an informal review by the PHA. The applicant must be given an opportunity at this review to submit written or oral objections to the decision. He or she may be represented by a lawyer. The PHA is required to provide a decision promptly in writing setting forth the reasons for its decision. Even if the hearing officer makes a determination in favor of the applicant, HUD regulations provide that the PHA and HUD will not be bound by decisions that exceed the authority of the hearing officer, or that are contrary to local, state, or federal laws and regulations.

Unfortunately, there are long waiting lists for housing assistance programs. Allocations of available funds are made by HUD to PHAs proportionately. Congress has mandated that assistance be primarily targeted to those with incomes totalling 50 percent or less of the local median income, and secondly to those with incomes equalling 51 to 80 percent of the median. This means that many otherwise qualified individuals will not receive assistance.

Chapter 6

Consumer Issues

Basics

- According to the House Subcommittee on Health and Long-term Care, although seniors account for roughly 12 percent of all consumers, they number 30 percent of victims of consumer fraud.

- Seniors should comparison shop not only among products but also merchants since they will be the first resources in resolving problems later on.

- The Uniform Commercial Code, a model law adopted in substance in all states, gives buyers rights that don't always appear in the contract. They may add to or even replace particular contract terms.

- A federal law called the Magnuson-Moss Warranty Act regulates warranties given by manufacturers to consumers.

- Both state and federal laws prohibit the use of deceptive acts or practices in the sale of goods and services. The federal law is enforced mostly by the Federal Trade Commission.

- In mediation or arbitration of a trade dispute a third party intervenes between the consumer and the merchant or service provider to try to reach a resolution. While the mediator cannot impose a resolution, an arbitrator typically can.

- A person making a claim in small claims court need not have legal representation. In fact, in most jurisdictions neither party is allowed to bring in a lawyer.

- The Equal Credit Opportunity Act prohibits discrimination in credit-granting based on age.

- Personal bankruptcy is an extreme step. It is a formidable bar to claims by most creditors, but it should be a senior's last resort since it will seriously affect the senior's ability to get any credit for at least a decade.

Introduction

The term *consumerism* came into vogue in the 1970s. Early advocates were concerned about access to information about product safety and performance as well as delivery on the goods and services promised. The fight goes on in the 1990s and seniors are in the front lines.

According to the American Association of Retired Persons, seniors are at a disadvantage in today's marketplace for several reasons. Seniors tend to engage in less comparative shopping and make less informed choices than younger consumers. They are also less likely to recognize unfair or deceptive marketing practices. Finally, seniors are less likely to take effective steps to remedy their complaints. These observations are borne out by a statistic cited by the House Subcommittee on Health and Long-term Care, that although seniors account for roughly 12 percent of all consumers, they number 30 percent of victims of consumer fraud.

Many of the consumer issues of special concern to seniors have been considered elsewhere in this book. Medigap and long-term care insurance policies, life care communities, and the like are discussed in Chapters 4 and 5. The reader should refer to those sections for a complete discussion. What follows is a consideration first of basic principles of good consumerism and the remedies available when things don't work out. This discussion is followed by areas that especially concern seniors. The second section concerns the availability of consumer credit and a brief discussion of personal bankruptcy laws.

Be a Smart Consumer

No discussion of consumer remedies should begin without touching on the elements of good consumerism. By avoiding problems at the outset through an inappropriate or unwise purchase, a senior can save him or herself the frustration of lost time and energy.

Research the Purchase

Seniors, along with all consumers, should look carefully before they leap into any purchase. Comparison shopping can save a senior from a "bargain" that simply doesn't exist. Consumer advocates across the country advise us that if a price seems too good to be true, it probably is, but a senior can't be sure until he or she has compared the product to others on the market.

In some cases, seniors may be able to consult consumer publications that compare products. *Consumer Reports* is a monthly magazine that contains reports about products as diverse as video recorders and long-term care insurance. Their reports are also available on the Prodigy™ online database. Where such publications are unavailable or not helpful, it is wise to go to several different merchants, if possible, to get their views on different products. It might be helpful to keep notes of these conversations. Seniors should also ask their friends who have purchased the same or similar products recently for their views.

Comparison shopping should go beyond products and include merchants as well, since they are the ones to turn to first if a product turns out to be inadequate or defective. In the case of purchases of services, this is particularly important. Community resources such as local Better Business Bureaus, chambers of commerce, and consumer action groups monitor complaints about businesses in the community. They may provide information about the reputation of a particular shop or office.

Analyze Advertisements

Often with advertising, it's what is not said rather than what is said that is important. Advertisers play on wishes, hopes, and fears to get consumers to buy their products or services without much thought. A prudent consumer should step back from the emotional or psychological elements of the advertisement and defuse such appeals. If the advertisement says the product is "better," for example, consumers should ask "than what?"

A healthy skepticism about the truth of any advertiser's claim—even for those involving charities—will be the safest consumer route.

Read the Contract or Warranty

Once the senior has researched the purchase it is extremely important that he or she carefully read the contract and any associated warranties, guarantees, and other materials carefully. In each state, the legislatures and courts have created a law of contracts that regulates transactions between businesses and individuals. Federal laws apply as well. One of the common elements of all of these laws is the contract between the business and the consumer. The contract of sale provides the starting point for any analysis of the agreement between a business and a consumer.

A senior should understand every term in the contract before signing it. He or she should also read any warranty before making the purchase. Two important questions every senior should ask himself or herself are whether the contract or warranty contains all of the terms that the salesperson has claimed, and whether the contract or warranty contains different terms than the salesperson mentioned.

If something is missing or conflicting with the senior's understanding, he or she should ask the business to modify the document and initial the change. For example, if the salesperson has said that the product may be returned for any reason for up to 30 days, but the contract says 14, the contract should be modified to reflect the 30-day policy. Likewise, if a written warranty says it is good for 90 days, but the salesperson has said one year, the senior should clarify the terms of the sale in writing.

The contract, however, is only the beginning point for analysis. Many state and federal consumer laws provide additional rights to consumers that don't necessarily appear in the contract. Chief among these are the Uniform Commercial

Code (more commonly known as the UCC), the Magnuson-Moss Warranties Act, and state and federal unfair or deceptive acts or practices laws (sometimes called UDAP laws).

THE UNIFORM COMMERCIAL CODE

The UCC gives buyers rights that don't always appear in the contract. They may add to or even replace particular contract terms. The UCC has been the model for state consumer laws across the country. It establishes three major types of warranties or "guarantees": express warranty, implied warranty of merchantability, and implied warranty of fitness for a particular purpose. In the context of the average consumer, interpretations of this law heavily favor the consumer over the seller.

An express warranty can be almost any written or oral representation about the quality of the product. The implied warranty of merchantability means that the product must be at least reasonably suitable for its normal use. The implied warranty of fitness for a particular purpose applies when the consumer has relied on the merchant to choose a product suitable for the consumer's need. In that case, the law gives the consumer special rights if the product later proves inappropriate.

Merchants and manufacturers can try to prevent consumers from acquiring rights under implied warranties by putting disclaimers in a contract. Depending upon the state law, however, disclaimers may not protect these companies.

MAGNUSON-MOSS WARRANTY ACT

A federal law called the Magnuson-Moss Warranty Act (or the Federal Trade Comission Improvement Act of 1975) regulates warranties given by manufacturers to consumers. It also applies to service contracts (sometimes called "extended warranty" or "breakdown insurance"), unless those contracts are regulated by state insurance laws.

The Magnuson-Moss Warranty Act requires that product warranties meet certain minimum requirements. They must be available prior to sale, and be clear and understandable. If a manufacturer offers a warranty, it cannot disclaim the implied warranties arising under the state's UCC law (see above).

Warranties must be labeled as either "full" or "limited." In order to qualify as a full warranty, it must meet the following requirements:

1. It cannot restrict the warranty rights of a subsequent owner during its stated duration.

2. It must promise to remedy defects within a reasonable time without charge.

3. It cannot limit the duration of any implied warranty.

4. It cannot limit consequential damages unless such exclusion or limitation conspicuously appears on the face of the warranty.

5. It must permit the consumer to elect a refund or replacement of the defective product or part after a reasonable number of attempts to fix the problem.

6. In most cases, the consumer has no duty under the warranty other than notification of the defect.

As a result of these stringent requirements, consumers find far fewer "full" than "limited" warranties.

UNFAIR OR DECEPTIVE ACTS OR PRACTICES (UDAP) ACTS

Both state and federal laws prohibit the use of deceptive acts or practices in the sale of goods and services. The Federal Trade Commission enforces many of the federal cases. In the UDAP statutes, the term "deceptive" is used broadly to mean any act that might mislead the consumer. There is generally no requirement to prove that the seller acted in bad faith. Ambiguous though literally true statements can be subject to censure under UDAP statutes.

Save Receipts and Warranties

Once the purchase is made, it is a good idea to keep a file of the pertinent documents to the sale: the sales receipt, charge slip, any contract, and warranties and guarantees of any kind, even if they are part of the packaging materials.

Register the Product with the Manufacturer

Consumers should register purchases with the manufacturer if a card is supplied. If a product is recalled for defects or useful improvements or accessories become available, the manufacturer can communicate directly with the consumer. Alternatively, consumers may have to contact the Consumer Product Safety Commission in Washington, D.C., about product recalls.

Use the Product according to Instructions

Finally, seniors should take care to use the product according to its operating instructions. A device that is used for purposes that were not intended can become dangerous, and the company's liability may be limited in these cases.

What To Do If a Problem Develops

Even the best purchases can turn out badly. Although the law provides various rights to consumers, the best first steps are not to the courts but back to the merchant and manufacturer to attempt to resolve the problem. If the salesperson is unable to help, a store manager or customer service representative may be of some assistance. If the problem is not resolved at the location where the senior purchased the product or service, the senior should ask for the name and address of the company owner or an appropriate individual at the corporate headquarters with whom to lodge a complaint.

The senior should keep records of whom he or she has talked to, when they spoke, and exactly what they said or did to resolve the problem. This serves two purposes: to ensure that the senior does not retrace his or her steps, and to demonstrate clearly the steps that a senior has taken.

If informal attempts to resolve the problem are unsuccessful, it may be necessary to draft a formal letter of complaint. A complaint letter should accurately state when and where the product was acquired or the services were performed. The letter should then provide details concerning the consumer's problem and how he or she would like it resolved. The best complaint letters give the merchant, service provider, or manufacturer a stated time period within which to resolve the problem before the senior pursues "other action." Seniors should remember to put their names, addresses, and telephone numbers on their letters.

Consumer Resources

Sometimes informal attempts to resolve consumer problems are unsuccessful. Before steaming ahead to the nearest courthouse, seniors should investigate government and community resources available to assist consumers. In addition, many private, non-profit consumer organizations will assist seniors in resolving problems with goods and services.

Federal Government Agencies

Numerous offices within the federal government can assist consumers. The *Consumer Resource Handbook,* a free publication available from the Consumer Information Center in Pueblo, Colorado, provides a comprehensive listing of these offices and their responsibilities.

There are three agencies that represent most general assistance. They are: the Federal Trade Commission (FTC), the Consumer Product Safety Administration (CPSA) , and the Food and Drug Administration (FDA).

THE FEDERAL TRADE COMMISSION

The FTC has broad responsibilities to consumers. Among its responsibilities are regulation of consumer advertising and warranties, and it issues numerous publications on consumer topics. The main offices of the FTC are located in Washington, D.C., but there are branch offices throughout the country.

THE CONSUMER PRODUCT SAFETY COMMISSION

The Consumer Product Safety Commission is responsible for enforcing federal laws concerning product safety. Consumers may contact the commission to report a hazardous product or a product-related injury, or to inquire about product recalls.

THE FOOD AND DRUG ADMINISTRATION

The FDA regulates advertising of food, drugs, and cosmetics and has been active in the area of health care quackery. It also has publications available to consumers.

A National Resource: The U.S. Postal Service

Although it is commonly mistaken for a government agency, the U.S. Postal Service is not operated by the federal government. It is nonetheless among the resources available nationwide to consumers who experience difficulty when ordering merchandise or conducting business through the mail.

If a senior suspects that he or she has been a victim of fraud or misrepresentation through the use of the mail, he or she should contact the local postmaster or postal inspector. Postage-free consumer service cards for this purpose are available in local post offices or from letter carriers.

Where use of the mail or telephones is involved, federal and state "RICO" claims may be brought against businesses that defraud consumers. RICO, which stands for Racketeer Influenced and Corrupt Organizations, is more commonly associated with prosecutions of organized crime, but it has been used to attack fraudulent business practices.

State and Local Government Agencies

Many states have consumer affairs offices that parallel those in the federal government. In addition, state attorneys general often have broad responsibilities in the consumer area to investigate consumer complaints and file lawsuits against those individuals and businesses engaging in misleading or fraudulent practices.

Media "Hotlines"—Consumer Reporters

Another resource for consumers with a problem are the numerous consumer reporters in the print and (more particularly) the electronic media. Merchants and manufacturers are generally anxious to avoid bad publicity. Sometimes a reporter looking for a story may succeed where the consumer alone has not.

Dispute Resolution

When all else has failed to secure the result the senior wishes, there is still recourse to dispute resolution mechanisms. Many people think immediately of a lawsuit, but this can be a very expensive means of solving a consumer dispute, once one takes into account court and attorney fees. Two alternatives, alternative dispute resolution and small claims court, can meet the need of the individual to reach a satisfactory settlement.

ALTERNATIVE DISPUTE RESOLUTION: ARBITRATION OR MEDIATION

In mediation or arbitration a third party intervenes between the consumer and the merchant or service provider to try to reach a resolution of the dispute. In mediation, the third party acts as a go-between to aid the parties in reaching their own resolution. The mediator has no power to force a settlement. By contrast, in an arbitration, the arbitrator does have the power to decide the terms of a resolution between the parties.

Some local governments fund alternative dispute resolution clinics. Most typically, the availability of services is limited to certain types of disputes. Alternatively, private mediation and arbitration services may be available.

SMALL CLAIMS COURT

Small claims court is a particularly useful mode of settling consumer disputes. The small claims courts were established to resolve disputes concerning small debts and accounts. Disputes are brought before a judge in a courtroom setting to be resolved on an expedited basis. A person making a claim in small claims court need not be represented by a lawyer, and, in fact, in most jurisdictions, neither party is allowed to bring in a lawyer.

The key difference between regular courts and small claims courts is that there is a maximum claim that can be brought. This maximum differs state to state, but it generally ranges up to between $1,000 and $3,000. Several states allow claims to range as high as $10,000. Court procedures are simple, quick, informal, and inexpensive. Some state or local governments publish guidebooks to assist consumers in filing their own complaints.

Special Issues

Mail Order Rights

The FTC has issued special rules that apply to solicitations by mail. First, if materials arrive unsolicited, the consumer is not under any obligation to buy—or to return—the merchandise. The FTC rules in effect make such merchandise a gift to the consumer from the company.

Second, when merchandise is ordered by mail, FTC regulations require that it must be delivered within the time specified by the seller's advertisements or 30 days if no time period is indicated. The seller has the right to notify the consumer if it cannot meet the deadline, and the consumer has the absolute right to cancel the purchase for a full refund. Some states have stricter laws.

Charity Solicitations

High-pressure sales tactics are not limited to merchandisers. Unfortunately, some unscrupulous individuals have used such methods in the name of "charity" as well. In at least one case reported in a recent FTC hearing, only 5 percent of donations to one so-called charity actually made it into the hands of cancer researchers.

It is a good idea for seniors to research charitable expenditures as they do their acquisitions. Not only does this ensure that the appropriate parties receive the funds, but it safeguards the senior's tax deduction. The National Charities Information Bureau is a private, nonprofit watchdog organization for charities. It maintains files on national charities and has issued accountability standards for these groups. The address for this organization is 19 Union Square West, New York, NY 10003.

Emergency Assistance Lines

Recently there has been a proliferation of services to seniors who fear they might become incapacitated and unable to call for help. Good consumer habits of shopping around can save money and ensure that once a service is selected the senior can afford to maintain it. Many of these services have a large up-front fee for the equipment. Most charge an additional monthly fee to maintain the services. Some hospitals have similar services for a minimal monthly fee.

Funeral and Burial Services

In response to perceived misleading marketing practices among funeral and burial service businesses, the FTC issued rules regulating the way in which funeral homes provide certain information to consumers. Funeral homes are required to:

1. Communicate pricing information over the phone or in person.

2. Provide itemized price information.

3. Obtain express approval from a family member or authorized person regarding embalming for a fee.

4. Refrain from misrepresenting specific aspects of the funeral transaction (such as claiming that embalming is required by law when it is not).

5. Refrain from requiring purchase of a casket or other items as a condition of funeral sale.

6. Make all disclosures in a clear and conspicuous manner.

Door-to-Door Sales

The FTC and many state laws provide safeguards for consumers making purchases as a result of door-to-door sales. Such sales contracts must provide a three-day cooling-off period during which the consumer can cancel the transaction and get a

full refund. The sales contract must provide notice of cancella-
tion rights.

Consumer Credit

Another issue that arises in the context of consumer transactions
is consumer credit. In the past, seniors with long credit histories
were astonished to find that creditors seemed to look at them
differently once they attained higher ages or retired. Credit arrangements were reduced or terminated and new credit denied.

The Equal Credit Opportunity Act, first enacted in 1974
and subsequently amended in 1976, prohibits discrimination in
credit-granting based on sex, marital status, race, color, religion,
national origin, or receipt of public assistance, and, significantly,
age. Creditors are prohibited from:

- Denying credit or offering less credit simply based on
  the age of the applicant

- Ignoring a senior's retirement income in rating the
  application

- Closing a consumer's credit account or requiring him
  or her to reapply for it based on the consumer's age
  or retirement

- Denying credit or closing a senior's account because credit
  life insurance or other credit-related insurance is not
  available due to the individual's age

  Creditors may:

- Use age as one of the factors in a credit-scoring system,
  provided that applicants who are 62 or older are not
  disadvantaged solely on the basis of their age relative to
  persons under 62

- Consider information related to age, such as how long
  until the applicant retires or how long his or her income
  will continue

If a creditor violates the law, a senior may sue the creditor. If the senior prevails, he or she can receive compensation for actual damages as well as punitive damages up to $10,000. The court may also order an unsuccessful defendant to pay the senior's court costs and attorney's fees.

Bankruptcy

Most people have heard of bankruptcy in the context of failing companies. Individuals may also file for bankruptcy, however, and it may be a good option for seniors overcome by debt. It should not be considered as the best way to stop harassment by creditors.

It should be emphasized at the outset that personal bankruptcy is an extreme step. It is a formidable bar to claims by most creditors, but it should be a senior's last resort because of the long-lasting devastation it wreaks on one's credit rating. Before filing for bankruptcy, seniors should investigate credit counseling through an organization such as the National Foundation for Consumer Credit.

Types of Bankruptcy

There are two types of bankruptcy of general application to individuals, denoted by the sections of the Federal Bankruptcy Code from which they derive: Chapter 7 and Chapter 13. The relief provided by the bankruptcy law is not a right; the court has discretion to deny petitions for bankruptcy.

Chapter 7, which accounts for roughly 70 percent of all filings, provides for the liquidation of the debtor's property to pay creditors. The bankruptcy court appoints an individual called a "trustee" to sell off all of the non-exempt property of the senior filing for bankruptcy. What constitutes "exempt" property varies from state to state. In some states such as Florida, for example, the home is fully exempt subject to acreage limitations. In others, only a limited exemption is provided. Absent extenuating circumstances, after liquidation of the properties, the trustee pays as many creditors as possible and the court "discharges" or cancels the remaining unpaid but dischargeable debt.

Chapter 7 results in an obvious loss of control. If a senior has assets with which he or she does not wish to part, this may not be the best option.

In contrast to Chapter 7 bankruptcy, under Chapter 13 seniors preserve their property from liquidation by establishing a repayment plan. Individuals filing under Chapter 13 may be given up to three or five years to repay creditors, and the creditors are prohibited from taking any legal action against them during this period. At the end of the period, the individual who filed for bankruptcy returns to court, and any unpaid but dischargeable debt is discharged.

Chapter 13 is only available to seniors with no more than $100,000 in unsecured debts and $350,000 in secured debt. A "secured" debt is one in which the creditor has retained an interest in the property acquired with the borrowed funds. For example, a home mortgage is a secured debt.

Most consumer debts can be discharged in bankrupty. These include:

- Rent

- Credit and charge account bills

- Loans from friends and family

- Legal, medical, and accounting bills

While personal bankruptcy can discharge some debts, it may not get rid of them all. Debts that must still be paid include most federal, state, and local taxes (including all tax fines and penalties) as well as child support and alimony.

Chapter 7

Issues in Family Law

Basics

- The process of dividing one household into two, and of dividing the property, income and child-rearing responsibilities between two former spouses is the subject of nearly one-half of all civil litigation in state courts.

- A marriage that is annulled is considered to have never taken place in the eyes of the law. Annulment occurs where the parties are not legally capable of entering into a valid marriage.

- During a separation the couple is still legally married, and the legal rights involved in the marriage contract, such as those related to inheritance, remain intact. After all, the couple may agree to resume their marriage.

- Today, all states have some form of "no-fault" divorce, although fault-related grounds may still be asserted in many jurisdictions.

- There are three theories of property division that govern in the various states: the equitable distribution approach, the community property approach, and the common law rule. The equitable distribution approach is the most prevalent.

- In the last ten years all 50 states have enacted statutes that provide grandparents with visitation rights. The statutes usually require that visitation only be awarded where it is in the "best interests" of the child.

Introduction

Anyone who has been married understands the deep significance of entering into that relationship. In the eyes of the law, marriage is a civil contract between two people, and the government has an interest in preserving the permanency of such relationships. The promises each person makes to the other form the basis of that contract. Of course, marriage is much more than just the sum total of the terms of that contract.

Most people do not think of divorce when they marry. However, 40 percent of all marriages in the United States end in divorce. Most divorces occur after at least seven years of marriage.

Legally speaking, a marriage can only be terminated through a divorce, also called a dissolution in some jurisdictions. If marriage is more than a civil contract, a divorce is more that just a termination of that contract, especially when children are involved. Many seniors know all too well the problem faced by grandparents in maintaining relationships with grandchildren when their sons and daughters divorce.

This chapter will discuss some of the key aspects of family law with a focus on matters concerning divorce. The specifics are determined by state law. A senior seeking to end a marriage should consult a knowledgeable attorney familiar with the local law as well as the important tax aspects of divorce before proceeding.

Divorce and Annulment

Most commonly, if a marriage is ended by a court, it is ended in a divorce. Annulment, because of its special nature, is only available in certain limited circumstances.

Annulment

A marriage that is annulled is considered to have never taken place in the eyes of the law. This occurs where the parties are not legally capable of entering into a valid marriage. For example, an individual who is already married may not enter into a valid marriage. Another ground for annulment is fraud, where one party is dishonest and conceals from his or her intended spouse information that would have caused the other party not to marry him or her. This is the more common reason for annulment.

An individual who suffers from a mental disability may not have the capacity to marry. One highly publicized case illustrates the difficulty the courts may have in determining mental capacity when outsiders want a marriage annulled on these grounds. During early 1987, the tabloids were full of stories about Sir Rudolf Bing, a famous author who married Carroll Douglas. His family objected to the marriage, arguing that Mr. Bing was incompetent. Six months after the marriage the Surrogate Court of the State of New York determined that Mr. Bing was incompetent. The conservator appointed to take care of Mr. Bing and his assets moved to have the marriage annulled but was rebuffed by the court, which stated that the conservator could not seek an annulment on behalf of Mr. Bing. Instead, a guardian *ad litem* had to be appointed to seek the annulment on Mr. Bing's behalf (see Chapter 2 for a detailed discussion of guardianship).

The advantage of an annulment is that it tends to be a relatively quicker and (therefore) less expensive court proceeding than divorce. Some argue that it may allow an individual to avoid the stigma of a failed marriage. Nevertheless, where the couple has lived together for a period of time, acquired joint property, or had children, many of the issues resolved in an annulment proceeding are the same as those in a divorce. The procedure for granting an annulment is similar to that described below for divorces.

Legal Separation

Often the first step to divorce is a legal separation. In a legal separation, the married couple lives apart under the terms of a binding contract called a separation agreement. Legally, the couple is still married, and the couple may agree to resume their marriage at any time.

Typically, the separation agreement is negotiated by the couple (and their legal representatives). Its terms set forth, among other things, who will live in the family home, who will be responsible for paying which bills, whether any support payments will be made, who will have custody of any minor children, and how visitation rights will be worked out during the separation.

Upon a petition of one or both parties, a court will issue a separation decree and ratify the separation agreement. Some states require proof of grounds for a legal separation; others seek proof of an actual separation for a specified period.

A separation agreement often provides the basis for the couple's final agreement in a divorce proceeding.

Divorce

Grounds for divorce are determined solely by state law. Formerly, an individual suing for divorce had to show that the other spouse was at fault for the failure of the marriage. Grounds for divorce included, for example, adultery, abandonment, and cruelty. Fault was also a great determiner in the court's decisions about property divisions and alimony payments. Today, all states have some form of "no-fault" divorce.

Several issues arise during a divorce: division of property, division of income, and the custody and support of minor children. These issues provide the basis of most divorce litigation these days. They affect not only the nuclear family that is being divided but also the extended family.

NO-FAULT DIVORCE

Although all states have some form of no-fault divorce, other grounds based on fault still exist in some jurisdictions. "No-fault" means that neither party need be found to have caused the marriage to fail, and the parties can concentrate on the business of settling the financial and familial aspects of their parting. In some jurisdictions, fault is still relevant in considering the way property is divided, but usually only to the extent that one or the other spouse has dissipated the family assets. For example, if a senior's husband has lost the family nest egg through gambling, some courts would take that into account in dividing the property that remains.

No-fault means different things in different jurisdictions. Essentially there are two approaches:

1. Some states simply provide that incompatibility, irreconcilable conflict, or irretrievable breakdown of the couple's relationship may be cited as the reason for the divorce.

2. Other states allow couples who have been voluntarily separated for a specified period (for example, two years) to dissolve the marriage. Some of these states require that a couple be legally separated pursuant to a court decree.

Division of Property

As indicated above, the central focus of most divorce proceedings has become the division of the family's property. There are three theories of property division that govern in the various states: the equitable distribution approach, the community property approach, and the common law rule. These principles are included in a state's domestic relations laws. The laws or principles are interpreted and develop over time through decisions by judges in cases.

Equitable Distribution

Most states follow the equitable distribution rule in divorce proceedings. In these jurisdictions the court is empowered under state law to divide property between partners based on equitable considerations. These may include:

• The duration of the marriage

• The age and health of the parties

• The couple's pre-separation standard of living

• The contributions of each partner to the acquisition or appreciation of marital property, including both tangible and intangible resources

- The present and prospective earnings of each party based upon their education, training, and experience

- Whether there are minor children and who will serve as the custodial parent

Depending upon state law, a court may look at all of a couple's property or only at property acquired during the marriage (often called marital property). Basically, marital property means all property acquired during the marriage, with certain limited exceptions. It can include traditional assets such as real estate, jewelry, or cash accounts. More recently, courts have begun to take into account so-called intangible assets such as professional degrees, rights to unvested pension assets, and the like. A recent New York case took into account the value of an opera singer's future career. Some jurisdictions explicitly exclude inheritances and gifts from the definition of marital property.

Separate property is what was acquired before the marriage, or property that the spouses have agreed to hold separate, by the terms of a prenuptial agreement, for example. In some jurisdictions it also includes property acquired by one of the spouses through bequest, devise, descent, or a gift from a third party, even if it is acquired during the marriage.

The definition of separate property applies to property that is acquired in exchange for separate property. For example, if a senior receives a cash inheritance, the cash itself would be separate property. If he or she uses that cash to purchase a car, the car would be considered separate property as well.

Community Property

To date, nine states (Arizona, California, Idaho, Louisiana, Nevada, New Mexico, Texas, Washington, and Wisconsin) have adopted the community property approach.

Under this theory, the marriage of two adults is considered to create a "community" in which each spouse is an equal member. The law takes the view that the couple was an economic unit, cooperating to achieve certain financial goals. All property acquired during the marriage with community assets is therefore owned equally. For example, real estate acquired with savings amassed from only one partner's wages during the marriage is deemed to be owned jointly.

Statutes set forth rules determining how property may be divided. Formerly, states with community property statutes divided community (or marital) property equally in cases of divorce. More recently, some have begun to take into account some of the same factors considered in states with equitable property division principles, blurring the line between these two approaches.

Common Law

The common law approach looks back to historical principles of property ownership. Under this approach, whoever holds title to the property is entitled to retain the property. Obviously the common law method can result in substantial inequities since it altogether ignores the relative worth of the parties' contributions to the economic unit. More recently courts have begun to moderate this approach by applying equitable principles.

Division of Income: Alimony and Support

Alimony (also called maintenance) is awarded at the discretion of the court on the basis of need and ability to pay. It may be awarded to ex-wives or ex-husbands, depending upon the economic circumstances.

The nature of alimony has changed over time. Formerly, when divorces were more commonly based upon fault grounds, alimony was also awarded on those grounds. Thus, only the "innocent" spouse (and almost always, only the wife) was entitled to alimony. Alimony was customarily paid for life, or until the spouse remarried.

Today the trend is toward "rehabilitative alimony" and relatively larger property settlements. Rehabilitative alimony is designed to provide income support for the spouse until he or she is able to become economically independent. Payments are provided over a set period, corresponding to the length of time it will take for the ex-spouse to resume a career or earn a degree to allow him or her to enter the paid work force. Alimony could be ordered by a court with the stipulation that the amount may be increased or decreased at some later time, depending upon changes in the recipient spouse's situation.

Obviously, the appropriateness of rehabilitative alimony will depend upon many factors, including the age of the ex-spouse or the presence of minor children. Certain factors weigh in favor of more traditional awards of alimony to an older spouse. For example, a woman who assumed the responsibilities of being a full-time homemaker for all or part of the marriage could argue that alimony represents delayed compensation for sacrificing her earnings potential.

Support generally refers to child support. True child support (concerning the care and feeding of children) is generally only awarded until the children reach the age of majority. In divorces between older couples, the cost of higher education is the chief concern, and is often the subject of negotiation in a settlement agreement.

Special Issue: Rights under Federal Law

Pension Plan Benefits

Accumulations in retirement plans often represent one of the most valuable assets a couple owns. It can represent economic security for the couple and for the widow or widower, if he or she should outlive the retiree. In case of divorce, however, there is no sharing of this important asset, and no requirement that a survivor benefit be provided—or even offered—to an ex-spouse, absent an agreement between the employee and his or her spouse, or a settlement imposed by the court.

Federal law regulates the manner in which such benefits may be divided between divorcing spouses, by requiring, in the case of private plans, the information that must be included in a court order dividing the pension. An employee or retiree can give all of his or her benefits under a private plan to his or her spouse, or only a portion. Typically, only a portion of the benefit is assigned to a spouse.

In the case of public plans, statutes regulate how and when pension assets may be divided between a retiree and spouse. For example, a benefit from the military retirement system is only divisible in a divorce proceeding if the couple was married for at least ten years, during which time the military employee was credited with active service. No more than 50 percent of his or her benefit may be assigned to the spouse. By contrast, veterans' disability benefits are not subject to division by court order at all.

Federal law provides two basic rights that divorcing seniors should keep in mind. These rights are not dependent upon any settlement agreement reached between the divorcing spouses.

Continuation of Medical Benefits

As discussed in Chapter 4 (page 71), a federal law called COBRA allows certain individuals to continue coverage in their or their spouse's employer's group health plan. In the case of divorce, an ex-spouse is entitled to up to 36 months of coverage dating from his or her divorce as long as the premium payments are made. It is the obligation of the ex-spouse to notify the employer within 60 days of the divorce that he or she seeks this coverage. As noted in Chapter 4, eligibility for coverage ends when the individual becomes entitled to Medicare benefits, among other events.

Social Security—Divorcee Benefits

As described in Chapter 3, an individual who has been married for at least ten years is entitled to benefits under the Social Security Act as a dependent spouse.

Custody and Visitation

Custody and visitation rights most commonly arise in divorce, but they can arise in other contexts as well, such as after the death of a parent or his or her incarceration. Not only parents, but grandparents, other relatives, and even unrelated adults may have rights under a given state's laws.

Generally speaking, the standard that the court uses to determine all custody and visitation issues is what is in the "best interests" of the child. As the standard suggests, no two cases are exactly alike, and courts are charged with considering a multiplicity of factors. Notwithstanding this ideal, custody decisions also necessarily take into account the interests of other parties, notably the individual petitioning for custody or visitation rights.

Traditionally, U.S. courts have awarded custody of minor children to the mother unless the court is convinced that she is unfit. In recent years, there has been a trend away from this predisposition. Awards of so-called joint custody are more common. Exactly what constitutes "joint" custody depends upon the state law and upon the parties. It may mean that children live with one or the other parent for periods of time, or simply that both parents will continue to participate in decisions concerning the children's care, education, and general welfare even though the children live with one parent. This division is sometimes called legal (who makes the decisions) versus physical (who the children live with) custody.

When a court makes decisions regarding custody in the context of a divorce, they are generally modifiable.

Special Issue: Grandparent Rights

Under the traditional common law, only the parents were considered to have rights regarding their relationship with the children. Courts rarely granted visitation to others if the custodial parent objected.

In the last decade all 50 states have enacted statutes that provide grandparents with visitation rights. Generally, the statutes require that visitation only be awarded where it is deemed to be in the best interests of the child.

The statutes differ from state to state in certain important respects. Most apply only in situations where the child's nuclear family is not intact due to legal separation, divorce, or death. A minority of states allow a grandparent to petition for visitation without such a familial breakdown. However, it is less common that a grandparent can secure visitation rights in cases where the grandchild's parents are still married. Circumstances are delineated specifically in the statute. The law is then applied to the particular situation in question.

Factors that courts consider in these cases include:

1. Whether the child has ever lived with his or her grandparents and for how long.

2. The need for continuity in the relationship (generally considered to be more important in divorce situations).

3. The effect of visitation on a child's physical and emotional health.

4. The child's preference (in some states).

Most courts will reject the argument that the custodial parent's hostility to visitation ought to be considered, even though this factor could significantly affect the child's emotional health.

Thus, visitation "rights" are hardly guaranteed. In a recent New York case, an appeals court rejected a grandparents' request to visit with their grandchildren. New York law provides that visitation can be ordered "where appropriate." Many experts have interpreted this to mean that visitation could be ordered even when a grandchild's nuclear family is intact. This was the situation in this case. Unfortunately, both the grandchildren's natural parents objected to visitation, and consequently the grandparents had not seen either of the grandchildren in several years. The court said that the parents had a constitutional right to raise their children as they wished—even if that meant denying the grandparents a relationship with their grandchildren. It indicated that the situation would be different if the family were not intact.

Most state laws set forth the procedure for seeking visitation rights. Grandparents might have the right to intervene in a divorce action, for example, so that their visitation rights can be incorporated into the court's orders. Alternatively, grandparents may be able to petition the appropriate court (usually a family court) directly. It is up to the person(s) seeking visitation to prove that visitation is appropriate under the state law. The court has complete discretion and its decision may be reversed on appeal to a higher court only when it has abused its discretion.

The Divorce Process

A divorce is more of a process than an event. True, there is a formal proceeding in a court to end the marriage officially where the court issues orders about how the household assets, income, and liabilities are to be divided, and about the custody, visitation, and care of any minor children. Relatively few divorces go to full-blown trials. More commonly, the parties and their legal representatives come to their own terms on many of the important matters, and the court ratifies their agreement, so long as it finds the terms are appropriate and then determines the resolution of any issues still in dispute.

A senior seeking, or subject to, a divorce proceeding should seek the assistance of an attorney (see Chapter 1, page 6, for recommendations on finding an attorney). The end of a marriage involves many complex issues and court proceedings. Most particularly, these concern the financial well-being of the parties after the divorce. Do-it-yourself divorce kits may result in a party's valuable rights being overlooked. Although it may be tempting for both parties to use the same attorney, it is generally not prudent to do so. The inherent conflict of interest between spouses getting a divorce makes it difficult for a lawyer to represent both parties well.

Lawyers have different approaches to divorce. Some will take a combative posture. Others prefer a more low-key, cooperative approach. In part, a lawyer's stance will be dictated by the manner of the other attorney. A senior should choose a lawyer with whom he or she is most comfortable.

Once a senior finds a lawyer, he or she should be prepared to provide detailed information about his or her family's economics. Many practitioners have extensive questionnaires that ask detailed questions about:

- Family assets, including where and when purchased, and with what funds (including real estate, stocks, bonds, and bank accounts).

- Family income, both present income and during the marriage (including salaries, trusts, investments, and pensions).

- Any employee benefit plans under which the family receives coverage (including health, life, and accidental death or dismemberment insurance).

- Family living expenses before the separation.

- The individual's expected or actual living expenses after separation.

- Copies of key documents such as deeds, trust agreements, stock and bond certificates, bank records, and statements of employee benefits or summary plan descriptions. These are most helpful in assessing family resources.

Some states require that such questionnaires be provided to the court to assist it in making its determination concerning property settlements.

Court Procedures

Procedures vary from state to state, and depend in part on whether the couple chooses to use divorce mediation as a method toward resolving some issues (see below). One or both spouses file a complaint (sometimes called a petition) asking the court to grant a divorce. There is usually a fee for filing this document, although it may be waived if the parties are indigent. The petition sets forth the background of the marriage and the reason the divorce is being sought.

If only one spouse is seeking the divorce, the other is required to be given notice of the filing. This is called service of process. Usually only the spouses are parties to the divorce. In some states, a guardian *ad litem* may be appointed for minor children. *Ad litem* simply means for the purposes of the litigation, in this case, a guardian who will act as a representive for the child(ren) in court. As indicated above, other parties (such as grandparents) may be able to intervene as well.

Some states impose a mandatory cooling-off period following the time a divorce petition is filed. This is usually no longer than two or three months, unless there are children involved. This period is designed to give the parties an opportunity to consider the seriousness of the steps being taken.

Following (and in some cases, during) this interval, there is a period of investigation, negotiation, and preparation for the court proceeding. As indicated above, few divorce cases actually go to a formal trial, unless there is a custody issue. During this period the court may at the request of either party issue "orders" to the parties concerning the use of family property, or temporary support and alimony payments, among other things. If there has been violence between the spouses, the court may enter protective orders that prohibit or restrict contact between them. The court's goal in making any orders is to maintain a status quo until the final disposition.

If there is a trial it is not usually before a jury. A judge (usually one who hears only family law cases) will listen to the arguments from both sides, consider the testimony of their witnesses and whatever documentary evidence is submitted, and make a determination. If the parties have come to agreement on some issues, the judge will most commonly only take court time to hear evidence on unresolved issues.

At the end of the trial, the judge enters a decree of divorce or a domestic relations order that resolves all issues in controversy. The court orders will set forth the division of property, any alimony and support payments, and custody and visitation arrangements. If the wife desires, the court will also order that her legal name be changed. In most states, the divorce decree is effective immediately. Some states provide that it does not take effect for some stated period.

Divorce Mediation

Many communities offer support services for couples seeking to divorce. These include alternative dispute resolution options such as mediation. In mediation, a third party (sometimes an attorney) assists the couple in working out the terms of the separation or divorce. The mediator has no power to compel the parties to agree. The mediator's role is simply to facilitate communication between the parties involved.

Mediation is designed to be an informal and cooperative approach to dispute resolution. The mediator will meet with both parties together for the most part. Individual sessions may occur throughout the process with one or the other spouse.

Lawyers for the parties may, but usually do not, attend mediation sessions.

The advantage of mediation is that the couple is sometimes able to arrive at more creative alternatives for meeting their needs than a court could. A judge may be constrained by legal precedents. Mediation is obviously not appropriate where one party dominates the other so that true negotiations are not possible.

Even where arbitration or mediation is sought, each individual should have his or her own lawyer to provide counsel during the resolution process and to review the final settlement agreement. Fair and effective negotiations require that both parties understand their rights under the state domestic relations law.

Mediators can be found by looking in the telephone book under "Mediators." Alternatively, seniors may contact the American Arbitration Association (see page 168), Divorce Mediation Research Services, or the Academy of Family Mediators' national referral service (see page 198).

Chapter 8

Issues in Estate Planning

Basics

- Each state's law is different, so a senior who is considering his or her estate plan should consult a lawyer or other legal advisor for assistance.

- When an individual dies without a will, the law calls it dying "intestate." At least one-half of all people die intestate.

- A will is a legal document that directs how an individual's money and property are to be distributed after death.

- Although the senior making a will has a great deal of discretion with regard to the disposition of his or her property at death, the law does impose some limits. For example, state laws make it difficult or impossible to disinherit one's spouse.

- Probate is a court-supervised process for winding up the affairs of the individual who has died. The decedent's debts and taxes are paid and his or her property divided among the designated heirs.

- Joint ownership of property is probably the most common way to avoid probate. Some commentators have called it "the poor man's will."

- Life insurance can serve two purposes in an estate plan: to replace income the deceased person was bringing into the family, and to provide a ready source of cash to pay any large financial obligations of the deceased, including estate and inheritance taxes.

- A trust involves transferring legal ownership of property to another person who manages that property for the benefit of someone else. Because someone else legally owns the property, the ownership does not change at the death of the person who creates the trust, and the property is not part of the probate estate, although it may be part of the taxable estate.

Introduction

Estate planning issues arise in two separate, though related, contexts. First, we all know that "you can't take it with you" when you die. So the first way in which estate issues arise is in planning for how your property will be distributed after your death. The second way estate issues arise is when a spouse, relative, or close friend dies and the business of winding up or "settling" that person's estate begins.

This chapter is designed to give a brief overview of the concepts and process of estate planning. Some of the important issues have already been discussed in other chapters. For example, living wills and advance directives concerning health care are an important part of any estate plan (see Chapter 2). This chapter will focus primarily on transfers of property upon death. Each state's law is different, so a senior who is considering his or her estate plan should consult a lawyer or other legal advisor for assistance in interpreting it.

This chapter will largely avoid the subject of federal and state taxes on estates in favor of a more general discussion of estate planning principles. The taxation of estates is quite complicated. Many high-powered estate and financial planners base their livelihood on assisting people with large assets in minimizing estate taxes through careful planning. Seniors who have substantial assets ($600,000 or more) should consult with an estate planner to see what might be done in their case.

Wills and Intestacy

Everyone Should Have a Will

Lawyers and other professionals who assist people with estate planning often say that everyone has a will—some people just allow the state to write theirs. Individuals die "intestate" when they neglect to draw up legal wills. It is estimated that at least half of all people die intestate.

In cases of intestacy state law determines who gets the deceased person's property. Most commonly these laws give the property to the immediate family of the person who died: his or her spouse, children, and parents first. If there is no family, sometimes the property goes to the state. This is called escheat. So perhaps the first issue a senior should consider in whether or not to make a will is whether he or she will be satisfied with the way the state will divide his or her property. Many people are not.

Another issue that a senior should consider is that a will might help the family avoid disputes after the senior's death. It is not uncommon for more than one person to claim that the same property was intended for them. A will is the final word in these matters. In addition, surviving spouses and family members often take comfort in having done what "John would have wanted."

What a Will Is

Very simply, a will is a legal document that directs how an individual's money and property should be distributed after death.

Wills can be rewritten, amended, or revoked at any time up until the death of the will maker assuming he or she is competent to do so. In fact, many lawyers who specialize in estate planning recommend that seniors review their wills periodically to see that they still reflect the intention of the individual. For example, the birth of a new grandchild or the acquisition of new property may warrant a change in the will. A will that is valid in one state will generally be recognized by another, but a senior who relocates should review the new state's law to be sure.

There are basically three types of wills: formal, handwritten (also called holographic), and oral. A formal will is accepted under all states' laws. Twenty states will also accept handwritten wills. Fewer accept oral wills, and even then only in very specific circumstances such as when the deceased was in a life-threatening situation in military service and did not survive to formalize a will. State law will set forth the conditions.

A formal will is one that complies with all of the requirements of the state law. Generally, there are four requirements:

1. The will must be written. Although it may be handwritten, most wills are typed. Any form of legible, fairly permanent writing will suffice.

2. The will must be signed by the will maker. Any mark such as an "X," a check mark, or the individual's full signature will do. In some jurisdictions, and only in certain limited circumstances, it may be signed by another person at the direction of the will maker.

3. The person making the will must declare it to be his or her "last will and testament" to those witnessing the will. This is sometimes called "publication," although the will maker is not required to reveal the terms of the will.

4. The signing of the will must be witnessed. All states require at least two witnesses to be present when the will is signed. The witnesses could be called upon after the death of the will maker to support the validity of the will (for example, to testify that the will maker had the mental capacity to make a will). It is generally not a good idea for a person who is a beneficiary under the will to be a witness. Some states' laws disqualify these individuals.

A written will that does not meet the formalities under state law is called a "holographic" will. Some states do not recognize this type of will at all; others do in certain circumstances.

If an individual dies without a will that is valid under state law, then the individual is considered to have died intestate.

How the Law Determines Who Can Make a Valid Will

Anyone who has attained the age of majority can make a will unless they lack the mental capacity to do so. A senior has the capacity to make a will if he or she understands:

- The nature of the act of making a will

- The nature, situation, and extent of the property held and subject to disposition under the will

- The individuals who would be his or her legal heirs absent a will (the courts call this the "natural objects of his or her bounty")

- Whose interests are affected by the will

What Should Be Included in a Will

Certain factors are appropriately included in a will; others are not. Factors that should be included are:

1. Nomination of a personal representative. A personal representative (often called an executor or executrix) is the person (or persons) who technically manages the probate process. The property of the deceased is placed in the care and custody of the personal representative for as long as it takes to pay the deceased's debts and distribute the property according to the will.

2. Provisions for special types of property, such as stock investments, businesses, and the like, which may require the personal representative to make complicated decisions. The will must give the personal representative power to manage and sell these investments as appropriate. The choice of personal representatives should be made carefully and with some thought as to whether the individual nominated will be able to do the job.

3. Gifts of tangible personal property. When the individual making a will wants a particular piece of jewelry

or furniture to go to a specific person, that may be set forth in the will. This is called a "bequest." Some practitioners recommend that only gifts of property with substantial value be included in the will to avoid complicating the will. Basically, when the person who makes the will dies, his or her property will be divided into two groups. The first consists of properties designated to go to particular persons. The second consists of properties that are not specifically given, or "devised." These properties are called "residue." Taxes and other debts are paid first out of the residue and last out of specific bequests.

4. Dispositions of real estate. Real estate presents special issues. If the personal representative is to sell the properties, the will should grant him or her specific powers. A surviving spouse usually has some rights to the family home that cannot be taken away by a will. These are generally referred to as "dower" or "curtesy."

5. Gifts of cash or income. Sometimes, instead of giving a specific property, an individual wishes to give income to an individual under his or her will. This can be accomplished in many ways, both under and outside of the will (see the discussion of life insurance and other survivor incomes on page 142). One decision facing a senior making such a gift is whether to specify the source of the income, for example, a simple gift of $1,000, or a gift of $1,000 to be made from the proceeds of the sale of XYZ Corporation stock. If the property is sold before the senior dies, the beneficiary of a specific gift gets nothing. On the other hand, as in the case of specific bequests of property, the beneficiary whose gift comes out of the residue runs a greater risk of losing all or a part of his or her bequest if the deceased left many debts.

6. The creation of trusts. Rather than leaving property or cash to heirs outright, some people create a trust for them. When the will creates the trust it is called a "testamentary trust." Legal ownership of the property

passes to the trustee who manages it for the benefit of the individual(s) the deceased designates. How much and what types of control the trust beneficiaries exercise depends upon the terms of the trust. Trusts are discussed more fully in Chapter 2 and on page 144 in this chapter).

7. Provisions for minor or incompetent children. The will may provide for the legal custody of minor or incompetent children through designating a guardian. The same person or another may be made trustee or conservator of resources to provide for them.

Limitations on What Can Be Accomplished in a Will

Although the senior making a will has a great deal of discretion in the disposition of his or her property, the law does impose some limits. First, state laws make it difficult or impossible to disinherit one's spouse. If the will does not make provision for the spouse, then he or she is generally entitled to claim a share of the estate as determined by state law. A senior who wishes to disinherit children should specifically do so in the will. In some states, children who are not mentioned in the will may be entitled to inherit the portions of the estate that would have been granted to them if the deceased parent was intestate.

Another factor to keep in mind is that creditors of a deceased person are entitled to be paid before heirs inherit any property. This includes not only private debts but public debts such as claims against the estate for Medicaid benefits mistakenly paid or overpaid to the senior during his or her lifetime.

How a Will Is Changed or Revoked

When an individual executes a new will, it is extremely important that he or she specifically revoke the old one. This is to prevent any ambiguity about whether the second will is intended to amend the first or to replace it entirely. If a senior only wants to change certain limited terms he or she may do so with a document called a codicil. A codicil is designed to affect only certain portions of the will.

Any symbolic destruction of the old will may be used as evidence of its revocation. This includes tearing it up, burning it, striking through the text, or writing "revoked" across the top of the document. The will maker can do this him or herself or may direct another person to do so.

What a Senior Should Bring to an Estate Planning Session

A senior should bring any and all documents concerning income, assets, former estate plans, and family. Good estate planning requires the will maker's full disclosure of pertinent information to his or her estate planner.

Specifically, the will maker should bring:

- Any existing wills, including codicils

- Life insurance policies

- Retirement benefit statements about payments the senior is currently receiving or is entitled to receive

- Any business agreements, including buy/sell or stock redemption agreements

- Trust agreements

- Income and gift tax returns for the past five years

- Any pre- or post-nuptial agreements, separation agreements, and divorce papers

- Documents showing the basis of assets (such as stock or bonds) that belong to the senior

- Documents creating joint tenancies of specific assets

- Evidence supporting a claim of separate property (in community property states)

- The names, addresses, phone numbers, birth dates, and Social Security numbers of all intended beneficiaries and the senior's spouse

- A complete inventory of valuable property, including some estimate of its value and where it is located

Probate

The process of probating a will has gotten a lot of bad press throughout the years. It is generally assumed to be costly, time consuming, and best avoided. This is not always the case, and avoiding probate "at all costs" may mean you will incur just that. As discussed below, joint ownership of property—the so-called poor man's will—has its own risks.

Simply put, probate is nothing more than a court-supervised process for winding up the affairs of the individual who has died. The decedent's debts and taxes are paid, and his or her property divided among the designated heirs. Relatively few wills are "contested," meaning that the authenticity or validity of their provisions is challenged.

Currently it is estimated that costs for probating an estate of $100,000 or less run between 8 and 9 percent of the gross assets in the estate. These costs are partly determined by the nature of the assets in the estate. Depending upon the court and its case load, probating an estate can take anywhere from six months to one year.

The Process in a Nutshell

The probate process differs from state to state and court to court, but all jurisdictions have the following steps in common:

APPLICATION OR PETITION FOR PROBATE

Someone, usually the deceased person's personal representative or spouse, will petition the court to have the will accepted as the last will and testament. If there is no will, an heir or the deceased person's spouse will petition the court for "administration" of the estate. The probate court sets a hearing date and notice is given to all persons who are or who would be heirs under the laws of intestacy.

HEARING

If someone is contesting the will as being invalid, he or she steps forward at this point in the process. The most common claim is that the will maker lacked the capacity to make a valid will, or was subject to undue influence. For example, a disinherited son may argue that his sister who lived with their father in his later years forced him to change the will by threatening to leave him alone. Other claims may center on ambiguities in the will.

Typically, the hearing (if there is one) proceeds unencumbered by a contest. More commonly the personal representative and perhaps some members of the decedent's immediate family appear for the hearing. In some states, a hearing is only scheduled if an objection to the will is filed. The result is that the will is verified, a personal representative is appointed pursuant to the will and given authority to settle the estate, and a notice is issued to all creditors to present their claims against the estate by the end of a period set forth in the state's estate law. If the will is found to be invalid, the estate will be administered as if the individual died intestate. The court appoints an administrator for this purpose.

COLLECTION OF ESTATE ASSETS AND SETTLEMENT OF CLAIMS

With a court order to give evidence of his or her authority, the personal representative sets about collecting the assets of the deceased individual. This means changing the ownership of assets temporarily to "the estate of Jane Doe." Some states require that the personal representative provide the court with an inventory of the decedent's estate showing its fair market value.

Certain assets, such as real estate, stock, and other business interests may require a personal representative to take special care to ensure that they retain their value during the period the estate is being settled.

Once the deceased person's assets have been valued, the personal representative must pay the legitimate claims of creditors. Typical debts include outstanding loans, credit card balances, and household bills. Where a senior has taken advantage of property tax deferrals (see Chapter 3, page 55), the state or local government may also submit a claim. In some states, benefits paid under Medicaid may result in a claim against the estate. If the personal representative is unclear as to whether a claim is proper, he or she may seek the guidance of the probate court.

Numerous taxes must also be paid out of the estate. A complete discussion of state and federal estate and inheritance taxes is beyond the scope of this chapter. Briefly, federal estate taxes generally apply when the deceased person's estate is valued at $600,000 or more. However, state inheritance and estate taxes typically apply at lower levels. An inheritance tax technically taxes the individual receiving the property, although the tax is paid before the transfer. Generally the amount of such taxes is determined according to the individual's relationship to the deceased person. For example, in Pennsylvania, property left to a child or parent is taxed at a rate of 6 percent, while property left to other nonfamilial beneficiaries is taxed at 15 percent. An estate tax taxes the deceased person's right to transfer property and it comes out of the estate before it is distributed to heirs.

FINAL ACCOUNTING

The personal representative or administrator makes a final accounting to the court, setting forth the debts and taxes paid prior to beginning distributions to beneficiaries. This provides the heirs an opportunity to object to claims that might affect the size of their inheritance.

DISTRIBUTION OF ASSETS TO BENEFICIARIES

Once the personal representative has assembled the deceased person's assets and paid the appropriate debts, expenses, and taxes, he or she is able to distribute the remaining assets according to the will, or the state intestacy laws if there is no valid will.

FINAL REPORT TO THE COURT

After the distribution to beneficiaries, the personal representative typically submits a sworn statement to the court, claiming that the business of the estate is concluded.

An Alternative: Small Estate Administration

An alternative available in some states for smaller-sized estates is administration by affidavit (also called summary administration or small estate administration). Where it is available, transfers of property pursuant to a will or under the laws of intestacy are accomplished by filing a written, sworn statement (called an affidavit) with the court. Generally, the affidavit states that all debts have been paid and details the deceased person's remaining property and the parties to whom it will be transferred. Forms for this purpose are sometimes supplied by the court. There is usually no court proceeding accompanying this type of administration and settlements are typically quicker than the formal proceeding described above.

Small estate administration is only available in certain circumstances determined under state law. For example, in the state of Connecticut, the deceased person's total probate assets may not exceed $10,000 and may not include real estate.

When Legal Assistance Is Necessary

One source of costs in the probate process is obviously legal fees. Since court proceedings are involved, it is often advisable to involve a lawyer in settling an estate. It is probably more important to do so when the deceased person's estate is large or when it contains complex assets such as stock, an interest in a closely held business, or real estate.

The choice of lawyers falls to the personal representative. There are no hard and fast rules about whom he or she should select. In some cases, it is helpful to hire the lawyer who helped the deceased person write the will. For example, if it appears that the will might be challenged, often the assistance of the deceased person's own lawyer can be helpful in uncovering the meaning of the terms of the will. The personal representative's own lawyer can often be helpful. Whoever is chosen, the personal representative remains responsible for the administration of the estate. The lawyer is the personal representative's employee—and not the reverse.

Much of the time-consuming work of settling an estate can be done by a determined and patient layperson. Even if legal counsel is necessary or advisable, the expense can be minimized by the personal representative by his or her doing the legwork with the guidance of counsel.

"Avoiding" Probate—Non-Probate Assets

Certain types of assets are not required to go through the probate process in order to reach their intended beneficiaries. This does not mean these assets are not subject to taxation—quite the contrary. The deceased person's share of any jointly owned assets is included in the estate and taxed as part of the estate. They do avoid the delay of the probate process, however. Non-probate assets include:

- Assets owned jointly with the right of survivorship, which will become the sole property of the joint owner.

- Assets held in trusts, which will pass according to the trust agreement.

- Life insurance proceeds, which will be paid to the beneficiaries designated in the policy or beneficiary form.

- Pension, profit-sharing, deferred compensation or other corporate death benefits, and Individual Retirement (IRA) or Keogh accounts, which will be paid to the beneficiaries designated in the beneficiary form.

JOINTLY OWNED PROPERTY

Joint ownership of property (also known as "the poor man's will") is probably the most common way to avoid probate. There are several forms of joint ownership; those of most importance for estate planning purposes include a "right of survivorship." A "right of survivorship" means that when one of the joint owners dies, the remaining joint owner (or owners) acquires the deceased's interest in the property. The joint owners have no rights to pass the property to any other beneficiary at their death. The mechanics of establishing joint ownership is determined by state law.

A statutorily mandated form of joint ownership exists between spouses in community property states. All property acquired during the marriage with community assets (wages and investment) is the property of both spouses, share and share alike. Any property that one or the other partner owned outside of the marriage is separate property. Separate property may be transferred by will. Property in a joint ownership that was begun with another partner before a marriage is only inherited by the surviving partner if there was a "right of survivorship."

Joint ownership can be used with many different types of property: real estate and bank accounts being among the most common. Even U.S. Savings Bonds have their own form of joint ownership. A senior who purchases a bond may put it in his or her own name, but stipulate "Paid on Death" (POD) to another person.

From an estate administrator's perspective, the benefit of joint ownership with the right of survivorship is that it doesn't take action by a probate court to determine the new owner of the property. The assets are immediately available to the survivor. A joint bank account, for example, could allow a relative or close friend to assist a senior in getting the bills paid when he or she is in the hospital or a nursing home.

There are drawbacks to joint ownership, however. The joint owner acquires rights to determine how the property is used. He or she may prevent its sale, for example, even if the original owner wishes to sell the property. In the case of a joint bank account, the other person could withdraw all of the money. It can be difficult to undo the joint ownership. Finally, when a joint owner dies, he gives up all control of the property to the other owner. So, for example, a family homestead could be passed outside of the family by the surviving joint owner, while a will or trust could prohibit such a transfer.

LIFE INSURANCE

Life insurance can serve two purposes in an estate plan. First, it can be used to replace income the deceased person had been bringing (and was anticipated to continue to bring) into the family. This is perhaps its most common use. Second, life insurance proceeds can also provide a ready (and cost-effective) source of cash to pay any large financial obligations of the deceased. These include estate and inheritance taxes, outstanding debts, and anticipated expenses such as the children's college tuition.

Unless the insured person names his or her estate as beneficiary, the probate court is not involved in getting funds to the beneficiary. However, the proceeds are generally included in the taxable estate of the deceased unless the insured person is successful at transferring ownership of the policy more than three years before death. For example, a senior can make a gift of ownership of the policy to a daughter. Thereafter, the daughter may exercise any rights under the policy such as changing beneficiaries or pledging the policy as collateral.

Another attractive factor of life insurance is that proceeds payable on account of death of the insured are exempt from income tax. If the beneficiary elects to have payments made on an installment basis with interest, then the death benefit only, not the interest, is tax-free. For example, a $30,000 benefit payable over 10 years in installments of $4,500 each year would result in $1,500 in taxable income each year ($30,000 divided by 10 equals $3,000; the balance of each annual payment ($1,500) is taxable interest income).

Types of Life Insurance

There are many different types of life insurance. Basically they are either "term" or "permanent" (also called cash value) life insurance, or they combine some features of each.

Term insurance pays a benefit only upon the death of the insured person. Premiums for term insurance are generally less expensive than cash value policies when an individual is younger. However, since premiums generally increase as the individual becomes older, term insurance can become prohibitively expensive for seniors.

Cash value policies, such as "whole" or "universal" policies, combine death benefits with an investment feature. As premiums are paid over time, the policy builds up a reserve that the insurance company invests over the years to fund the insurance benefit for the policyholder later on and to provide the cash value at the policy's maturity date. This cash value may be available to the policyholder through policy loans or by cash-in features set forth in the policy. When the policy "matures" the cash value is paid to the policyholder if the insured person is still alive. In effect, the policyholder pays the insurance company to invest his or her money and provide a benefit at a certain point whether he or she is alive or deceased.

SURVIVOR ANNUITIES AND QUALIFIED RETIREMENT PLAN BENEFITS

Survivor benefits under ERISA-qualified retirement plans (see Chapter 3) also pass outside of probate. The type of payments provided under a given plan depends upon the terms of the plan and the participant's choices pursuant to the plan. Most qualified plans are required to provide benefits in a stream of payments called an "annuity" to a surviving spouse unless another form of payment is chosen by the plan participant with the consent of his or her spouse.

Survivor benefits are considered part of the taxable estate of the deceased person.

TRUSTS

A trust involves transferring legal ownership of property to another person who manages (or, in legal language, "holds") that property for the benefit of someone else. The person who holds the property is called the trustee. Because someone else legally owns the property, the ownership does not change at the death of the person who creates the trust. The property avoids probate because the trust, not the will, determines who owns the property.

The trust agreement sets forth the terms under which the trustee holds, manages, and distributes property. The two most common types of trusts are *inter vivos* and testamentary trusts. In addition, a trust can be said to be revocable or irrevocable. A revocable trust may be terminated by the person who makes it. An irrevocable trust cannot. A trust may be revocable to begin with and become irrevocable at a later time—such as the incapacity or death of the trust maker.

The essential difference between an *inter vivos* and testamentary trust is the document that creates them. A testamentary trust is created by a will and goes into effect only after the person who made it dies. An *inter vivos* trust is created and "exists" while the trust maker is alive. As discussed in Chapter 2, it can be quite useful in providing for management of the trust maker's property in cases of incapacity.

A trust is used to conserve the underlying property of the trust, while providing benefits to trust beneficiaries. In an estate planning context, it allows the trust maker to control the use of the property held in trust (sometimes called the principal or the *res*) even after his or her own death, or the deaths of trust beneficiaries. The beneficiary's rights to the trust property are strictly limited by the stipulations of the trust.

What the Trust Agreement Should Say

The trust agreement is the "constitution" that determines what happens to the trust property. The agreement should be as complete as possible. No two people establishing a trust are exactly alike and neither should their trusts be. Trust agreements are complicated legal documents, and they should be drafted, or at least reviewed, by a lawyer.

The trust agreement should include:

1. Information as to the amount and type of property that will be contained in the trust.

2. A statement concerning the length of the trust agreement.

3. Instructions for management of the trust property.

4. Conditions under which beneficiaries will receive benefits.

5. How assets should be used if trust conditions are not met or circumstances change.

6. Designation of an individual or institution to act as trustee.

7. Guidelines as to who should receive trust assets when the trust terminates.

Individuals and institutions that act as trustees are subject to complicated laws concerning fiduciary duty. Basically, the trustee has the duty to act with great care, skill, and diligence in administering the trust. He or she must safeguard, preserve, and protect the estate. In doing so, the trustee may not engage in acts that result in a benefit to him or herself. If mismanagement occurs, the trustee may be sued by trust beneficiaries.

References for Part One

ABA. Commission on Legal Problems of the Elderly and Young Lawyers Division. Committee on Delivery of Legal Services to the Elderly. *Guardianship of the Elderly: A Primer for Attorneys*. Washington, DC: ABA, February 1990.

ABA. Committee on the Mentally Disabled. *Involuntary Civil Commitment: A Manual for Lawyers and Judges*. Washington, DC: ABA, 1988.

American Association of Retired Persons (AARP). Consumer Affairs Section. Program Department. *A Consumer's Guide to Probate*. Washington, DC: AARP, December 1989.

Burke, Thomas P., and Rita S. Jain. "Trends in Employer-provided Health Care Benefits." *Monthly Labor Review* 114 (February 1991): 24–30.

Bysiewicz, Shirley R., ed. and comp. *Attorney's Elderly Law Desk Manual*. 2d ed.: Connecticut Bar Association, 1987.

Clark, Homer H. *The Law of Domestic Relations in the United States*. Vol. 2. 2d ed. St. Paul, Minnesota: West Publishing Company, 1987.

Commerce Clearing House Tax Law Editors. *Federal Estate & Gift Taxes Explained*. Chicago: Commerce Clearing House, 1990.

Cooney, George A., Jr. "Drafting Powers of Attorney for Success." *The Practical Lawyer* 36 (October 1990): 59–63.

Fairbanks, Joan E. "Home Equity Conversion Programs: A Housing Option for the 'House-Rich, Cash-Poor' Elderly." *Clearinghouse Review* 23 (Summer 1989): 481–487.

Gano, Ralph, and Morey S. Rosenblum. *The Tools and Techniques of Estate Planning*. 8th ed. Cincinnati: The National Underwriter Company, 1990.

Hearings on Issues Affecting Older Americans before the Federal Trade Commission, 16 March 1988.

147

Ingulli, Elaine D. "Grandparent Visitation Rights: Social Policies and Legal Rights." *West Virginia Law Review* 87 (1985): 295–334.

Kane, Rosalie A., and Cheryl D. King, eds. *Deciding whether the Client Can Decide: Assessment of Decision-making Capability*. Minneapolis: University of Minnesota Long-Term Care DECISIONS Resource Center, August 1990.

Kess, Sidney, and Bertil Westlin. *CCH Estate Planning Guide*. Chicago: Commerce Clearing House, 1989.

Legal Counsel for the Elderly. *Organizing Your Future: A Guide to Decisionmaking in Your Later Years*. Legal Counsel for the Elderly, January 1990.

Leonard, Robin. *Money Troubles: Legal Strategies To Cope with Your Debts*. Berkeley, CA: Nolo Press, 1991.

Lubasch, Arnold H. "Court Denies Grandparents Visitation Rights." *The New York Times*, 30 September 1990, 36.

Myers, Teresa Schwab. *How To Keep Control of Your Life after 60: A Guide for Your Legal, Medical, and Financial Well-Being*. Lexington, MA: Lexington Books, 1990.

Nader, Ralph, and Wesley Smith. *Winning the Insurance Game*. New York: Knightsbridge, 1990, 538.

National Committee to Preserve Social Security and Medicare. *Buying Your Medigap Policy*. Washington, DC: The National Committee to Preserve Social Security and Medicare, 1990.

The National Underwriter Company. *All about Medicare*. Cincinnati: The National Underwriter Company, 1990.

Neuman, R. Emil. *The Complete Handbook of U.S. Government Benefits*. Leucadia, CA: United Research, 1989.

Practising Law Institute. *Counseling the Elderly Client*. New York: Practising Law Institute, 1989.

Raper, Ann Trueblood, Anne C. Kalicki, and American Association of Homes for the Aging, eds. *National Continuing Care Directory: Retirement Communities with Nursing Care*. 2d ed. Glenview, IL: Scott, Foresman and Co., 1988.

Rosmarin, Yvonne W., and Jonathan Sheldon. *Sales of Goods and Services*. 2d ed. Boston: National Consumer Law Center, 1989.

Rudy, Theresa Meehan, and HALT. *Small Claims Court, Making Your Way through the System: A Step-by-Step Guide*. New York: Random House, 1990.

Sack, Steven Mitchell. *The Complete Legal Guide to Marriage, Divorce, Custody & Living Together*. New York: McGraw-Hill, 1987.

Segal, Ellen C., and Naomi Karp, eds. *Grandparent Visitation Disputes: A Legal Resource Manual*. Washington, DC: ABA Commission on Legal Problems of the Elderly, 1989.

Sheldon, Jonathan. *Unfair and Deceptive Acts and Practices*. 2d ed. Consumer Credit and Sales Legal Practice Series. Boston: National Consumer Law Center, 1990. Includes a cumulative supplement.

Soled, Alex J. *The Essential Guide to Wills, Estates, Trusts, and Death Taxes*. 2d ed. Glenview, IL: Scott, Foresman and Co., 1987.

Sommer, Henry J. *Consumer Bankruptcy Law and Practice*. 3d ed. Washington, DC: National Consumer Law Center, 1988.

Talley, Louis Alan. *Federal Income Tax Treatment of the Elderly*. Washington, DC: Congressional Research Service Reports, 5 March 1991.

"Update: The New Medigap Plans." *Consumer Reports* 56 (September 1991): 616–617.

U.S. Department of the Treasury. *Tax Information for Older Americans*. IRS Publication no. 554. Washington, DC: Department of the Treasury, 1990.

U.S. Department of Veterans Affairs. *Federal Benefits for Veterans and Dependents*. Washington, DC: Department of Veterans Affairs, January 1991.

U.S. Office of Consumer Affairs. *Consumer's Resource Handbook*. Washington, DC: U.S. Government Printing Office, 1990.

U.S. Senate. Special Committee on Aging. *A Matter of Choice: Planning Ahead for Health Care Decisions*. Washington, DC: U.S. Senate Special Committee on Aging, 1986.

Vierck, Elizabeth. *Paying for Health Care after Age 65*. Choices and Challenges series. Santa Barbara, CA: ABC-CLIO, 1990.

PART
TWO

Resources

Chapter 9

Directory of Organizations

This selected list of organizations is broken down by categories that correspond closely to the structure of the preceding chapters: legal issues, personal autonomy, income security, health care, housing, consumer issues, family law, and estate planning. An additional subheading "General" begins the directory and includes organizations whose areas of concern transcend chapter headings.

The entry for each organization includes an address and phone number, a contact name, and a brief description of the organization's objectives and specific areas of interest. If the contact person listed is no longer with the organization, seniors should ask for someone with expertise in the issue which concerns them. The information was current at the time of publication. If any of these organizations has moved, other organizations concerned with the particular issue may be able to supply the new address or phone number.

General

Government Agencies

Administration on Aging (AoA)
U.S. Department of Health and Human Services
330 Independence Avenue, SW
Washington, DC 20201
(202) 619-0724

The AoA develops federal programs and coordinates community services for elder Americans. AoA sponsors programs on legal aid, housing, employment, transportation, consumer affairs, counseling, and nutrition. AoA also has special programs for older Native Americans.

PUBLICATIONS: The quarterly *Aging Magazine: Where To Turn for Help for Older Persons,* and the *Nationwide Network of State and Area Agencies on Aging.*

Select Committee on Aging, U.S. House of Representatives
Richard A. Veloz, Majority Staff Director
712 House Office Building Annex I
Washington, DC 20515-6361
(202) 226-3375

The Select Committee on Aging is responsible for studying problems encountered by seniors, encouraging the development and coordination of appropriate public and private programs, and reviewing recommendations from the president and the White House Conference on Aging. The committee focuses on issues such as income maintenance, housing, health, welfare, employment, and education. Subcommittees include: (1) the Subcommittee on Health and Long-term Care, (2) the Subcommittee on Housing and Consumer Interests, (3) the Subcommittee on Human Services, (4) the Subcommittee on Retirement Income and Employment, (5) the Task Force on Rural Elderly, and (6) the Task Force on Social Security and Women.

Special Committee on Aging, U.S. Senate
Portia Mittelman, Majority Staff Director
Dirksen Senate Office Building, Room SD-G31
Washington, DC 20510-6400
(202) 224-5364

The Senate's Special Committee on Aging reports annually on its continuing study of problems such as health, income, employment, housing, and other issues as necessary. Legislation is not referred to the committee, and the committee is not empowered to report by bill or exercise other legislative jurisdiction. The committee has no subcommittees.

State Units on Aging

Alabama
Commission on Aging
Oscar D. Tucker, Executive Director
770 Washington Avenue, Suite 470
Montgomery, AL 36130
(205) 242-5743

Alaska
Older Alaskans Commission
Connie Sipe, Director
Department of Administration
Pouch C—Mail Station 0209
Juneau, AK 99811-0209
(907) 465-3250

Arizona
Aging and Adult Administration
Department of Economic Security
Richard Littler, Director
1400 West Washington Street
Phoenix, AZ 85007
(602) 542-4446

Arkansas
Division of Aging and Adult Services
Arkansas Department of Human
    Services
Herb Sanderson, Director
P.O. Box 1417, Slot 1412
7th and Main Streets
Little Rock, AR 72201
(501) 682-2441

California
Department of Aging
Chris Arnold, Director
1600 K Street
Sacramento, CA 95814
(916) 322-5290

Colorado
Aging and Adult Service
Department of Social Services
Rita Barreras, Manager
1575 Sherman Street, Tenth Floor
Denver, CO 80203-1714
(303) 866-3851

Connecticut
Department on Aging
Edith Prague, Commissioner
175 Main Street
Hartford, CT 06106
(203) 566-3238

Delaware
Division on Aging
Department of Health and Social
    Services
Eleanor Cain, Director
1901 North DuPont Highway
New Castle, DE 19720
(302) 421-6791

District of Columbia
Office on Aging
E. Veronica Pace, Executive Director
1424 K Street, NW, Second Floor
Washington, DC 20005
(202) 724-5626

Florida
Program Office of Aging and Adult
    Services
Department of Health and
    Rehabilitative Services
Larry Polivka, Assistant Secretary
1317 Winewood Boulevard
Tallahassee, FL 32301
(904) 488-8922

Georgia
Office of Aging
Fred McGinnis, Director
878 Peachtree Street, NE, Room 632
Atlanta, GA 30309
(404) 894-5333

Hawaii
Executive Office on Aging
Office of the Governor
Jeanette Takamura, Director
335 Merchant Street, Room 241
Honolulu, HI 96813
(808) 548-2593

Idaho
Office on Aging
Charlene Martindale, Director
Statehouse, Room 108
Boise, ID 83720
(208) 334-3833

Illinois
Department on Aging
Victor L. Wirth, Director
421 East Capitol Avenue
Springfield, IL 62701
(217) 785-2870

Indiana
Choice/Home Care Services
Department of Human Services
Geneva Shedd, Director
251 North Illinois Street
P.O. Box 7083
Indianapolis, IN 46207-7083
(317) 232-7020

Iowa
Department of Elder Affairs
Betty Grandquist, Executive Director
Jewett Building, Suite 236
914 Grand Avenue
Des Moines, IA 50319
(515) 281-5187

Kansas
Department on Aging
Esther Valladolid Wolf, Secretary
Docking State Office Building, 122-S
915 Southwest Harrison
Topeka, KS 66612-1500
(913) 296-4986

Kentucky
Division of Aging Services
Cabinet for Human Resources
Sue Tuttle, Director
CHR Building, Sixth West
275 East Main Street
Frankfort, Kentucky 40621
(502) 564-6930

Louisiana
Office of Elderly Affairs
Vickey Hunt, Director
4550 North Boulevard, Second Floor
P.O. Box 80374
Baton Rouge, LA 70806
(504) 925-1700

Maine
Bureau of Elder and Adult Services
Department of Human Services
Christine Gianopoulos, Director
State House, Station Number 11
Augusta, ME 04333
(207) 626-5335

Maryland
Office on Aging
Rosalie Abrams, Director
State Office Building
301 West Preston Street, Room 1004
Baltimore, MD 21201
(301) 225-1100

Massachusetts
Executive Office of Elder Affairs
Andrew Bader, Acting Secretary
38 Chauncy Street
Boston, MA 02111
(617) 727-7750

Michigan
Office of Services to the Aging
Nancy Crandall, Director
P.O. Box 30026
Lansing, MI 48909
(517) 373-8230

Minnesota
Board on Aging
Gerald Bloedow, Executive Director
444 Lafayette Road
St. Paul, MN 55155-3843
(612) 296-2770

Mississippi
Council on Aging
Division of Aging and Adult Services
Billie Marshall, Director
421 West Pascagoula Street
Jackson, MS 39203-3524
(601) 949-2070

Missouri
Division on Aging
Department of Social Services
Edwin Walker, Director
P.O. Box 1337
615 Howerton Court
Jefferson City, MO 65102-1337
(314) 751-3082

Montana
The Governor's Office on Aging
Hank Hudson, Aging Coordinator
State Capitol Building
Capitol Station, Room 219
Helena, MT 59620
(406) 444-3111

Nebraska
Department on Aging
Connie Bratka, Acting Director
P.O. Box 95044
301 Centennial Mall-South
Lincoln, NE 68509
(402) 471-2306

Nevada
Division for Aging Services
Department of Human Resources
Suzanne Ernst, Administrator
340 North 11th Street, Suite 114
Las Vegas, NV 89101
(702) 486-3545

New Hampshire
Division of Elderly and Adult Services
Richard Chevrefils, Director
6 Hazen Drive
Concord, NH 03301-6501
(603) 271-4680

New Jersey
Division on Aging
Department of Community Affairs
Lois Hull, Director
CN807
South Broad and Front Streets
Trenton, NJ 08625-0807
(609) 292-4833

New Mexico
State Agency on Aging
Michelle Lujan Grishan, Director
La Villa Rivera Building, Fourth Floor
224 East Palace Avenue
Santa Fe, NM 87501
(505) 827-7640

New York
Office for the Aging
Jane Gould, Director
New York State Plaza
Agency Building Number 2
Albany, NY 12223
(518) 474-4425

North Carolina
Division of Aging
Alfred B. Boyles, Assistant Secretary
693 Palmer Drive
Raleigh, NC 27603
(919) 733-3983

North Dakota
Aging Services
Department of Human Services
Larry Brewster, Administrator
State Capitol Building
Bismarck, ND 58505
(701) 224-2577

Ohio
Department of Aging
Judith Brachman, Director
50 West Broad Street, Ninth Floor
Columbus, OH 43266-0501
(614) 466-5500

Oklahoma
Aging Services Division
Department of Human Services
Roy Keen, Division Administrator
P.O. Box 25352
Oklahoma City, OK 73125
(405) 521-2327

Oregon
Senior and Disabled Services Division
Richard Ladd, Administrator
313 Public Service Building
Salem, OR 97310
(503) 378-4728

Pennsylvania
Department of Aging
Linda Rhodes, Secretary
231 State Street
Harrisburg, PA 17101-1195
(717) 783-1550

Rhode Island
Department of Elderly Affairs
Maureen Maigret, Director
160 Pine Street
Providence, RI 02903-3708
(401) 277-2858

South Carolina
Commission on Aging
Ruth Seigler, Director
400 Arbor Lake Drive, Suite B-500
Columbia, SC 29223
(803) 735-0210

South Dakota
Office of Adult Services and Aging
Gail Ferris, Executive Director
Kneip Building
700 North Illinois Street
Pierre, SD 57501
(605) 773-3656

Tennessee
Commission on Aging
Emily Wiseman, Executive Director
706 Church Street, Suite 201
Nashville, TN 37243-0860
(615) 741-2056

Texas
Department on Aging
Polly R. Sowell, Director
P.O. Box 12786, Capitol Station
1949 IH 35, South
Austin, TX 78741-3702
(512) 444-2727

Utah
Division of Aging and Adult Services
Department of Social Services
Percy Devine III, Director
120 North—200 West
Box 45500
Salt Lake City, UT 84145-0500
(801) 538-3910

Vermont
Aging and Disabilities
Lawrence G. Crist, Commissioner
103 South Main Street
Waterbury, VT 05676
(802) 241-2400

Virginia
Department for the Aging
Thelma Bland, Commissioner
700 Centre, Tenth Floor
700 East Franklin Street
Richmond, VA 23219-2327
(804) 225-2271

Washington
Aging and Adult Services
    Administration
Department of Social and Health
    Services
Charles Reed, Assistant Secretary
OB-44A
Olympia, WA 98504
(206) 586-3768

West Virginia
Commission on Aging
David K. Brown, Executive Director
Holly Grove, State Capitol
Charleston, WV 25305
(304) 348-3317

Wisconsin
Bureau of Aging
Division of Community Services
Donna McDowell, Director
217 South Hamilton Street, Suite 300
Madison, WI 53707
(608) 266-2536

Wyoming
Commission on Aging
Scott Sessions, Director
Hathaway Building, Room 139
Cheyenne, WY 82002-0710
(307) 777-7986

Guam
Division of Senior Citizens
Department of Public Health and
    Social Services
Florence P. Shimizu, Administrator
Government of Guam
P.O. Box 2816
Agana, GU 96910

Private, Nonprofit, and Community Organizations

American Association of Retired Persons (AARP)
Horace B. Deets, Executive Director
601 E Street, NW
Washington, DC 20049
(202) 434-2277

Founded in 1958, AARP is perhaps the foremost membership and advocacy organization for seniors. AARP's large headquarters staff includes experts on virtually every issue of concern to older Americans, including housing, legal rights, minority concerns, consumer affairs, Social Security and SSI, health care, age discrimination, and women's issues. Local AARP chapters also sponsor their own programs on topics such as consumer protection and income tax preparation. AARP operates a wide variety of programs, distributes information on relevant issues, offers exclusive group services for members, serves as an advocate for seniors, and organizes volunteer programs. AARP's National Gerontology Resource Center offers access to a wide range of publications, reference services, Ageline and other materials. AARP sponsors the nonprofit Legal Counsel for the Elderly (LCE). For details on LCE, see the entry under "Legal Services."

PUBLICATIONS: Numerous publications include the monthly *AARP News Bulletin* and the bimonthly magazine *Modern Maturity*.

American Bar Association (ABA)
Commission on Legal Problems of the Elderly
Nancy Coleman, Associate Staff Director
1800 M Street, NW, Suite 200 South
Washington, DC 20036
(202) 331-2297

Formed in 1978, the ABA is a professional organization comprising lawyers and other legal professionals. It serves as a clearinghouse for information on lawyers and about legal topics. The ABA is divided into numerous "sections" by areas of law. These include sections on taxation, estates, labor, and employment law, to name just a few.

The Public Education Division of the ABA produces many publications, films, and newsletters; manages numerous programs and conferences; and conducts outreach activities to make the law more comprehensible to U.S. citizens. It can be reached by contacting the American Bar Association Public Education Division, 750 North Lake Shore Drive, Chicago, IL 60611, (312) 988-5725

The ABA's interdisciplinary Commission on Legal Problems of the Elderly analyzes issues of concern to seniors. The commission conducts research, compiles information, offers publications, and supports community agencies that provide low-cost legal services to seniors. It has developed continuing education programs on topics such as grandparent visitation laws (Naomi Karp is the contact person); guardianship (Erica Wood is the contact person); personal and estate planning, health law, and long-term care (Charles Sabatino is the contact person); Social Security (Joan Fairbanks is the contact person); housing; mediation; the Older Americans Act; and the participation of the private bar in legal proceedings affecting seniors.

PUBLICATIONS: The commission publishes the quarterly journal *BIFOCAL* and technical and more general references for lawyers and other interested parties.

American Law Institute (ALI)
Paul A. Wolkin, Executive Vice President
4025 Chestnut Street
Philadelphia, PA 19104
(215) 243-1600

> The ALI comprises jurists, scholars, and practicing lawyers and publishes resource books known as "restatements" that set forth basic principles of law and catalog decisions interpreting those principles in various jurisdictions. In addition, the ALI promulgates model and uniform laws to be enacted by the states. The ABA and the ALI cosponsor a program of continuing legal education. One of their recent programs, "Estate, Financial, and Health-Care Planning Opportunities for Aging America" (presented 14 June 1990), is available on audiocassette, along with materials prepared by the speakers.

American Society on Aging (ASA)
Gloria Cavanaugh, Executive Director
833 Market Street, Suite 512
San Francisco, CA 94103
(415) 882-2910

> Founded in 1954 as the Western Gerontological Society and expanded to a national group in 1989, the nonprofit ASA has nearly 8,000 members. ASA emphasizes analyzing and influencing public policy, conducting professional education courses, offering publications on aging, and undertaking special projects. ASA sponsors more than 20 conferences and seminars each year, and the annual meeting brings together professionals and other interested parties to share knowledge and forge professional ties. The society also supports forums on business and aging and on religion and aging.

PUBLICATIONS: The highly regarded quarterly *Generations,* which focuses on a different subject each issue, including law and aging, housing, home health care, coercive placement of elders, and autonomy and long-term care practice. Also publishes the bimonthly newspaper *Aging Today* (formerly *The Aging Connection*), which discusses current topics, and a series of monographs from special conferences on particular issues. ASA's Answers, an information clearinghouse, provides access to information on print and audiovisual resources on issues such as long-term care, employment, women's health concerns, and retirement planning.

Asociacion Nacional por Personas Mayores (ANPPM) [National
Association for Hispanic Elderly]
Carmela G. Lacayo, Executive Director
3325 Wilshire Blvd., Suite 800
Los Angeles, CA 90010
(213) 487-1922

> The association and its eight regional offices serve as advocates
> for Hispanic elderly on a broad range of federal, state, and local
> public policy issues, including employment and social services
> programs. The ANPPM furnishes research, technical assistance,
> and training to community groups and seniors.

PUBLICATIONS: The quarterly *Legislative Bulletin: Bibliographic
Research and Resource Guide to the Hispanic Elderly,* video and audio
materials, and public service announcements. English and Spanish
versions of articles are available on Social Security, Medicare, health
topics, and the start-up of volunteer groups to serve low-income older
people.

The Center for Social Gerontology (CSG)
Penelope A. Hommel, Executive Director
117 North First Street, Suite 204
Ann Arbor, MI 48104
(313) 665-1126

> Founded in 1971 as the International Center for Social Gerontol-
> ogy, the nonprofit CSG is devoted to promoting the legal well-
> being of seniors by conducting research, education, technical
> assistance, and training programs. CSG's particular areas of con-
> cern are (1) guardianship and alternative protective services; (2)
> legal rights, including issues such as age discrimination, Social
> Security, housing, and elder abuse; (3) the delivery of legal ser-
> vices; and (4) the care of Alzheimer's patients. The CSG main-
> tains a reference library on legal and policy issues, conducts
> periodic training courses, and develops training materials for
> legal advocates, nonlawyers who work with seniors, and older
> consumers.

PUBLICATIONS: The quarterly *Best-Practice Notes on Delivery of
Legal Services to Older Persons,* the quarterly *Law and Aging: A
Coordinated Bulletin of the AoA-Funded National Legal Support*

System, and manuals such as the *Comprehensive Guide to Delivery of Legal Assistance to Older Persons.*

Gray Panthers
Todd Gossert, Systems Manager
1424 16th Street, NW, Suite 602
Washington, DC 20036
(202) 387-3111
Fax: (202) 387-2492

> Founded in 1970, the Panthers have evolved into a nonprofit group representing 70,000 national members-at-large and an active local membership of 8,000 people in more than 80 local chapters in 24 states. The group's activities include litigation, research and education, and publication of materials on topics such as access to health care, age discrimination, housing, Social Security, and transportation. An information and referral service guides the public on resources for older Americans. The group also operates a speakers' bureau.

PUBLICATIONS: The quarterly newspaper *Network,* the bimonthly newspaper *Health Watch,* and the bimonthly newsletter *Gray Panthers Washington Report.*

Institute on Law and Rights of Older Adults
Rose Dobraf, Executive Director
Brookdale Center on Aging, Hunter College
425 E. 25th Street
New York, NY 10010
(212) 481-4433

> Funded by Hunter College, Brookdale is an academic gerontology center that furnishes advice and professional training to social service professionals serving seniors. Brookdale's Institute on Law and Rights of Older Adults serves as an advocate for seniors, conducts seminars, and represents clients appealing a reduction or termination of health care or income benefits. The center also maintains current information on aging research and offers technical assistance to communities establishing respite care services for caregivers of Alzheimer's disease patients.

PUBLICATIONS: The quarterly *Senior Rights Reporter,* a *Directory of Legal Services for Older Adults,* and a *Benefits Checklist.*

Jewish Association for Services for the Aged
Bernard Warach, Executive Director
40 West 68th Street
New York, NY 10023
(212) 724-3200

> The association provides community services to older adults by using 23 community service offices and 26 local senior citizens' centers in New York City, Nassau, and the Suffolk County area. Among its many programs, the group furnishes information and referrals on government benefits and entitlements, financial assistance, housing and long-term care, and legislative issues. The association also sponsors housing for seniors.

PUBLICATIONS: *Senior Citizens Advocate* and *Aspects of Aging,* a quarterly newspaper.

National Alliance of Senior Citizens
Lawrence Bivins, Executive Director
2525 Wilson Boulevard
Arlington, VA 22201
(703) 528-4380

> The alliance is a consumer advocacy group that furnishes information about government programs for older Americans and lobbies federal and state governments on issues such as health-related legislation and retirement benefits.

PUBLICATIONS: The monthly *Senior Guardian* and the bimonthly *Our Age.*

National Association of Retired Federal Employees (NARFE)
Daniel Griffin, Executive Director
1533 New Hampshire Avenue, NW
Washington, DC 20036
(202) 234-0832

> NARFE addresses the interests of current and future federal retirees and their spouses and survivors. The association's 500,000 national members can receive assistance with pensions, health insurance, Social Security, and veterans' benefits. NARFE intercedes with federal agencies on behalf of its members and lobbies on relevant issues.

National Association of State Units on Aging (NASUA)
Theresa Lambert, Associate Director for Development
2033 K Street, NW, Suite 304
Washington, DC 20006
(202) 785-0707

> Founded in 1964, this national public interest association repre-
> sents a variety of state aging organizations that older persons or
> their advocates may want to contact directly (for example, see
> the "State Units on Aging" entry in this section). NASUA will be
> of most use to readers who cannot locate a current contact ad-
> dress or phone number for one of their member groups. NASUA's
> members include (1) state offices of aging, which are responsible
> for developing programs and policies benefitting older people;
> (2) legal services developers, who work with law schools, bar
> associations, private lawyers, and public legal services providers
> to increase the number of lawyers serving seniors; and (3) long-
> term care ombudsmen, who are responsible for improving the
> quality of life for nursing-home residents. Sponsors the National
> Clearinghouse on State and Local Older Worker Programs.

PUBLICATIONS: Publishes working tools for state units and for other
interested parties.

National Caucus and Center on Black Aged
Samuel J. Simmons, President
1424 K Street, NW, Suite 500
Washington, DC 20005
(202) 637-8400

> The nonprofit National Caucus and Center on Black Aged lob-
> bies Congress and the federal government about issues of concern
> to lower-income seniors, particularly black seniors. The Caucus
> operates a program employing 2,000 seniors in 14 states and
> sponsors rental housing and transportation programs for seniors.
> The group advises community groups, works to strengthen na-
> tional and community-based groups, and conducts educational
> programs on nursing home administration, long-term care, and
> housing management.

PUBLICATIONS: The Caucus publishes the quarterly newsletters
Golden Age and *COBAS Newsletter*.

National Council on the Aging, Inc. (NCOA)
Dr. Cynthia Creyke, President
409 3rd Street, SW, Suite 200
Washington, DC 20024
(202) 479-1200

> Founded in 1950, NCOA is a private, nonprofit membership organization. NCOA represents a primary national resource for information, training, technical assistance, advocacy, publications, and research on every aspect of aging. To achieve its goal of serving as a national information and consultation center, NCOA sponsors conferences and workshops, conducts research, supports demonstration projects, and maintains a comprehensive library of materials on aging, emphasizing the psychological, economic, and social aspects of aging.
>
> NCOA also serves as an umbrella organization for numerous special institutes, such as the National Center on Health Promotion and Aging, the National Association of Older Worker Employment Services, the National Center on Rural Aging, the National Institute of Senior Housing, the National Institute of Community-Based Long-term Care, and the National Voluntary Organizations for Independent Living for the Aging.

PUBLICATIONS: A quarterly annotated bibliography, *Current Literature on Aging,* which features books and articles on issues of interest to seniors; *Perspective on Aging,* a bimonthly magazine; and *NCOA Networks,* a bimonthly newspaper. NCOA also publishes the quarterly *Older Worker News, Senior Housing News, Rural Aging Roundup, Community Care Quarterly, Update on Aging for the Voluntary Sector,* and *Aging and Work.*

National Council of Senior Citizens
Lawrence Smedley, Executive Director
1331 F Street, NW
Washington, DC 20004-1171
(202) 347-8800

> The nonprofit National Council of Senior Citizens comprises 4,800 autonomous senior citizens' clubs, councils, and other community groups, totaling 4.5 million individual members across the nation. The NCSC (1) serves as an advocate for seniors on issues such as income security; (2) maintains a resource library

on topics such as Medicare, Social Security, and federal employment, housing, and other programs; and (3) sponsors the National Senior Citizens Education and Research Center.

PUBLICATIONS: Numerous publications, including the monthly *Senior Citizen News*.

National Hispanic Council on Aging
Dr. Marta Sotomayor, Director
2713 Ontario Road, NW
Washington, DC 20009
(202) 265-1288

> The private, nonprofit council represents the interests of older Hispanics, conducts demonstration projects to provide health care and social services, develops and publishes educational materials, and sponsors training institutes, workshops, and conferences for professionals in the field.

PUBLICATIONS: The quarterly *Noticias* and materials on topics such as access and use of services, long-term care, and the needs of elderly Hispanic women.

National Indian Council on Aging
David Baldridge, Executive Director
6400 Uptown Boulevard, Suite 510-W
Albuquerque, NM 87110
(505) 888-3302

> Sponsored by the Administration on Aging (see entry above), the nonprofit council tries to ensure that older Indian and Alaskan Native Americans have equal access to legal assistance, high-quality and comprehensive health care, and social services. The council furnishes support, technical assistance, and training to tribal organizations and functions as an information clearinghouse.

PUBLICATIONS: The monthly *Elder Voices* and other publications.

NOW Legal Defense and Education Fund
Helen Newborne, Executive Director
99 Hudson Street, Twelfth Floor
New York, NY 10013
(212) 925-6635

Founded in 1971 by the National Organization for Women, the NOW Legal Defense and Education Fund is the public litigation and education arm of the national women's rights group. It conducts research and publishes its findings concerning the legal, economic, and educational situation of women.

PUBLICATIONS: The *State by State Guide to Women's Legal Rights,* a very helpful and substantive compilation of divorce, family, and estates law by jurisdiction.

Older Women's League
Joan Kuriansky, Director
666 11th Street, NW, Suite 700
Washington, DC 20001
(202) 783-6686

Founded in 1980, this nonprofit membership group focuses on the special needs and concerns of older women, advocating appropriate public policy and legislation on issues such as adequate health care and insurance, Social Security, pension rights, equal access to social services, and age discrimination in employment. The league operates a speakers' bureau, supports economic improvements for older women, prepares educational materials, and monitors topics of interest to older women.

PUBLICATIONS: The monthly *OWL Observer* and other materials on topics such as health care in retirement.

Legal Services

American Arbitration Association (AAA)
Robert Coulson, President
140 West 51st Street
New York, NY 10020
(212) 484-4000

The AAA constitutes the preeminent U.S. option for alternative dispute resolution. AAA members include businesses, unions, trade and educational associations, law firms, arbitrators, and others interested in arbitration, mediation, and other resolution mechanisms. The AAA maintains a panel of arbitrators and mediators for referrals and conducts educational seminars and conferences to promote alternative dispute resolution techniques.

PUBLICATIONS: The quarterly *Arbitration Journal.*

American Civil Liberties Union (ACLU)
Ira Glasser, Executive Director
132 West 43rd Street
New York, NY 10036
(212) 944-9800

> The ACLU is well known for activities supporting the individual civil liberties guaranteed by the Constitution regardless of an individual's race, color, sexual orientation, national origin, political opinions, or religious beliefs. Through referrals to private attorneys and its local chapters, the ACLU directly assists people seeking to vindicate their rights in court or at any level of government.

PUBLICATIONS: In addition to numerous policy statements, handbooks, and pamphlets, the ACLU publishes the quarterly journal *Civil Liberties* and the monthly newsletter *Civil Liberties Alert.*

Legal Assistance to the Elderly (LAE)
Howard Levy, Executive Director
1453 Mission Street, Suite 500
San Francisco, CA 94103
(415) 861-4444

> LAE provides free legal services to San Francisco residents over 60, regardless of income, on all matters, including pension benefits, Social Security, and Medicare.

Legal Counsel for the Elderly (LCE)
Wayne M. Moore, Director
601 E Street, NW, A Bldg., 4th Floor
Washington, DC 20049
(202) 833-6720

> AARP (see entry above) sponsors the nonprofit Legal Counsel for the Elderly, which addresses all concerns of seniors, including pensions, Social Security and SSI, landlord-tenant disputes, medical care, Medicare, guardianship, powers of attorney, and taxes.

On the local level, LCE operates a full-service law office for low-income elderly residents of the District of Columbia, including outreach services for the homebound. LCE's extensive national services include training for state legal services and aging advocates, and it conducts demonstration programs to test innovative ways of using volunteers to provide legal services to older Americans. In addition, LCE furnishes technical assistance on increasing funding for legal services to the low-income elderly and on operating legal services delivery systems. LCE manages an SSI application assistance project, a national representative payee and bill-payer project, a state model project for money management, a national support project in protective services law, and a national volunteer lawyers project.

As part of its mission to serve seniors, LCE operates statewide telephone hotlines now serving Florida, Texas, Pennsylvania, Ohio, Michigan, Maine, Arizona, New Mexico, and the District of Columbia. The hot-lines offer free legal advice to older Americans involved in minor legal disputes. They also refer callers to free legal services programs and to private practice attorneys who furnish reduced-rate legal services.

PUBLICATIONS: LCE's numerous publications are designed for legal professionals and for lay readers. They address legal rights late in life, nursing home advocacy, Medicare practice, and other relevant topics. LCE manuals cover protective services, disability issues, and training on seven substantive legal topics. They include the bimonthly *Elder Law Forum* newsletter, which updates legal issues of concern, and *Trainingworks*.

Legal Services Corporation (LSC)
Ellen Smead, Director
Office of Field Services
750 First Street, NE
Washington, DC 20024
(202) 336-8800

The LSC furnishes professional staff to the Administration on Aging (see entry above) to help develop legal services. The LSC funds a variety of programs that offer free legal assistance to older Americans who cannot afford the services of an attorney.

Legal Services for the Elderly (LSE)
Edgar Pauk, Deputy Director
130 West 42nd Street, 17th Floor
New York, NY 10036-7803
(212) 391-0120

> Funded by the Legal Services Corporation since 1968, LSE serves legal services lawyers by furnishing advice, pleadings, memoranda of law, briefs, and *amicus curiae* briefs. LSE does not represent elderly clients directly. The organization's concerns include issues such as Medicaid and Medicare, Social Security, SSI, unemployment insurance, disability, voluntary and involuntary commitment, involuntary committee appointment, conservatorship, intestacy, age discrimination, pensions, elderly rent-increase exemptions, rent control and housing, and nursing home care. Although LSE services focus on litigation assistance and legal information for advocates, LSE does offer nearly two dozen free publications that cover topics such as Social Security hearings, transportation benefits, age discrimination, entitlements, Medigap, and LSE's work with Exxon's pro bono lawyers.

National Academy of Elder Law Attorneys (NAELA)
Thomas G. Goddard, Executive Director
655 North Alvernon Way, Suite 108
Tucson, AZ 85711
(602) 881-4005

> The National Academy of Elder Law Attorneys is an association of attorneys, law professors, and other professionals who specialize in legal issues of concern to seniors. The NAELA sponsors seminars and publishes practice manuals to assist lawyers and paraprofessionals. The NAELA does not make referrals on behalf of its members.

PUBLICATIONS: The organization produces a brochure, "Questions and Answers When Looking for an Elder Law Attorney."

National Bar Association
Maurice Foster, Director
1225 11th Street, NW
Washington, DC 20001-4217
(202) 842-3900

The National Bar Association's Black Elderly Legal Assistance Project emphasizes delivery of legal services to minority elderly, involving the minority bar association, and recruiting black pro bono attorneys.

PUBLICATIONS: The monthly *NBA Magazine,* which each June since 1989 has devoted an issue to seniors and the law.

National Clearinghouse for Legal Services
Michael Leonard, Executive Director
407 Dearborn, Suite 400
Chicago, IL 60605
(312) 939-3830

The National Clearinghouse furnishes extensive legal research and informational support to poverty law advocates.

PUBLICATIONS: Available Clearinghouse resources include legal briefs, publications, and case law abstracts. Such resources can be accessed online through the LEXIS and WESTLAW services and in print in the monthly *Clearinghouse Review.*

National Legal Aid and Defender Association (NLADA)
Clinton Lyons, Executive Director
1625 K Street, NW, Eighth Floor
Washington, DC 20006
(202) 452-0620

The association furnishes technical support and assistance to— and lobbies the federal government on behalf of—local organizations that offer legal services to the poor. NLADA acts as a clearinghouse for information on legal aid and extends litigation support by generating a legal-brief bank, reports, and handbooks.

PUBLICATIONS: *Cornerstone,* a technical newsletter for attorneys, issued five times a year, and a directory of civil and criminal legal defense programs for the poor, biennially.

National Resource Center for Consumers of Legal Services
William A. Boldger, Executive Director
P.O. Box 340
Gloucester, VA 23061
(804) 693-9330

The center is a clearinghouse for information and research needed by individuals and groups seeking to establish or evaluate legal service plans or other delivery mechanisms.

PUBLICATIONS: The center publishes a biweekly newsletter, *Legal Plan Letter,* and model plan documents and other papers.

National Senior Citizens Law Center (NSCLC)
Burton Fretz, Executive Director
1815 H Street, NW, Suite 700
Washington, DC 20006
(202) 887-5280

Neal S. Dudovitz, Deputy Director
1052 West 6th Street, 7th floor
Los Angeles, CA 90017
(213) 482-3550

Established in 1972, the NSCLC helps older Americans by practicing law in support of legal services programs and on behalf of poor elderly clients and client groups. The NSCLC primarily serves legal assistance providers (under the Older Americans Act or the Legal Services Corporation Act), state and area agencies on aging, and private attorneys representing low-income clients. Center services include the provision of litigation assistance, research and consulting support, representation of eligible clients before Congress and federal agencies, manuals and materials, and on-site training courses.

The NSCLC also maintains a staff of attorneys who offer assistance on a broad spectrum of legal issues, and on developing and evaluating legal assistance delivery mechanisms. The center's attorneys can offer purely supportive or advisory services or can serve as active co-counsel or as lead counsel.

PUBLICATIONS: A legislative newsletter and a wide range of handbooks, guides, and updates targeted primarily at legal advocates serving seniors.

Personal Autonomy

American Bar Association Commission on the Mentally Disabled
John Parry, Director
1800 M Street, NW
Washington, DC 20036
(202) 331-2240

One of many special interest sections of the ABA, the commission gathers and disseminates information on federal and state legislation, regulation, and case law affecting people with mental and physical disabilities. The commission addresses issues such as civil commitment, institutional rights, and discrimination.

PUBLICATIONS: Services include a computer database (ABA Disability Law Network), a quarterly publication (*Disability Law Briefs*), and special-issue publications such as *Guardianship: An Agenda for Reform* and *Involuntary Civil Commitment: A Manual for Lawyers and Judges.*

Choice in Dying
Joel Roselin, Director of Communications
200 Varick Street
New York, NY 10014
(212) 366-5540

Choice in Dying is a nonprofit group whose goal is advocating a patient's right to make autonomous health care decisions in the event of a terminal illness. The group sponsors interdisciplinary educational programs for medical, legal, and other professionals and operates a speaker's bureau and a library. It furnishes sample living wills and advanced directives tailored to meet the requirements of an individual's state of residence. The organization also offers a Living Will Registry; for a one-time fee of $35, a copy of an individual's living will or advanced directive is maintained, and the individual receives a wallet-sized notification card.

Hastings Center, Institute of Society, Ethics, and the Life Sciences
Ronnie Brown, Associate Director of Public Information
255 Elm Road
Briarcliff, NY 10510
(914) 762-8500

The Hastings Center is a nonprofit and nonpartisan organization that conducts research in biomedical ethics. It periodically sponsors conferences for public participation. For example, in March 1991 it sponsored a conference on long-term care ethics as the culmination of a three-year research project.

PUBLICATIONS: Of its two publications, it is perhaps best known for *The Hastings Center Report,* which publishes papers on biomedical ethics. The *Report* is available for $46 for individuals, and $60 for institutions.

Kennedy Institute of Ethics, Center for Bioethics
Reference Librarian, Georgetown University
Washington, DC 20057
(800) MED-ETHX

> The Kennedy Institute conducts research in bioethics, including issues such as euthanasia, right to health care, and living wills. It conducts an annual one-week intensive seminar on bioethics and serves as a clearinghouse for research on bioethical issues.

PUBLICATIONS: In addition to its annual publication, *Bibliography of Bioethics,* the institute publishes *ScopeNotes,* which summarizes the debate on a particular issue and provides an annotated bibliography. *ScopeNotes* is available free, and staffers will copy full texts of documents upon request for a copying charge.

Income Security

Government Agencies

Commission on Civil Rights
Alfredo Gonzales, Staff Director
1121 Vermont Avenue, NW, Room 800
Washington, DC 20425
(202) 376-8514

> The commission investigates and holds public hearings in cases of discrimination or denial of equal opportunity. The commission's library is open to the public and includes materials on discrimination against seniors and the handicapped, employment discrimination, women and minority issues, voting rights, and civil rights education.

Department of Labor Pension and Welfare Benefits Administration (PWBA)
200 Constitution Avenue, NW
Washington, DC 20210
(202) 523-8921

The PWBA is the branch of the Department of Labor charged with enforcing the federal private pension law that affects plan participants most directly. The PWBA's Division of Technical Assistance and Inquiries provides general information about private pension laws. A Public Disclosure Room supplies copies of summary plan descriptions and annual financial reports of individual plans upon request for a copying charge. The Division of Public Information can furnish copies of free publications such as *How To File a Claim for Your Benefits, What You Should Know about the Pension Law,* and *Often-Asked Questions about Employee Benefits.* The PWBA has 15 field offices investigating pension fund mismanagement and other breaches of federal pension law.

Equal Employment Opportunity Commission (EEOC)
Evan Kemp, Chairman
1801 L Street, NW
Washington, DC 20507
(202) 663-4900
(800) 872-3362 (Information Service)

The EEOC's mandate is to eliminate all types of discrimination in hiring, promoting, firing, and all other conditions of employment. The EEOC enforces the Age Discrimination in Employment Acts by investigating charges, attempting conciliation or settlement, and if necessary initiating court actions. The EEOC also offers seminars for employers and unions. The toll-free information number accesses recorded messages that describe EEOC programs and direct callers to the appropriate field office to obtain more information or to file a complaint.

Internal Revenue Service
Employee Plans Technical and Actuarial Division
1111 Constitution Avenue, NW, Room 6526
Washington, DC 20224
(202) 566-6783

The IRS is responsible for interpreting the minimum standards imposed by the Internal Revenue Code and for ensuring that company and union pension plans comply with such laws. The Employee Plans Technical and Actuarial Division answers questions about interpretation of the Internal Revenue Code provisions between 1:30 and 4 P.M. (Eastern Standard Time), Monday through Thursday. The IRS does audit individual plans from time to time to ensure compliance with the law, and will consider cases brought to its attention by taxpayers. Such reports should be made to the nearest key district office of the Employee Plans/ Exempt Organizations Division.

Internal Revenue Service
Toll-Free Taxpayer Assistance
1111 Constitution Avenue, NW
Washington, DC 20224
(800) 829-1040

Although it is not always a happy circumstance to hear from "the tax man," seniors may find it helpful to pose their tax questions directly to the IRS if secondary sources are insufficient. The toll-free number listed above is often busy (particularly in the early spring), but persistence is advisable. The IRS also publishes a number of official and helpful publications regarding tax issues, including one directed at seniors (IRS Publication 554) which describes tax benefits available to older Americans. There is no charge for individual copies of these documents. Call (800) 829-3676 to order IRS publications.

Pension Benefit Guaranty Corporation (PBGC)
Public Affairs
2020 K Street, NW
Washington, DC 20006-1806
(202) 778-8800
(202) 778-8859 (TTY/TTD)

The PBGC is one of three U.S. agencies that oversee private pension plans (the others are the IRS and the Department of Labor). Approximately 112,000 private-sector pension plans pay annual premiums to the PBGC for "insurance" to protect guaranteed benefits for participants when a private defined-benefit pension plan terminates.

PUBLICATIONS: PBGC publishes two pamphlets, *Your Guaranteed Pension* and *Your Pension: Things You Should Know about Your*

Pension Plan, which provide general information about participants' rights in private pension plans.

Social Security Administration (SSA)
Gwendolyn King, Director
U.S. Department of Health and Human Services
Room 4J5, West High Rise
6401 Security Boulevard
Baltimore, MD 21235
(800) 772-1213

> The SSA is responsible for payments under (1) the Social Security retirement, survivors, and disability program and (2) the SSI program. SSA services are supplied through a network of district offices, branch offices, and tele-service centers. Questions and applications for benefits can be handled by telephone. Local offices are listed under "U.S. Government" in the telephone directory and can furnish general information and assist in filing claims, obtaining earnings records or benefit statements, and resolving associated problems.

PUBLICATIONS: SSA offers a number of free publications on Social Security, SSI, and Medicare.

U.S. Department of Veterans Affairs
Edward Derwinski, Secretary of Veterans Affairs
810 Vermont Avenue, NW
Washington, DC 20420
(202) 233-2356

> This department administers benefits for veterans and their dependents, supplies information and assistance to applicants, and operates a network of regional offices. Counselors at the regional centers can help benefits applicants by gathering relevant information, obtaining evidence to support the benefit claim, and assisting with reapplications if benefits are denied. The toll-free telephone numbers for such Veterans Assistance Service projects are listed in local telephone directories under "U.S. Government."

PUBLICATIONS: *Federal Benefits for Veterans and Dependents,* a free document describing VA medical, educational, vocational, loan, and insurance benefits.

Private, Nonprofit, and Community Organizations

American Association of Retired Persons (AARP)
Worker Equity Department
Martin Sicker, Director
601 E Street, NW
Washington, DC 20049
(202) 662-4892

> AARP programs address a number of income security issues. The
> Worker Equity Department provides information on age dis-
> crimination and pensions. In addition, AARP's SSI Outreach
> Project helps low-income people understand how to obtain SSI
> benefits, and the Personal Financial Security program has infor-
> mation on Social Security issues. The Tax-Aide Department helps
> older Americans file income taxes. The Women's Initiative sup-
> plies information to women with income security and employ-
> ment questions. The Legal Counsel for the Elderly, described in
> the "Legal Services" section, also offers advice on income secu-
> rity and age discrimination issues.

Center on Social Welfare Policy and Law
Henry Freedman, Executive Director
275 Seventh Avenue, Sixth Floor
New York, NY 10001-6708
(212) 633-6967
1029 Vermont Avenue, NW, Suite 850
Washington, DC 20005
(202) 347-5615

> The center is a legal services corporation national support center
> for litigation concerning cash public assistance programs. The
> majority of its work concerns Aid to Families with Dependent
> Children and general assistance; however, it does handle some SSI
> matters. The center does not take on clients directly, but will act
> as co-counsel or provide support to local legal services programs.

Displaced Homemakers Network
Jill Miller, Executive Director
1625 K Street, NW, Suite 300
Washington, DC 20005
(202) 467-6346

The nonprofit Displaced Homemakers Network uses more than 900 local programs to furnish employment counseling and educational assistance to women whose source of income has been lost because of divorce, separation, the death or disability of a spouse, or termination of public assistance.

PUBLICATIONS: The quarterly *Network News* and pamphlets describing the network's operations, its minority outreach program, and the job-search process.

Employee Benefit Research Institute (EBRI)
Dallas Salisbury, President
2121 K Street, NW, Suite 600
Washington, DC 20037
(202) 659-0670

> EBRI is fundamentally a lobbying organization that consults with Congress and various federal agencies about public policy on employee welfare and retirement benefits. EBRI sponsors research projects, publications, and educational programs for its members (principally corporations, banks, consulting firms, and insurance companies). EBRI is a good source of information on current trends, legislative and regulatory activity, and policy issues affecting employee benefits.

PUBLICATIONS: In addition to its monthly *Issue Briefs* (which explores a single topic in depth) and *Employee Benefit Notes* (which tracks federal and state regulation of employee benefits), EBRI publishes consumer education pamphlets for participants in employee plans.

Food Research and Action Center (FRAC)
Robert J. Fersh, Executive Director
1875 Connecticut Avenue, NW
Suite 540
Washington, DC 20009
(202) 986-2200

> Founded in 1970 as a nonprofit law firm and advocacy group, FRAC furnishes legal and nonlegal research assistance to organizations working to make federal food assistance programs accessible to lower-income people. It does not provide any direct services to seniors. It maintains a library, sponsors research and

educational programs, and serves as a resource to advocates interested in hunger issues. FRAC also supports local and statewide anti-hunger activities.

PUBLICATIONS: Issue reports and analyses of federal food assistance programs. *Foodlines,* a bimonthly newsletter, is available for an annual fee of $20.

International Foundation of Employee Benefit Plans
John A. Altobelli, Chief Executive Officer
18700 W. Bluemound Road
P.O. Box 69
Brookfield, WI 53008
(414) 786-6700

> The International Foundation comprises benefits professionals from all walks of life—plan sponsors and administrators, consultants, bankers, attorneys, accountants, and actuaries. The foundation conducts research in all areas of employee benefits, leaning toward practical applications and public policy, and cosponsors a certification program and curriculum for benefits professionals. The foundation has an extensive subject and periodical file.

PUBLICATIONS: Among its publications are the bimonthly newsletter *Employee Benefits Basics, Employee Benefits Quarterly,* and the *Legal-Legislative Reporter News Bulletin,* a monthly publication that summarizes legal and legislative developments affecting employee benefits.

National Association of Meal Programs (NAMP)
Michael Giuffrida, Administrative Director
204 E Street, NE
Washington, DC 20002
(202) 547-6157

> The association furnishes support and technical assistance to agencies that provide home-delivered or congregate meals to the disabled and seniors. The NAMP maintains resource files on nutrition and statistics, conducts training seminars, and operates a speakers' bureau.

PUBLICATIONS: The bimonthly *Between the Lines* and various publications on operating a volunteer-based meals program.

National Association of Nutrition and Aging Services Programs
Connie Benton Wolfe, Executive Director
2675 44th Street, SW, Suite 305
Wyoming, MI 49509
(616) 531-8700

> The association sponsors quarterly meetings and generates publications for its members concerning the Older Americans Act and national standards for congregate and home-delivered meals. It maintains a database concerning the aging network and nutrition programs for seniors across the United States.

National Committee to Preserve Social Security and Medicare
Martha McSteen, President
2000 K Street, NW, Suite 800
Washington, DC 20006
(202) 822-9459

> The National Committee is a lobbying and educational organization.

National Organization of Social Security Claimants' Representatives (NOSSCR)
6 Prospect Street
Midland Park, NJ 07432
(800) 431-2804

> The NOSSCR offers educational and referral opportunities for its 2,000 members, comprised of attorneys seeking to represent individuals in disability claims. The organization sponsors two national education conferences. At least a portion of the organization's operating funds come from fees paid by members for referrals through the 800 number phone-in service.

PUBLICATIONS: *Social Security Disability* and *SSI Claims: Your Need for Representation.*

Pension Rights Center
Karen Ferguson, Director
918 16th Street, NW, Suite 704
Washington, DC 20006
(202) 296-3778

The nonprofit Pension Rights Center's stated goal is to promote a retirement system that is fair, adequate, and responsive for both retirees and the economy. The center focuses on three objectives—educating the public, protecting workers' pension rights, and developing solutions to retirement income problems. Staff of the center lobby in Washington on behalf of workers and retirees. In addition, the center has developed a National Pension Assistance Project, which refers retirees and beneficiaries to free or low-cost legal assistance from a national network of 360 lawyers.

PUBLICATIONS: The center furnishes information to consumers through a national clearinghouse on pensions and divorce and publishes a variety of fact sheets and booklets. A recent pamphlet, *Your Pension Rights in Divorce,* is one example.

Public Voice for Food and Health Policy
Ellen Haas, Executive Director
1001 Connecticut Avenue, NW, Suite 522
Washington, DC 20036
(202) 659-5930

Public Voice is a national research, education, and advocacy group that promotes interest in public and private decisions about food, nutrition, agriculture, and related health issues. The nonprofit Public Voice encourages communication on such topics by conducting innovative public education programs and regulatory and legislative programs.

Health Care

Government Agencies

LONG-TERM CARE OMBUDSMEN

In each state there is a long-term care ombudsman who acts as an advocate for nursing home residents. The ombudsmen are listed by state below.

State Long-Term Care Ombudsmen

Alabama
Marie Tomlin
Commission on Aging
136 Catoma Street, Second Floor
Montgomery, AL 36130
(205) 242-5743

Alaska
William O'Connor
Office of the Older Alaskans
  Ombudsman
3601 C Street, Suite 260
Anchorage, AK 99503-5209
(907) 279-2232 (accepts collect calls
  from older persons)

Arizona
Rozz Webster
Aging and Adult Administration
P.O. Box 6123-950A
1400 West Washington Street
Phoenix, AZ 85007
(602) 542-4446

Arkansas
Raymon Harvey
Division of Aging and Adult Services
1417 Donaghey Plaza South, POB 1437
7th and Maine Streets
Little Rock, AR 72203-1437
(501) 682-8952

California
Sterling Boyer
California Department on Aging
1600 K Street
Sacramento, CA 95814
(916) 323-6681; (800) 231-4024

Colorado
Virginia Fraser
The Legal Center
455 Sherman Street, Suite 130
Denver, CO 80203
(303) 722-0300; (800) 332-6356

Connecticut
Ida Arbitman
Connecticut Department on Aging
175 Main Street
Hartford, CT 06106
(203) 566-7770

Delaware
Marietta Z. Wooleyhan
Division on Aging
1113 Church Avenue
Milford, DE 19963
(302) 422-1386; (800) 223-9074

District of Columbia
Bruce Vignery
Legal Counsel for the Elderly
1909 K Street, NW
Washington, DC 20049
(202) 833-6720

Florida
Barbara Pogge
State LTC Ombudsman Council
Office of the Governor
154 Holland Building
Tallahassee, FL 32399-0001
(904) 488-6190

Georgia
Joanne Mathis
Office of Aging
Department of Human Resources
878 Peachtree Street, NW, Room 632
Atlanta, GA 30389
(404) 894-5336

Hawaii
Sandy Rongitsch
Hawaii Executive Office on Aging
335 Merchant Street, Room 241
Honolulu, HI 96813
(808) 548-2539

Idaho
Arlene Davidson
Office on Aging
State House, Room 114
Boise, ID 83720
(208) 334-3833

Illinois
Neyna Johnson
Department on Aging
421 East Capitol Avenue
Springfield, IL 62701
(217) 785-3140

Indiana
Robin Grant
Division of Aging
Department of Human Services
251 North Illinois, P.O. Box 7083
Indianapolis, IN 46207-7083
(317) 232-7020; (800) 622-4484

Iowa
Carl McPherson
Department of Elder Affairs
Jewett Building, Suite 236
916 Grand Avenue
Des Moines, IA 50319
(515) 281-5187

Kansas
Myron Dunavan
Department on Aging
Docking State Office Building, 122-S
915 S.W. Harrison
Topeka, KS 66612-1500
(913) 296-4986; (800) 432-3535

Kentucky
Gary Hammonds
Division for Aging Services
Cabinet for Human Resources
CHR Building, Sixth Floor West
275 East Main Street
Frankfort, KY 40621
(502) 564-6930; (800) 372-2291

Louisiana
Hugh Eley
Governor's Office of Elderly Affairs
4528 Bennington Avenue, Box 80374
Baton Rouge, LA 70898-3074
(504) 925-1700

Maine
Joan Sturmthal
Maine Commission on Aging
State House, Station 127
Augusta, ME 04333
(207) 289-3658; (800) 452-1912

Maryland
Condict Stevenson
Office on Aging
301 West Preston Street, Room 1
Baltimore, MD 21201
(301) 225-1083

Massachusetts
Susan McDonough
Executive Office of Elder Affairs
38 Chauncy Street
Boston, MA 02111
(617) 727-7273

Michigan
Hollis Turnham
Citizens for Better Care
1627 East Kalamazoo
Lansing, MI 48912
(517) 482-1297; (800) 292-7852

Minnesota
Bruce Johnson
Board on Aging
Office of Ombudsman for Older
    Minnesotans
444 Lafayette Road
St. Paul, MN 55155-3843
(612) 296-3969; (800) 657-3508

Mississippi
Cinda Henderson
Council on Aging
421 West Pascagoula
Jackson, MS 39203
(601) 949-2070

Missouri
Carol Scott
Division of Aging
Department of Social Services
P.O. Box 1337
2701 West Main Street
Jefferson City, MO 65102
(314) 751-3082

Montana
Doug Blakley
Seniors' Office of Legal and
    Ombudsman Services
P.O. Box 232, Capitol Station
Helena, MT 59620
(406) 444-4676; (800) 332-2272

Nebraska
Geri Tucker
Department on Aging
P.O. Box 95044
301 Centennial Mall South
Lincoln, NE 68509-5044
(402) 471-2306; (402) 471-2307

Nevada
Steve Empey
Division of Aging Services
Department of Human Resources
State Mailroom Complex
Las Vegas, NV 89101
(702) 486-3545

New Hampshire
Doris Beck
Division of Elderly and Adult Services
6 Hazen Drive
Concord, NH 03301-6508
(603) 271-4375; (800) 442-5640

New Jersey
Thomas Brown
Office of the Ombudsman for the
    Institutionalized Elderly
28 West State Street, Room 305,
    CN808
Trenton, NJ 08625-0807
(609) 292-8016; (800) 624-4262

New Mexico
Tim Covell
State Agency on Aging
LaVilla Rivera Bldg, Fourth Floor
224 East Palace Avenue
Santa Fe, NM 87501
(505) 827-7640

New York
Dave Murray
Office for the Aging
Agency Building, Number 2,
    Empire State Plaza
Albany, NY 12223
(518) 474-7329

North Carolina
Debbie Brantley
Department of Human Resources
Division of Aging
693 Palmer Drive
Raleigh, NC 27603
(919) 733-8400

North Dakota
Jo Hildebrant/Ramona Ehrmantraut
Aging Services Division
Department of Human Services
State Capitol Building
Bismarck, ND 58505
(701) 224-2577; (800) 472-2622

Ohio
Roland Hornbostel
Department of Aging
50 West Broad Street, Ninth Floor
Columbus, OH 43266-0501
(614) 466-9927; (800) 282-1206

Oklahoma
Esther Allgood
Division of Aging Services
Department of Human Services
P.O. Box 25352
Oklahoma City, OK 73125
(405) 521-6734

Oregon
Meredith Cote
Office of Long-Term Care Ombudsman
2475 Lancaster Drive, Building B,
    Number 9
Salem, OR 97310
(503) 378-6533; (800) 522-2602

Pennsylvania
Linda Jackman
Department of Aging
Barto Building, 231 State Street
Harrisburg, PA 17101
(717) 783-7247

Rhode Island
Rhode Island Department of Elderly
    Affairs
160 Pine Street
Providence, RI 02903-3708
(401) 277-6883

South Carolina
Mary B. Fagan
Office of the Governor
Division of Ombudsman and Citizens'
    Service
1205 Pendleton Street
Columbia, SC 29201
(803) 734-0457

South Dakota
Rolland Hostler
Office of Adult Services and Aging
Department of Social Services
Richard F. Kneip Building
700 North Illinois Street
Pierre, SD 57501-2291
(605) 773-3656

Tennessee
Jane Bridgman
Commission on Aging
706 Church Street, Suite 201
Nashville, TN 37219-5573
(615) 741-2056

Texas
John Willis
Department on Aging
P.O. Box 12786 Capitol Station
1949 IH 35, South
Austin, TX 78741-3702
(512) 444-2727; (800) 252-9240

Utah
Sally Brown
Division of Aging and Adult Services
Department of Social Services
120 North—200 West, Box 45500
Salt Lake City, UT 84145-0500
(801) 538-3924

Vermont
Camille George
Office on Aging
103 South Main Street
Waterbury, VT 05676
(802) 241-2400; (800) 642-5119

Virginia
Mark Miller
Department for the Aging
700 East Franklin Street, 10th Floor
Richmond, VA 23219-2327
(804) 225-2271; (800) 552-3402

Washington
Kary Hyre
South King County
Multi-Service Center
1200 South, 336 Street
Federal Way, WA 98003
(206) 838-6810; (800) 422-1384

West Virginia
Carolyn Riffle
Commission on Aging
State Capitol Complex
Charleston, WV 25305
(304) 558-3317

Wisconsin
George Potaracke
Board on Aging and Long Term Care
214 North Hamilton Street
Madison, WI 53703
(608) 266-8944

Wyoming
Debra Alden
Wyoming State Bar Association
900 8th Street
Wheatland, WY 82201
(307) 322-5553

Health Care Financing Administration, Office of Beneficiary Services
(HCFA)
U.S. Department of Health and Human Services
6325 Security Boulevard
Baltimore, MD 21207
(301) 966-3000

> The HCFA (1) coordinates federal participation in Medicaid and
> Medicare; (2) sets Medicare eligibility requirements, develops
> claim procedures, and regulates Medicare claims processors; (3)
> sponsors quality assurance programs such as the Second Surgical
> Opinion Hotline, which helps people considering nonemergency
> surgery to locate a doctor for a second opinion; and (4) super-
> vises HMOs that participate in federal programs, including
> Medicare and Medicaid. HCFA's Office of Beneficiary Services
> furnishes information about Medicare and Medicaid, explains
> how to qualify and obtain needed services, and identifies state
> and federal management responsibilities.

PUBLICATIONS: The yearly *Medicare and Medicaid Data Book and
Health Care Financing Review*, the quarterly *Current Publications
Listing*, and a pamphlet on second surgical opinions, which is available
from the hotline.

National Institute on Aging, National Institutes of Health,
Public Health Service, U.S. Department of Health and Human Services
C. F. William, Director
Federal Building, Room 6C12
9000 Rockville Pike
Bethesda, MD 20892
(301) 496-1752

> The National Institute on Aging focuses on conducting and sup-
> porting professional research, producing technical reports, and
> promoting health education and disease prevention.

PUBLICATIONS: The institute's publications primarily address the aging process but include some useful documents on legal issues—for example, the two-page "Getting Your Affairs in Order," one of the concise Age Page series of flyers that provide brief and pragmatic overviews of health topics for older people. Publications can be obtained by writing to P.O. Box 8057, Gaithersburg, Maryland 20898-8057.

Private, Nonprofit, and Community Organizations

American Health Care Association (AHCA)
Dr. Paul Willging, Executive Vice President
1201 L Street, NW
Washington, DC 20005
(202) 842-4444

> This professional association represents the interests of licensed nursing homes and long-term care facilities before Congress, federal agencies, and other professional groups. AHCA furnishes consumer information about long-term care, nursing homes, and guardianship and offers continuing education programs.

American Hospital Association (AHA)
Dr. Carol McCarthy, President
840 North Lake Shore Drive
Chicago, IL 60611
(312) 280-6000; (800) 242-2626 (publications service)

> A professional organization, the AHA represents hospitals and other operations furnishing medical care. The association conducts research, issues policy papers on hospital issues affecting seniors, connects hospitals with other community groups serving older Americans, and offers continuing education programs.

PUBLICATIONS: An annual survey of hospitals, the weeklies *AHA News and Hospitals,* and *A Patient's Bill of Rights.*

Concerned Relatives of Nursing Home Patients
Nursing Home Advisory and Research Council
Mary A. Mendelson, Executive Director
P.O. Box 18820
Cleveland Heights, OH 44118
(216) 321-0403

This organization is a subsidiary of the Nursing Home Advisory and Research Council. It serves the families, friends, and guardians of nursing home residents by advocating residents' rights.

PUBLICATIONS: A bimonthly newsletter, *Insight,* and several other publications, including *Selecting a Nursing Home.*

Foundation for Hospice and Home Care
Val Halamandaris, President
519 C Street, NE
Washington, DC 20002
(202) 547-7424

The foundation comprises community agencies that furnish homemaker and home health services. The group also helps individuals in locating approved homemaker and home health services.

PUBLICATIONS: Publishes the annually updated *Directory of Accredited/Approved Homemaker-Home Health Aide Services.*

Health Insurance Association of America (HIAA)
Dr. Carl J. Schramm
P.O. Box 41455
Washington, DC 20018
(202) 223-7780; (800) 423-8000 (information services)

The HIAA provides information on U.S. health insurance companies and answers general questions about health and disability insurance coverage, including supplementary Medicare insurance.

PUBLICATIONS: HIAA publishes the annual *Source Book of Health Insurance,* which reviews companies' performance; *How To Use Private Insurance with Medicare,* and *A Consumer's Guide to Long-Term Care Insurance.*

Hospice Association of America (HAA)
Janet E. Neigh, Executive Director
519 C Street, NE
Washington, DC 20002
(202) 546-4759

The Hospice Association of America's members are hospices, home health care agencies, community service organizations, and other professionals committed to the concept of hospice care. The association operates a speakers' bureau and educational programs and offers hospice referral services and consultation on Medicare reimbursement problems.

PUBLICATIONS: A bimonthly newsletter, *Hospice Forum,* which features updates on research, state hospice programs, public policy, and regulatory developments.

National Center for State Longterm Care Ombudsman Resources
2033 K Street, NW
Suite 304
Washington, DC 20006
(202) 797-0657

The center is a central resource for state long-term care ombudsmen (see list above) authorized by the Older Americans Act. Its primary service to consumers is that it will provide a list of the long-term care ombudsmen in the inquirer's state or region.

National Citizens Coalition for Nursing Home Reform
Elma Holder, Executive Director
1224 M Street, NW, Suite 301
Washington, DC 20005-5183
(202) 393-2018

Founded in 1975, the consumer-based coalition has roughly 300 member groups in 45 states. The coalition emphasizes improving the quality of care and life for nursing home residents by working with individual consumers, resident and family councils, state and local long-term care ombudsmen, concerned professionals, and regulatory officials. The organization supports consumer and citizen action groups around the country that work on behalf of seniors and the institutionalized disabled. The coalition conducts seminars on nursing home issues, sponsors a speakers' bureau, and acts as a clearinghouse for information on nursing home care.

PUBLICATIONS: Upon request, the coalition will supply a free information packet, outlining resources in the requester's area and giving tips on choosing a nursing home. Publications include the bimonthly *Quality Care Advocate* and a number of pamphlets on nursing and boarding homes.

National Health Law Program (NHLP)
Laurence M. Lavin, Director
2639 S. La Cienega Boulevard
Los Angeles, CA 90034
(213) 204-6010
1815 H Street, NW, Suite 705
Washington, DC 20006
(202) 887-5310

> The National Health Law Program furnishes advice to attorneys and paraprofessionals in legal services programs about health problems of the poor, including Medicare and Medicaid. The NHLP offers referral services and consultation on litigation strategies.

PUBLICATIONS: The quarterly *Health Advocate* as well as manuals and guides for advocates of seniors. NHLP issues special reports and submits occasional law review articles authored by its staff.

National Hospice Organization (NHO)
John Mahoney, Director
1901 North Moore Street, Suite 901
Arlington, VA 22209
(703) 243-5900

> The NHO offers technical advice and training to local hospice groups and furnishes consumers with information on local hospice services.

PUBLICATIONS: The annual *Guide to the Nation's Hospices.*

National Legal Center for the Medically Dependent
Thomas Marzen, Managing Attorney
50 South Meridian, Suite 605
Indianapolis, IN 46244
(317) 632-6245

> A national support center of the Legal Services Corporation, this group provides research data and consultation services to advo-

cates for the indigent and disabled to ensure these groups' access to medical care. The center furnishes three types of services: (1) direct representation of individuals, (2) support to advocates, lawyers, paraprofessionals, and ombudsmen, and (3) a quarterly journal, *Issues in Law and Medicine.*

United Seniors Health Cooperative (USHC)
James Firman, President and Chief Executive Officer
1331 H Street, NW, Suite 500
Washington, DC 20005
(202) 393-6222

> The private, nonprofit USHC has nearly 8,000 members, most in the District of Columbia area. Members receive information for making better health care and financing decisions and discounts on a variety of services and products. USHC conducts seminars on Medicare benefits, legal issues such as living wills and durable powers of attorney, long-term care options, and medical recordkeeping. For a small fee, the cooperative's computerized Medigap checkup program can analyze individual coverage to ensure its adequacy. USHC also has developed benefits eligibility checkup software that is available to community groups and that is customized for each community. USHC's information on the 125 Medigap policies available in the District of Columbia, Maryland, and Virginia has wider applicability because the majority of the policies are sold nationally.

PUBLICATIONS: A bimonthly newsletter, *Long-Term Care: A Dollars and Sense Guide,* which furnishes details on home care, shared housing, nursing homes, and long-term care insurance and other materials on topics such as Medigap policies.

Housing

Government Agencies

Department of Housing and Urban Development (HUD)
Office of Public Affairs
451 7th Street, SW
Washington, DC 20410
(202) 755-6420

HUD is responsible for federal programs to satisfy housing needs, ensure fair housing opportunities, and improve and develop U.S. urban and rural communities. HUD distributes printed information about its programs, including the Elderly and Assisted Housing Program.

Private, Nonprofit, and Community Organizations

American Association of Homes for the Aging (AAHA)
Sheldon Goldberg, President
901 E Street, NW, Suite 500
Washington, DC 20005
(202) 783-2242

> The association's members are nonprofit and governmental homes, housing, and health-related facilities for seniors and others interested in promoting long-term solutions to the housing problems of seniors. AAHA cooperates with Congress and the federal agencies in developing public policy, develops educational programs and materials, and promotes group purchasing and insurance programs. AAHA furnishes free information on long-term care and housing for seniors.

PUBLICATIONS: The biweekly *AAHA Provider News* and two biannuals, the *National Continuing Care Directory* and the *Continuing Education Update.*

National Center for Home Equity Conversion
Ken Scholen, Director
1210 East College Drive, Suite 300
Marshall, MN 56258
(507) 532-3230

> The center is an independent, nonprofit organization that provides research and consultation services to product and program developers, public policy makers, and consumer organizations, and serves as a clearinghouse of information on home equity conversions for seniors.

PUBLICATIONS: *Federal Research on Home Equity Conversion, Home Made Pension Plans,* and the *National Directory and Sourcebook,* a list of programs, consultants, and further resources on home equity conversion. A complete publications list is available.

National Voluntary Organizations for Independent Living for the Aging
National Council on the Aging
Cynthia Creyke, Program Coordinator
600 Maryland Avenue, SW, West Wing, Suite 100
Washington, DC 20024
(202) 479-1200

> The organization is one of the subsidiary groups of the National Council on the Aging. Its goal is to promote independent living for seniors through educating and assisting voluntary community-based groups in providing services to seniors.

PUBLICATIONS: A directory of national voluntary organizations as well as a newsletter, *Update on Aging for the Voluntary Sector.*

Consumer Issues

Government Agencies

Consumer Information Center (CIC)
P.O. Box 100
Pueblo, CO 81009

PUBLICATIONS: The General Service Administration's CIC publishes the popular quarterly *Consumer Information Catalog,* which lists and briefly describes more than 200 federal publications of interest to consumers on topics such as housing, employment, health, and money management.

Consumer Product Safety Commission
Dan Rumelt, Director
Office of Information and Public Affairs
5401 Westbard Avenue
Bethesda, MD 20207
(301) 492-6580

The Consumer Product Safety Commission is one of several key agencies charged with protecting consumers from dangerous products. It maintains information on product recalls.

Federal Trade Commission (FTC)
Public Reference Section
6th Street and Pennsylvania Avenue, NW
Washington, DC 20580
(202) 326-2222

> The FTC is charged with establishing trade regulations and protecting consumers from unfair or deceptive business practices. The FTC and its branch offices furnish information on request, investigate complaints, and manage programs that focus on unfair or deceptive advertising and labeling, fair credit reporting, product reliability and warranty performance, business practices of nursing homes, and door-to-door sales. The FTC cannot resolve individual consumer complaints but can take action against a company if evidence shows a pattern of deception, unfair practices, or statutory violations.

PUBLICATIONS: Consumer protection publications include a number of free pamphlets on topics such as home refinancing, fair debt collection, and the FTC funeral rule.

Food and Drug Administration (FDA)
Dr. David Kessler, Commissioner
5600 Fishers Lane
Rockville, MD 20857
(301) 443-3170

> The FDA regulates the safety, effectiveness, and purity of food, drugs, cosmetics, and medical devices and is active in combating health quackery. The Office of Consumer Affairs answers questions about the side effects, safe use, and effectiveness of vitamins, drugs, cosmetics, medical devices, and products that produce radiation.

PUBLICATIONS: The quarterly *FDA Consumer* and free publications on topics such as hearing aids, quack doctors, X-rays, and medical devices.

Interstate Commerce Commission
Office of Compliance and Consumer Assistance
Constitution Avenue and 12th Street, NW
Washington, DC 20423
(202) 275-7844

> The ICC advises consumers of known complaints against transportation services furnished by railroads, trucks, buses, and interstate movers. The ICC responds to requests for consumer information, offers advice and assistance when possible, and refers consumers to other groups if appropriate.

Private, Nonprofit, and Community Organizations

Consumers Union
Rhoda Carpatian, Executive Director
2001 S Street, NW, Suite 520
Washington, DC 20009
(202) 462-6262

> Consumers Union is perhaps best known for its respected *Consumer Reports* magazine. Consumers Union does its own tests, and rates and reports on competing consumer products. It also represents consumer interests in the legislature, the courts, and agencies.

PUBLICATIONS: In addition to *Consumer Reports* magazine, Consumers Union publishes a newsletter, reports, and books on consumer products as varied as insurance, food, and automobiles.

Council of Better Business Bureaus
4200 Wilson Boulevard, Suite 800
Arlington, VA 22209
(703) 276-0133

> The council represents the 170 local Better Business Bureaus (BBBs) and addresses complaints about national advertising and national charities. Local BBBs are sponsored by a city or region's businesses in an effort to self-police local merchants. A complete list of local BBBs or a reference in your area is available from the council.

National Consumers League
Linda Golodner, Executive Director
815 15th Street, NW, Suite 928
Washington, DC 20005
(202) 639-8140

> Founded in 1899, the private, nonprofit National Consumers League is the pioneer consumer group in the United States, working to educate consumers, bring consumer issues to the attention of government and industry decision makers, and bring citizens into the decision-making process. The league conducts research and advocacy projects on behalf of consumers and helps ensure that consumer and worker protection programs are enforced. Educational materials are available on topics such as the cost of medical care, Medicare, supplemental health insurance, food and drug safety, credit, and workplace safety. The NCL also plans to develop an information network on nursing home care, home health care, and other services for older persons.

PUBLICATIONS: The bimonthly *Bulletin,* the *Consumer Guide to Hospice Care,* and a variety of other consumer-oriented publications.

National Foundation for Consumer Credit
8701 Georgia Avenue
Suite 507
Silver Spring, MD 20910
301-589-5600; (800)-388-2227 (Consumer Credit Counseling Service)

> This nonprofit organization counsels individuals on credit problems. For an average fee of $9 it assists debtors in establishing a debt repayment plan, and in selling that plan to creditors. The organization has 550 locations nationwide.

Family Law

Academy of Family Mediators (AFM)
James C. Melamed, Executive Director
P.O. Box 10501
Eugene, OR 97440
(503) 345-1205

The academy comprises attorneys and mental health professionals who are trained in family mediation and, moreover, are committed to mediation as an alternative to adversarial court proceedings for resolving divorce and other family disputes. The AFM has developed standards of practice for its members (900 standards as of 1990), conducts workshops, and offers referral services.

PUBLICATIONS: An annual directory of members and two quarterly publications, *Mediation News* and *Mediation Quarterly*.

Foundation for Grandparenting
Arthur Kornhaber, M.D., President and Founder
P.O. Box 31
Lake Placid, NY 12946

> The foundation holds a broad concern about grandparenting issues, including visitation rights. One of its goals is establishing a national visitation policy.

Grandparents'/Children's Rights
Lee and Lucille Sumpter, Study Directors
5728 Bayonne Avenue
Haslett, MI 48840
(517) 339-8663

> Grandparents'/Children's Rights is a loose national coalition of self-help groups that provide mutual support and information to grandparents seeking the right to visit grandchildren. The organization functions as a clearinghouse for information about state laws and pending legislation across the country.

Estate Planning

American Council of Life Insurance (ACLI)
L. Charles FitzGerald, Secretary
1001 Pennsylvania Avenue, NW
Washington, DC 20004-2599
(202) 624-2000; (800) 942-4242 (Consumer Helpline)

> ACLI is one of several trade organizations for insurance companies that represent the companies' interests to policymakers in

Washington. The council also promotes consumer awareness of cost differences among policies. To facilitate these objectives, ACLI maintains the Insurance Industry's Citizen Action Network and publishes pamphlets and consumer booklets on topics such as Medigap.

National Association of Insurance Commissioners (NAIC)
Sandra Gilfillan, Executive Vice President
120 West 12th Street, Suite 1100
Kansas City, MO 64105
(816) 842-3600

The NAIC is an association of insurance commissioners from various states. The organization's principal aim is promoting uniform legislation and encouraging consistent regulation of life, health, property, and casualty insurance among the jurisdictions by promulgating model laws and regulations (for example, model regulations on marketing Medigap insurance).

Chapter 10

Reference Materials

The first sections of this chapter list and summarize print references that supplement the information given in the chapters of Part One. The print reference sections are divided into the following topics: general references, legal services, personal autonomy, income security, health care, housing, consumer issues, family law, and estate planning.

The relevant print references for each of these topics are subdivided into loose-leaf services, books, booklets and pamphlets, and articles. Loose-leaf services are multi-volume works that typically provide primary source material (statutes, regulations, agency pronouncements, etc.) in addition to a treatise on the law. They are continually updated by the publisher to reflect changes in the law. No annotation appears after these listings because of this common format. Substantive annotations are provided for other materials. The annotations are intended to enable the reader to make an intelligent decision about the usefulness of the reference for his or her needs.

A strong emphasis was placed on the currency of the citations. The references are mostly targeted at a lay audience, but many may be of greater interest to various professionals who are not familiar with the issues in question.

The final section of this chapter reviews nonprint materials and sources of such materials—electronic databases, software, and audiovisual materials.

General References

The references in this section cut across several of the subjects analyzed in this book or offer general information on the law or on aging.

Books

Brown, Robert N. *The Rights of Older Persons: A Basic Guide to the Legal Rights of Older Persons under Current Law.* American Civil Liberties Union Handbooks. Carbondale, IL: Southern Illinois University Press, 1989. 413p. $9.45. ISBN 0-8093-1432-0.

> Designed for use by lay readers and professionals, this book uses a question-and-answer format to address seniors' basic legal rights to adequate income, health care, and freedom from restraints on life, liberty, and property. The book is one of a series of American Civil Liberties Union guides for identifying and protecting individual legal rights. The book focuses on benefits guaranteed by law (Social Security, Medicare, and other public assistance programs), protections against age discrimination, guardianship and civil commitment, and the right to refuse medical treatment, among other issues. It summarizes the roles of government agencies and suggests ways to deal with them.
>
> The guide's appendixes detail national legal and advocacy organizations for seniors; Congressional committees; state offices of aging, legal services developers, and long-term care ombudsmen; and the computation of Social Security and SSI benefits.
>
> Robert Brown is a law professor at the University of Detroit and is director of the University's Health Law Center.

Maddox, George L., ed. *The Encyclopedia of Aging.* New York: Springer, 1986. 890p. $96. ISBN 0-8261-4840-9.

> This broad-based reference book is designed for educated inquirers who need a brief, authoritative introduction to key topics and issues and to relevant organizations and legislation. The book's 500 entries are organized alphabetically. Entries are extensively cross-referenced, and citations from the lengthy 40-page bibliography are incorporated in the text of each entry as appropriate.

National Senior Citizens Law Center. *Representing Older Persons: An Advocate's Manual.* Washington, DC: National Senior Citizens Law Center, 1990. 142p. $85 for private attorneys; $45 for nonprofit organizations, legal services lawyers, and Older Americans Act attorneys. ISBN 0-932605-00-1.

> This manual is a collaborative effort of the staff of the National Senior Citizens Law Center. It provides advocates for seniors with basic information about key litigation issues, including statutory references and current developments on topics including age discrimination, pensions and retiree health, Social Security, SSI, Medicare, Medicaid, and the Older Americans Act. Many chapters provide helpful practice tips and suggest resources for further inquiry.

Reader's Digest Family Legal Guide: A Complete Encyclopedia of Law for the Layman. Pleasantville, NY: Reader's Digest Association, 1981. 1,268p. ISBN 0-89577-100-4.

> This reference book covers 2,600 topics organized alphabetically in an encyclopedic format and indexed using lay terminology. Entries define legal terms, include cross-references, and cite case histories as necessary to help understanding. The book includes 17 special articles (for example, on estate planning and making a will) and several dozen charts summarizing state laws on particular topics. The book in no way eliminates the need for a lawyer, but will help average citizens understand their rights and remedies, communicate more effectively with lawyers, and avoid legal problems. The age of the guide may limit its utility.

Regan, John J., and AARP Legal Counsel for the Elderly. *Your Legal Rights in Later Life.* Glenview, IL: Scott, Foresman, 1989. 321p. $13.95. ISBN 0-673-24884-4.

> Using nontechnical language, the author addresses a broad range of legal questions commonly asked by seniors. The book focuses on central topics such as meeting legal needs (yourself or with a lawyer's help), securing retirement income from public and private sources, providing for necessary health care, addressing landlord and tenant concerns, protecting consumer rights, understanding family law, planning for incapacity, estate planning and administration. The book also includes a useful glossary. Each

section is punctuated by helpful questions and answers, which serve to draw out key points.

Strauss, Peter J., Robert Wolf, and Dana Shilling. *Aging and the Law.* Chicago: Commerce Clearing House, 1990. 912 p. $100. 1991 Supplement $35.

> This comprehensive work is designed as a primer for law students and advocates studying to represent senior clients in the broad range of elder law issues. The text is updated by supplements that cover changes in the law since the book's original publication.

Articles

Frolik, Lawrence A., and Alison P. Barnes. "An Aging Population: A Challenge to the Law." *The Hastings Law Journal* 42 (March 1991): 683–718.

> This article is the first in a series concerning legal issues for seniors as discussed in the *Journal*'s "Symposium: Legal Issues Relating to the Elderly." After setting forth the basic demographics of America's aging population, the authors consider how the legal profession might serve seniors.

Legal Services

Books

American Bar Association (ABA). Commission on Legal Problems of the Elderly. *The Law and Aging Resource Guide.* Washington, DC: ABA, February 1990. 250p. (A large-print copy of an individual state entry is free.)

> Produced since 1980 and updated annually, this guide is designed to help the legal community and seniors identify and contact available legal resources. This guide furnishes an outstanding and timely overview of the legal resources available to seniors throughout the United States.
>
> The guide profiles each state and the District of Columbia, identifying available resources in the following categories: (1)

the legal services developer for seniors; (2) the state long-term care ombudsman; (3) legal services funded under the Older Americans Act; (4) state and local bar committees; (5) pro bono and reduced-fee legal assistance projects that employ the services of private attorneys; (6) educational projects serving the community, attorneys, law schools, and the media; and (7) special projects and activities, focusing on legislative projects. Organizations whose functions are not obvious are briefly described, and an address, phone number, and (frequently) a contact person are supplied for each organization.

Coombs, Richard. *The Lawsuit Handbook*. Irvine, CA: LawPrep Press, 1990. 168p. $24.95. ISBN 0-9623338-1-6.

> A senior should read this book before deciding whether to proceed with a lawsuit. The author, a litigator himself, explains the federal and state court system and the phases of the litigation process. It represents the potential costs and pitfalls of filing a lawsuit. A glossary of legal terms completes the book.

Corbin, John. *Find the Law in the Library: A Guide to Legal Research*. Chicago: American Library Association, 1989. 327p. $58. ISBN 0-8389-0502-1.

> Designed for consumers and nonlawyer advocates who want to conduct legal research, this textbook explains American law, the references that record such law, and how to locate relevant information. Among other specialties, the book focuses on law for seniors (including probate, insurance, and pensions), the family (including marriage and divorce, landlords and tenants), and the community (including torts, administrative law, taxation, contracts, and civil rights). John Corbin is a professor of law and law librarian at the Reynaldo G. Garza School of Law in Edinburgh, Texas.

Elias, Stephen. *Legal Research: How To Find and Understand the Law*. 2d ed. Berkeley, CA: Nolo Press, 1990. 220p. $14.95. ISBN 0-87337-020-1.

> For the senior who wants to find the answers him or herself, Nolo Press provides just the orientation needed. This book reviews the resources and tools available to perform legal research and provides guidance with respect to the concepts of statutory and

regulatory authority and legal precedent. It won't make the reader qualified to practice law, but it might empower him or her to understand it better.

Hommel, Penelope. *The Comprehensive Guide to the Delivery of Legal Services for Older Persons.* Ann Arbor, MI: Center for Social Gerontology, 1988. 500p. $35.

> This guide was developed to assist legal service providers, area agencies on aging, and other developers of legal services in the programmatic and administrative aspects of legal services for seniors. The guide consists of 12 chapters setting forth the history of legal assistance under the Older Americans Act, identifying common legal problems for seniors and charting the way for developing a legal services program. It includes information on funding and targeting seniors who need services.

Ostberg, Kay, and HALT. *Using a Lawyer . . . and What To Do If Things Go Wrong: A Step-by-Step Guide.* New York: Random House, 1990. 146p. $8.95. ISBN 0-679-72970-4.

> Written as a consumer guide, this book is easy to read, describes a sound strategy for addressing the client-attorney agreement as a business relationship, and offers practical advice on choosing a lawyer, monitoring progress on the case, identifying trouble spots, exercising cost control, and rectifying difficulties in the client-lawyer relationship. Appendixes include a model client-attorney agreement, a prepaid legal services plan contract, a diagram of the procedural stages of a lawsuit, a list of state bar programs for resolving complaints against lawyers, a glossary, and a brief bibliography.

Powers, Patricia R., and Karen Klingensmith, eds. *Aging and the Law: Looking into the Next Century.* Washington, DC: AARP, 1990. 239p.

> This collection of papers and discussions from a national conference on aging and the law furnishes a useful overview for policymakers, advocates, and interested lay readers. The conference focused on social, legal, and demographic trends; legal assistance for older persons now and in the future; and broad-based thinking about gerontology, law, and justice. Papers of particular interest address trends in poverty and elderly law and legal services delivery systems.

Booklets and Pamphlets

AARP, Consumer Affairs Section, and Federal Trade Commission, Office of Consumer and Business Education, Bureau of Consumer Education. *Money Matters: How To Talk to and Select Lawyers, Financial Planners, Tax Preparers, and Real Estate Brokers.* Washington, DC: AARP, 1989. 16p. Free.

> This guide offers advice on deciding when a professional's services are needed, assessing the qualifications of professionals, evaluating the quality of professional services rendered, formulating questions and keeping records of the relationship, registering complaints if necessary, and getting your money's worth from professionals.
>
> The guide includes brief sections specifically focused on lawyers, financial planners, tax preparers, and real estate brokers. The section on lawyers discusses alternative options (handling the problem yourself, using nonlegal resources), questions to ask before selecting a lawyer, and bases for calculating and negotiating fees.

ABA. Commission on Legal Problems of the Elderly, and Committee on Delivery of Legal Services to the Elderly, Young Lawyers Division. *Legal Services for the Elderly: Where the Nation Stands—A Role for the Private Bar.* 4th ed. Washington, DC: ABA, September 1988. 56p. Free.

> A smaller cousin of the commission's annual state-by-state guide (see above), this booklet is targeted more toward concerned groups, particularly bar associations. The first half of the book reviews the legal issues confronting seniors and the scope of available legal services (including the government, the private bar, and corporate law departments). Appendixes list (1) state and local bar committees addressing the legal needs of seniors, (2) state units on aging, (3) private attorney projects for seniors, (4) continuing legal education projects on law and aging, (5) funding sources for legal programs aimed at seniors, (6) criteria to use in the process of selecting an attorney, and (7) a brief reading list.

ABA. Public Education Division. *The American Lawyer: When and How To Use One.* You and the Law Series. Washington, DC: ABA, 1986. 40p. $2.

This booklet offers lay readers a lawyer's view on common legal matters such as wills, estates, home ownership, marriage and divorce, civil wrongs, financial matters, consumer matters, and taxes, and suggests when legal assistance may be appropriate. The booklet provides a framework for structuring the attorney-client relationship including selection of an attorney, and expected legal fees and expenses. It also addresses strategies to employ if a senior is not satisfied with his or her lawyer and suggests dispute resolution alternatives such as negotiation, resolution centers, and small claims courts.

National Academy of Elder Law Attorneys. *Questions and Answers When Looking for an Elder Law Attorney.* Tucson, AZ: National Academy of Elder Law Attorneys, 1990. 9p.

This brochure suggests how to find legal help for your needs, promoting the specialized services of an elder law attorney. As the authors point out, not even all elder law attorneys handle all issues of concern to seniors. The brochure stresses the importance of forging good communications with counsel.

Wood, Erica F., and Prudence B. Kestner. *Mediation: The Coming of Age—A Mediator's Guide in Serving the Elderly.* 2d ed. Washington, DC: ABA, November 1989. 37p. Free. ISBN 0-89707-549-8.

Noting the more than 350 community-based mediation and dispute-resolution projects throughout the country, the booklet seeks to inform mediators about the aging process, available aging networks, common law-related disputes, and the value of using seniors as mediators. The two appendixes list the state units on aging and the state ombudsmen and outline six stages of mediation.

Articles

Arnason, Sia. "The Legal Needs of the Elderly: Rights, Wrongs and Remedies." *Aging* 360 (1990): 14–17.

This is one of a series of articles in *Aging* focusing on legal services for seniors. The author promotes the value of alternative legal assistance through social workers and community education.

Moore, Wayne. "Expanding Access to Legal Services: The Legal Hotline Approach." *Aging* 360 (1990): 19–22.

This is another of the series of articles mentioned above. It evaluates the early experience of the Washington, DC, based Legal Counsel for the Elderly.

Wood, Erica. "Building Bridges to Bar Associations." *Aging 357* (1988): 2–5.

The article is intended to coach state and regional governmental agencies on tactics to involve local bar associations in concerns of the elderly. A broader audience will be interested in the author's assessment of how bar associations work.

Personal Autonomy

References in the "Health Care" and "Estates" sections (and to a lesser degree those in the "Income Security" section) also address topics relevant to personal autonomy issues.

Books

AARP. Legal Counsel for the Elderly. *Decision-Making, Incapacity, and Seniors: A Protective Services Practice Manual*. Washington, DC: AARP, December 1987. 200p. $XXX. ISBN 0-933945-00-0.

A product of the counsel's National Protective Services Support Center, this book is designed as a single source of practice materials on all aspects of protective services law. The book is divided into five sections: (1) counseling clients who have unimpaired decision-making capacities; (2) representing clients with impaired decision-making capacity; (3) special circumstances, including health care decision making and nursing home admission contracts; (4) illustrative case summaries; (5) tables of state statutory authorities governing durable power of attorney, living wills, guardianship and conservatorship, adult protective services, and health care decision making.

ABA. Commission on the Mentally Disabled. *Involuntary Civil Commitment: A Manual for Lawyers and Judges*. Washington, DC: ABA, 1988. 130p. $30.

This book focuses on involuntary civil commitment of adults, furnishing a framework for lawyers and judges to participate meaningfully in the process and to ensure full benefits to the respondent and to the mental health care system. Although designed for lawyers, this work may be useful to anyone who must deal with involuntary civil commitment of seniors and consequently must understand the civil commitment process.

The book evaluates the responsibilities of each of the parties in the court proceeding, including a discussion of basic procedural steps and strategies. Appendixes include sample practice forms and seven tables summarizing key provisions in state civil commitment laws.

ABA. Commission on the Mentally Disabled and Commission on Legal Problems of the Elderly. *Life Services Planning*. 3 vols. Washington, DC: ABA, 1989. approx. 275p. $40.

The three volumes comprising this work are the culmination of a two-year project undertaken by the ABA Commissions on Legal Problems of the Elderly and on the Mentally Disabled. The first volume reports on the details of the project itself and will probably not be of general interest.

Volumes 2 and 3 offer a profile of more than 100 organizations throughout the country that provide specialized services to seniors, the disabled, and their families as well as a comprehensive training manual for advocates on financial and estate planning, government benefits programs, mechanisms to plan for future incapacity, and residential concerns. Three appendixes include planning forms and client questionnaires. Copies of this well-written and thorough resource can be ordered from ABA Order Fulfillment, 750 N. Lake Shore Drive, Chicago, IL 60611.

Brakel, Samuel Jan, John Parry, and Barbara A. Weiner. *The Mentally Disabled and the Law*. 3d ed. Chicago: American Bar Foundation, 1985. 845p. $96. ISBN 0-910059-05-5.

This extensive book covers all aspects of interactions between the mentally disabled and the law. This edition incorporates the wide range of new legislation and policy that evolved during the decade before its publication. The book offers a thorough evaluation of all topics addressed, but the material should be updated to obtain a full understanding of relevant issues.

The book describes historical trends; involuntary institutionalization; voluntary admission; discharge and transfer; rights and treatment rights of institutionalized persons; incompetency, guardianship, and restoration; decision-making rights over persons and property; family laws; provider-patient relations (confidentiality and liability); rights and entitlements in the community; and mental disability and criminal law.

The book includes dozens of tables that summarize relevant laws by state and references to hundreds of legal cases that constitute relevant precedents. A brief bibliography also is provided.

Cantor, Norman L. *Legal Frontiers of Death and Dying.* Bloomington: Indiana University Press, 1987. 208p. $24.95. ISBN 0-253-33290-7.

Professor Cantor provides a thoughtful and thought-provoking treatment of what he calls the "frontier" issues of death with dignity and the consent of patients to life-sustaining medical procedures. The text explores the underlying constitutional and common-law principles at work in various court decisions, including the landmark decisions in the Quinlan and Conroy cases. Extensive footnotes provide resources for further inquiry. Considering the complexity of the issues covered in the book, it is surprisingly readable.

Center for Social Gerontology. *Guardianship and Alternative Legal Interventions: A Compendium for Training and Practice.* National Support Project in Law and Aging series, Penelope A. Hommel, Project Director. Ann Arbor: Center for Social Gerontology, October 1986. 254p.

Developed under a grant from the Administration on Aging, the manual was developed to train social service personnel in guardianship and protective services. It discusses the pros and cons of guardianship and the alternative options such as money management, joint property arrangements, powers of attorney, living wills, trusts, and representative payees. The manual includes sample forms for establishing direct deposit, powers of attorney, health care decision making, and representative payees; practice notes on guardianship and conservatorship; and a guide to the client interview. A dated but comprehensive annotated bibliography on guardianship and alternative legal interventions completes the work.

Clifford, Denis. *The Power of Attorney Book.* 3d ed. Self-Help Law Series. Berkeley, CA: Nolo Press, 1990. 270p. $19.95. ISBN 0-87337-123-2.

Written by an attorney for lay readers, this book furnishes a thorough discussion of the durable powers of attorney, offering standardized forms and instructions necessary to create a durable power of attorney and a living will. The use of durable powers of attorney for financial and asset management is detailed, including appropriate uses and advantages, legal limits, advice on selecting an attorney-in-fact, complexities of using the tool for this purpose, and factors involved in statutory durable power of attorney, along with sample forms and clauses to use in a contract. The application of durable powers of attorney for health care is described for Californians and other Americans. The book features numerous examples and also offers advice on effective legal research.

Colen, B. D. *The Essential Guide to a Living Will.* New York: Pharos Books, 1987. 112p. $5.95. ISBN 0-345-34887-7.

This book describes the living will option in detail, focusing on how to determine need for such a will, state laws regarding them, and how to prepare one in videotape format. The book lists several additional resources.

Myers, Teresa Schwab. *How To Keep Control of Your Life after 60: A Guide for Your Legal, Medical, and Financial Well-Being.* Lexington, MA: Lexington Books, 1990. 429p. $17.95. ISBN 0-669-19457-3.

The author focuses on how seniors—and the soon-to-be elderly—can plan ahead so that medical treatment, finances, and other important matters are handled according to one's wishes. The book is divided into four sections that address (1) planning ahead by considering wills, trusts, joint accounts, Medigap and long-term care insurance policies, living wills, powers of attorney, and paying for nursing home care; (2) maintaining control while in a hospital or nursing home, including information on patient rights and responsibilities, criteria for discharge, Medicare and Medicaid, and how to deal with problems and complaints; (3) making decisions for the incompetent—and limits on such decisions—by the use of guardians, conservators, and Social Security payments to parties other than the recipient; and (4) the need to formulate new and better policies. The 35 appendixes constitute roughly one-half of the book, but are difficult to access. They provide supplemental information such as charts, sample forms and documents, lists of relevant organizations and programs, and summaries of state and federal legal provisions.

Booklets and Pamphlets

AARP. *A Matter of Choice: Planning Ahead for Health Care Decisions.* Washington, DC: AARP, December 1986. 87p.

> Prepared at the request of the chairman and ranking member of the U.S. Senate Special Committee on Aging, this booklet is a succinct discussion of the public policy issues surrounding advance directives. The booklet examines the importance of making choices about personal health care, traditional approaches for protecting patients' rights, and the use of advance directives. The booklet includes a brief bibliography, a list of 17 relevant organizations, and a one-page checklist for advisers and admission offices. A series of appendixes provide useful background, detailing living will statutes by state, and including samples of documents creating a living will and a durable power of attorney for health care, among others.

ABA. Commission on Legal Problems of the Elderly and Young Lawyers Division, Committee on Delivery of Legal Services to the Elderly. *Guardianship of the Elderly: A Primer for Attorneys.* Washington, DC: ABA, February 1990. 79p. $7.95.

> This primer is targeted at attorneys for all parties in guardianship proceedings. It attempts to help attorneys adopt the least-restrictive alternative concept and to guide them through the guardianship process, offering a step-by-step approach to the system, hands-on tips, and suggested references. The primer describes the steps in the guardianship process and reviews relevant ethical issues and practice strategies. Appendixes include a list of state agencies on aging, a summary of state statutes governing guardianship, suggested resources, sample guardianship forms and a sample letter to guardians, and a summary of relevant national and state bar association projects. Order from ABA Order Fulfillment, 750 N. Lake Shore Drive, Chicago, IL 60611.

ABA. Commission on the Mentally Disabled. *Mental Disability: A Primer.* (By the editors of the *Mental and Physical Disability Law Reporter.*) Washington, DC: ABA, 1984. 61p. $10.

This booklet is divided into two sections, each replete with relevant case citations that were reviewed in the *Reporter*. A new edition of this useful but technical booklet is being compiled and should be available shortly. The first section includes definitions of key terms, why the mentally disabled need representation, a lawyer's concerns when representing the mentally disabled, and specialized resources available from the commission. The second section offers a more extensive description of, and cites significant cases and other guidelines on, a wide range of topics, including important federal statutes, civil commitment, criminal mental disability issues, rights within an institution , deinstitutionalization, decision-making rights and competency, exclusionary zoning, employment and other discrimination, education, private health insurance, confidentiality, liability, and Social Security and Medicaid eligibility and case studies.

Articles

Alexander, George J. "Time for a New Law on Health Care Advance Directives." *The Hastings Law Journal* 42 (March 1991): 755–778.

> The author reviews the history of advance directives and their use in other countries, and recommends that a single statute be adopted addressing living wills, durable powers of attorney, and family consent. The article also has extensive footnotes regarding state laws on these topics.

Bopp, James Jr., and Daniel Avila. "The Siren's Lure of Invented Consent: A Critique of Autonomy-based Surrogate Decision Making for Legally Incapacitated Older Persons." *The Hastings Law Journal* 42 (March 1991): 779–816.

> This article was written as a counterpoint to that written by Susan Martyn and Henry Bourguignon, summarized below. Both address the issue of surrogate decision making addressed in the *Cruzan* case. Bopp and Avila posit that a model based on substitute decision making is inherently flawed in that an incompetent person retains no autonomy. The article is forcefully argued and conveys a great deal of information about the underlying principles behind surrogate decision making.

Gottlich, Vicki. *Powers of Attorney: A Guide for Advocates.*
Washington, DC: National Senior Citizens Law Center, October 1990.
14p. Free. (Also available through the National Clearinghouse for Legal
Services, Document no. 45,470.)

> The memorandum is akin to a term paper on the effective use of
> powers of attorney for seniors. It reaches back into common-law
> history and brings the relevant concepts forward through recent
> case law examples. An advocate who feels the need for a ground-
> ing in the underlying policies surrounding powers of attorney
> will benefit from this piece.

Hommel, Penelope A., and Erica F. Wood. "Guardianship: There Are
Alternatives." *Aging* 360 (1990): 6–12.

> Part of a special issue devoted to legal services for seniors, this
> article considers the alternatives to full guardianship. The author
> uses a hypothetical case study approach to explore basic con-
> cepts of advanced directives, supportive services, trusts, and joint
> ownership of property in particular.

Katz, Robert. "Not a Pretty Picture." *Esquire* 115 (April 1991):
108–119.

> An account of the controversy surrounding the guardianship of
> Willem de Kooning, the famous abstract expressionist painter. In
> among the gossip, the reader can discern the process of institut-
> ing a guardianship.

Martyn, Susan R., and Henry J. Bourguignon. "Coming to Terms with
Death." *The Hastings Law Journal* 42 (March 1991): 817–858.

> This article was written as a counterpoint to that written by
> James Bopp and Daniel Avila, summarized above. It reviews the
> rationale behind the Supreme Court's decision in the *Cruzan*
> case, arguing that the court did more to bolster state interference
> with surrogate decision making than to aid it.

Topolnicki, Denise M. "The Gulag of Guardianship." *Money* 18
(March 1989): 140–152.

> Those who are curious about when and upon whom guardian-
> ship is imposed will want to read this article. The thesis of the
> piece, that guardianship should be avoided, is borne out by

numerous case histories and discussion about the risks of guardianship. Some alternatives to guardianship are discussed.

Income Security

Loose-Leaf Services

Employment Coordinator. New York: Research Institute of America.

Labor Law Reporter. Chicago: Commerce Clearing House.

Pension and Profit Sharing Plans. Englewood Cliffs, NJ: Maxwell Macmillan.

Pension Coordinator. New York: Research Institute of America.

Pension Plan Guide. Chicago: Commerce Clearing House.

Social Security Law and Practice. Rochester, NY: The Lawyers Co-operative.

Social Security Practice Guide. Albany, NY: Matthew Bender & Company.

Books

Age Discrimination: A Legal and Practical Guide for Employers. Washington, DC: Bureau of National Affairs, 1990. 625p. $95.

> This manual provides a comprehensive treatment of the Age Discrimination in Employment Act, noting differences between jurisdictions in its interpretation and application.

Coleman, Barbara. *Primer on ERISA*. 3d ed. Washington, DC: Bureau of National Affairs, 1989. 10p. $25. ISBN 0-87179-626-0.

> This handbook summarizes the major provisions of the Employee Retirement Income Security Act (ERISA), the federal law that regulates private employer-sponsored pension and welfare benefit plans. It sets forth the tax qualification and operating rules, reporting and document disclosure requirements, and the various plan participant guarantees. The agencies that partici-

pate in the regulation of these plans are also discussed. Copies of forms that plan administrators are required to file with the federal government are enclosed. A glossary of common terms completes the volume.

Commerce Clearing House. *State Tax Handbook*. Chicago: Commerce Clearing House, 1990. 684p. $19.

> This handbook, which is updated and reissued every year, reviews the current tax system of each state and the District of Columbia. The handbook includes (1) a brief description of statewide levies, the basis and rate for each tax, and the principal payment and return due dates; (2) charts on corporate and personal income tax that detail rates, deductions, exemptions, and reporting requirements in the 45 income tax states, the District of Columbia, and major cities; (3) a summary of each state's tax administration structure and the primary responsibilities of each organization or person; (4) a concise digest of the principal revenue provisions of each state's constitution and tax system; and (5) tax yields for principal taxes in fiscal year 1988 and the percentage of total state revenue that each tax constitutes.

Coulson, Robert. *Empowered at Forty. How To Negotiate the Best Terms and Time of Your Retirement*. New York: HarperCollins, 1990. 224p. $12.95. ISBN 0-88730-433-8.

> This book takes a positive approach to early retirement. By informing readers of their rights under the Age Discrimination in Employment Act (ADEA), the Employee Retirement Income Security Act, Social Security, and other federal laws, the author encourages seniors to bargain with their employers as to the terms of their retirement. He seeks to downplay litigation as a means of enforcing ADEA, favoring negotiation or other alternative dispute resolution techniques. The first few chapters inform readers of their rights. Later chapters address negotiation and alternative dispute resolution techniques. Part of this discussion is in a question-and-answer format, which makes it particularly readable.
>
> Negotiation may not be in the cards for every reader; however, the information in this book on federal employment laws will find a wider audience.

Department of Veterans Affairs. *Federal Benefits for Veterans and Dependents*. Washington, DC: Department of Veterans Affairs, January 1991. 92p.

> At best, this booklet is an abbreviated overview of veterans' benefits. The reader may find eligibility descriptions difficult to follow and benefit descriptions too brief. The last 27 pages list VA facilities nationwide where veterans can seek information, assistance, and benefits.

Food Research and Action Center (FRAC). *FRAC Guide to the Food Stamp Program*. Washington, DC: FRAC, 1990. 200p. $12.

> The *Guide* is a comprehensive work on the operations and policy behind the food stamp program, and an invaluable source to anyone doing advocacy on food stamps. It is geared toward professionals, but may prove helpful to a lay reader as well.

Fretz, Burton D. and Neal S. Dudovitz (National Senior Citizens Law Center). *The Law of Age Discrimination: A Reference Manual*. Chicago: National Clearinghouse for Legal Services, January 1987. 89p. $15. ISBN 0-941077-17-9.

> Written primarily for lawyers, this heavily footnoted treatise cites hundreds of cases and reviews related to the Age Discrimination in Employment Act of 1967, including coverage, administrative considerations, civil actions (types, jurisdictions, evidence burdens), defenses, remedies, and jury instructions. Fretz is the executive director of the National Senior Citizens Law Center. Neal Dudovitz is its deputy director.

Gelfand, Donald E. *The Aging Network*. 3d ed. New York: Springer, 1988. 340p. $22.95. ISBN 0-8261-3054-2.

> This is a book to be read from cover to cover as it outlines the full range of services provided to seniors as a result of federal legislation. Part I provides demographic background on seniors and on the programs that have evolved to serve them, emphasizing the Older Americans Act. The remaining sections discuss public and private benefits, specialized programs such as information and referral efforts and crime prevention, and service delivery systems, including senior centers, adult day care, and nursing homes. A bibliography at the end of each section gives resources, and two appendixes, one addressing national nonprofit resource groups, complete the volume.

Kingson, Eric R. *What You Must Know about Social Security &*
Medicare. New York: Pharos Books, 1987. 120p. $4.95. ISBN
0-345-34397-2.

> The author concisely describes the history and future of,
> and society's common stake in, Social Security and Medicare.
> Issues covered include how to determine eligibility, apply for
> benefits, and estimate the level of expected benefits; how re-
> tirement and survivor benefits work; steps to take upon be-
> coming disabled; recent program changes and their effects;
> and other public benefit programs. The author is a college pro-
> fessor who has worked with congressional committees and
> served on the National Commission on Social Security Reform.
> Printed in large type and easy to understand, this book is a good
> choice for anyone who wants to understand Social Security and
> Medicare.

Matthews, Joseph, with Dorothy Matthews Berman. *Social Security,*
Medicare, and Pensions. 5th ed. Berkeley, CA: Nolo Press, 1990. 250p.
$15.95. ISBN 0-87337-076-7.

> One of a series of self-help law books, this book is targeted for
> lay readers and includes examples to illustrate complex points.
> The book is comprehensive and very useful, particularly when
> coupled with updated information on Medicare and Social Se-
> curity. Subjects covered in detail include Social Security, SSI,
> Medicare, Medicaid, Medigap insurance, private pensions, and
> age discrimination. Federal employment, railroad, and veteran's
> benefits are also summarized, with help in defining eligibility,
> calculating benefits, and applying for benefits.

National Legal Aid and Defender Association and National Senior
Citizens Law Center (NLADA and NSCLC). *Social Security/SSI:*
Litigation Strategy Training Materials. Papers presented at the annual
meeting of NLADA/NSCLC, Berkeley, CA, July 1989. Washington, DC:
National Senior Citizens Law Center, 1989. 229p.

> This book is a collection of conference papers covering specific
> aspects of topics such as disability, SSI, work incentive, overpay-
> ments, representative payees, jurisdiction, the Equal Access to
> Justice Act, and potential SSI litigation issues. The book should
> be useful to professionals, policymakers, and consumers trying
> to understand current issues of concern in the field.

The National Underwriter Company. *Social Security Manual.* 30th ed. Cincinnati: The National Underwriter Company, 1990. 206p. $9.95 (paperback). ISBN 0-87218-470-6.

> This book is one of a series of up-to-date National Underwriter books on Social Security and Medicare. Relying on a question-and-answer format, the book is a well-indexed and comprehensible guide to Social Security, but is not especially tailored for the lay reader with no knowledge of Social Security. The book is most useful to professionals and as a supplement for people who have acquired a basic familiarity with the program.
>
> The book furnishes information about OASDI coverage, wages and self-employment income and their relation to benefits, eligibility and filing, benefit characteristics and levels, taxation of Social Security benefits, Social Security taxes on employers and employees, loss of benefits because of excess earnings (the retirement test), Medicare, and the survivor benefit plan. The book also includes a number of useful Social Security tables.

Neuman, R. Emil. *The Complete Handbook of U.S. Government Benefits.* Leucadia, CA: United Research, 1989. 325p. $9.95. ISBN 0-961-4924-2-2.

> This handbook contains information about the federal benefits available to Americans of all ages, among them, Social Security, Medicare, and other income support programs. Overall, the treatment given to any one benefit is brief, but it may serve to orient the reader to the basics of particular programs.

O'Meara, Daniel P. *Protecting the Growing Number of Older Workers: The Age Discrimination in Employment Act.* Labor Relations and Public Policy Series, no. 33. Philadelphia: The Wharton School, University of Pennsylvania, 1989. 384p. $35. ISBN 0-89546-069-6.

> This book is a copiously footnoted dissertation on the Age Discrimination in Employment Act (ADEA). The author traces the development of the case law through the years, elucidating the many exceptions and nuances of the statute. Major cases and provisions are explored from different perspectives. Sections IV and V explain procedures and remedies and should prove helpful to advocates new to the ADEA arena.

Booklets and Pamphlets

AARP, Tax-Aide Department. *Relocation Tax Guide*. Washington, DC: AARP, 1989. 7p. Free.

> This pamphlet provides basic information on state taxes as a starting point for elderly people who are thinking about moving from one state to another. The pamphlet includes a brief glossary and a list of state departments of revenue (including addresses and telephone numbers). Two charts list the state-by-state status of the following taxes: (1) personal income taxes, including full Social Security exemptions, state and federal public pension exemptions, private pension exemptions, special preferences for seniors, and source taxes; (2) sales taxes, including state rate, combined state-local rate, and exemptions; (3) property taxes, including "circuit breakers," homestead exemptions or credits, and deferral programs; (4) estate taxes (pick-up only; pick-up and estate); and (5) inheritance taxes (pick-up and inheritance).

AARP, Worker Equity Initiative. *Advantages of Qualified Pension & Profit-Sharing Plans*. Washington, DC: AARP, 1988. 48p. Free.

> This is a good introduction to basic pension terms and concepts. After a brief overview of common elements of qualified retirement plans, this booklet breaks out different types of retirement plans, using tabs to simplify research. A "special considerations" section at the end of each section identifies significant issues in each particular type of plan. Regrettably, there is no bibliography to facilitate further inquiry.

Coleman, Barbara. *Protecting Your Pension Money: A Pension Investment Handbook*. Washington, DC: Pension Rights Center, 1987. 28p. Free.

> This booklet is written in nontechnical terms for workers and retirees who belong to pension plans. Topics addressed include applicable pension plan rules and exceptions; sources of information to assess compliance with the rules; determining whether pension funds are invested wisely, whether investments are diversified, and whether associated costs are reasonable; and the way to respond if the rules have been broken. The booklet also lists relevant government agencies and sources of information.

National Senior Citizens Law Center. *Retirees' Right to Continued Receipt of Health Benefits from Employers and Pension Plans: Are Your Benefits Safe?* Washington, DC: National Senior Citizens Law Center, July 1987. 8p. Free.

> This pamphlet is a brief, informative discussion of employer-provided benefits to retirees and the retiree's rights under federal law. Using straightforward questions and answers, the book suggests a few resources for further inquiry. A short glossary of pension and health benefit terms completes the work.

Pension Benefit Guaranty Corporation. *Your Pension: Things You Should Know about Your Pension Plan.* Washington, DC: Pension Benefit Guaranty Corporation, 1989. 24p. Free.

> This booklet is a bare-bones explanation of (1) pension plan structures and operations, (2) the rights and options of participants, and (3) protections provided by federal law. A pension checklist is designed to help laypersons collect key information about their benefits, and a glossary of terms completes the booklet.

Pension Rights Center, National Pension Assistance Project. *Directory of Pension Assistance Resources.* Washington, DC: Pension Rights Center, 1990. 20p. Free.

> This first-edition directory is useful for identifying sources of information on pension rights and for seeking legal assistance to enforce those rights. The booklet is divided into two sections: (1) pension information resources, including a list of government agencies and private groups that furnish information on pensions, and (2) legal assistance resources. The booklet includes a brief paragraph on each organization that describes the group's focus, objectives, and services.

Pension Rights Center, National Pension Assistance Project. *A Guide to Understanding Your Pension Plan.* Washington, DC: AARP, 1989. 49p. Free.

> A joint project of AARP, the National Pension Assistance Project, and the Administration on Aging, this booklet reviews how pension plans function, how seniors can assess their pension benefits, and the rules and regulations governing pension plans. It lists relevant government agencies and legal assistance resources. The guide also briefly summarizes applicable pension laws and lists several useful publications on pensions.

U.S. Department of Labor, Pension and Welfare Benefits
Administration. *What You Should Know about the Pension Law.*
Washington, DC: Department of Labor, May 1989. 65p. Free.

> This booklet is an overview of the important provisions of the
> Employee Retirement Income Security Act (ERISA), with a focus
> on the provisions that most directly affect plan participants. The
> lay reader may find it somewhat pedantic, stripped as it necessar-
> ily must be from the terms of any particular plan.

U.S. Internal Revenue Service. *Tax Information for Older Americans.*
IRS Publication no. 554. Washington, DC: U.S. Department of the
Treasury, 1990. 96p. Free.

> Not everyone finds IRS documents readable, but this one is geared
> especially for seniors to describe tax provisions of general appli-
> cability, as well as those that apply to seniors alone. It covers is-
> sues such as pension income, Social Security benefits, life insurance
> proceeds, sales of a principal home, and the like. Worksheets
> abound, and at the back of the booklet, the IRS has provided tax
> forms in large print for draft preparation. This document is
> reissued each year to reflect changes in tax laws and IRS forms.

Wilson, Sally Hart. *Federal Income Tax Guide for Seniors.* Los Angeles:
National Senior Citizens Law Center, March 1990. 19p. Free. (Also
available through the National Clearinghouse for Legal Services,
Document no. 43,947.)

> Taking its organization from the federal income tax return itself,
> this guide was designed to assist seniors in filing their 1989
> returns. Although the forms themselves have changed somewhat,
> the discussion in the memorandum will still be useful.

Articles

Foran, Nancy J., and Barbara A. Theisen. "Tax Benefits for Elderly
Continue To Erode, but Tax Savings Strategies Are Still Available."
Taxation for Lawyers 19 (September/October 1990): 114–120.

> A quick and helpful presentation of federal tax provisions bene-
> fiting seniors, as well as strategies to take advantage of them.

Fretz, Burton D., and Donna Shea. "Untender Mercies: Layoffs and the
Older Worker." *Clearinghouse Review* 19 (February 1989):
1104–1106.

This article provides a good introduction to the concepts and case law surrounding the Age Discrimination in Employment Act (ADEA), particularly as it pertains to reductions in force (RIFs). It debunks the myth that a RIF is a bar to ADEA claims.

Kent, Don. "Supplemental Security Income: Filling the Information Gap." *Aging* 362 (1991): 6–13.

The author argues that 1.75 million seniors who could be receiving SSI (and possibly Medicaid) are not even aware that they are eligible. Although targeted toward a professional audience, the article provides good information for laypersons as well, including recommendations on which documents to bring to an initial interview and sources of further information.

Park, Marilyn E. "New Pension Laws Improve Retirement Benefits." *Aging* 360 (1990): 38–39.

The article is a brief review of changes brought about by the Tax Reform Act of 1986, which took effect in 1989. The most valuable part of the article is the last column describing pension disclosure rules. It refers readers to the Pension Rights Center for publications of interest.

Terrell, Pamela M. "Social Security: The Search for Fairness." *Congressional Quarterly's Editorial Research Reports* 13 (5 April 1991): 190–203.

This article is a clear, concise summary of the current public policy debate on Social Security. It also contains a chart summarizing the way in which benefits are calculated.

Health Care

References in the "Personal Autonomy" and the "Income Security" sections address related issues.

Loose-Leaf Services

Social Security Law and Practice. Rochester, NY: The Lawyers Co-operative.

Books

Budish, Armond D. *Avoiding the Medicaid Trap: How To Beat the Catastrophic Costs of Nursing-Home Care.* New York: Henry Holt, 1989. 232p. $22.50. ISBN 0-8050-1035-1.

> This book is an excellent source of information on the difficult and important topic of protecting lifetime savings and assets from being wiped out by Medicaid requirements for long-term custodial care coverage. Summary checklists are included throughout. It assists the reader to evaluate his or her current financial status, exempt assets, and the wisdom of strategies such as the purchase of private insurance, transfers of assets, and the use of advance directives. The book also addresses the role of legal counsel and suggests how to select a lawyer.
>
> The conclusion supplies a master checklist for protecting assets that defines a senior's options before long-term care is required, when a spouse enters a nursing home and leaves a spouse at home, and when an unmarried person enters a nursing home. Appendixes constitute more than half of the book and supply durable power of attorney forms and descriptions of five model Medicaid trusts.

Komlos-Hrobsky, Peter (National Senior Citizens Law Center). *An Advocate's Guide to Home Care for the Elderly.* Chicago: National Clearinghouse for Legal Services, 1988. 132p. $15. ISBN 0-941077-18-7.

> This guide is designed for advocates for seniors, supplying the basic information necessary for representing people who want to arrange home care. The guide touches on all relevant issues but focuses on legal issues of immediate concern to advocates. Topics covered include home care and its advantages, Medicare and Medicaid home health services, adult day health services, and home care financing and planning. Programs for nonmedical daily needs are cited, such as daily living services, the Medicaid personal care option, Medicaid waivers, services under the Older Americans Act, the Retired Senior Volunteer Programs, private volunteer programs, social services block grants under Title XX, and nutrition services. Statutory and constitutional mandates for home care are reviewed.

Landay, Eugene, ed. *The Complete Medicare Handbook.* A special publication of the U.S. Department of Health and Human Services. Rocklin, CA: Prima Publishing and Communication, 1990. 200p. $8.95. ISBN 1-55958-036-4.

> Written in lay language and designed as a handy reference, this handbook was recently updated and offers a horse's-mouth assessment of how to use Medicare effectively. The book focuses on benefits and patient rights and obligations, providing some brief historical discussion of the program.
>
> Supplements constitute more than half of the book and address coverage of kidney dialysis and transplants, hospice benefits, Medicare and employer health plans, Medicare and prepayment plans, health insurance for people with Medicare, Medicare carriers by state, state insurance regulators, and state agencies on aging. A sample form 1490S and a glossary of Medicare-related terms are included.

The National Underwriter Company. *All about Medicare.* Cincinnati: The National Underwriter Company, 1990. 69p. $6.95. ISBN 0-87218-471-4.

> This up-to-date book is one of a series of National Underwriter books on Social Security and Medicare. The book summarizes the Medicare program in comprehensible language, but is not especially tailored for the lay reader with no knowledge of Medicare. The book is most useful to professionals and as a supplement for people who are somewhat familiar with the program. It includes discussions of eligibility, benefits administration, and financing under Parts A and B. Appendixes include a table of Medicare benefits, a list of items not covered by the program, an example of Medicare benefits for a hypothetical patient, and the addresses (by state) to which Medicare claims should be sent.

Oshiro, Carl, Harry Snyder, and the editors of Consumer Reports Books. *Medicare/Medigap: The Essential Guide for Older Americans and Their Families.* Mt. Vernon, NY: Consumers Union, 1990. 212p. $12.95. ISBN 0-89043-329-1.

> After a relatively brief description of Medicare, the remainder of this book is devoted to strategies to cope with uncovered medical costs, unpaid claims, overzealous salesmen, and unresponsive medical care. The authors include several model letters for

communicating with physicians, insurance commissions, and law enforcement authorities, as well as sources of further information and a glossary. An additional plus to this handy volume is that a free supplement is offered by the authors to bring the reader up-to-date with changes since publication.

Raper, Ann Trueblood, and Anne C. Kalicki, in association with American Association of Homes for the Aging. *National Continuing Care Directory: Retirement Communities with Nursing Care.* 2d ed. Glenview, IL: Scott, Foresman, 1988. 449p. $19.95. ISBN 0-673-24885-2.

> This guide to continuing care or life care communities includes not only a directory arranged by state, but guidelines to potential consumers in the form of worksheets and checklists and essential information about the state of affairs in the CCRC world. A "Special Features Index" that follows the directory lists additional services provided by facilities in the index. This book will save consumers time by helping them to focus their priorities before making inquiries.

Vierck, Elizabeth. *Paying for Health Care after Age 65.* Choices and Challenges series. Santa Barbara, CA: ABC-CLIO, 1990. 291p. $39.50. ISBN 0-87436-095-1.

> This book is a comprehensive treatment of sources of funding for medical care for seniors, including a clear and concise description of Medicare, Medicaid, and private insurance coverages such as Medigap and long-term care policies. The book also introduces readers to the vocabulary of health care. The second section of the book is a selective, annotated list of references, including organizations, print and audiovisual materials, and computer databases covering issues raised in the book.

Booklets and Pamphlets

AARP, Health Advocacy Services, Program Department. *Medicare's Prospective Payment System: Knowing Your Rights.* Washington, DC: AARP, 1988. 19p. Free.

> A user-friendly guide to Medicare's prospective payment system. The booklet includes a patient checklist for steps to be taken before, during, and following a hospitalization.

Coleman, Barbara. *Consumer Guide to Hospice Care*. Washington, DC: National Consumers League, February 1985. 25p. Free.

> This booklet provides a concise overview of hospice care, including definitions of terminology, case studies, and a checklist for consumers. The booklet also (1) reviews hospice standards, state regulation, and accreditation by Medicare and national organizations, and (2) summarizes financing options, including private insurance and Medicare (by billing under the optional hospice benefit or under regular Medicare benefits for specific services). The booklet also includes a brief resource list.

Finberg, Jeanne. *Medicaid—New Transfer of Assets Provisions*. Washington, DC: National Senior Citizens Law Center, 20 March 1990. 6p. Free. (Also available from National Clearinghouse for Legal Services, Document no. 45,456.)

> This memorandum addresses questions concerning transfers of assets under Medicaid, defining exempt transfers and outlining the impact of non-exempt transfers. Legal services or pro bono advocates with questions are directed to call the author at (213) 482-3550, or Trish Nemore (202) 887-5280.

Finberg, Jeanne. *New Medicaid Division of Assets and Income Rules for Long-Term Care—Spousal Impoverishment*. Washington, DC: National Senior Citizens Law Center, 20 March 1990. 4p. Free. (Also available from National Clearinghouse for Legal Services, Document no. 45,459.)

> This memorandum, prepared by a National Senior Citizens Law Center staff member, provides a general outline of the protections against spousal impoverishment under Medicaid. It is written in a question-and-answer format.

Health Insurance Association of America. *A Consumer's Guide to Long-Term Care Insurance*. Washington, DC: Health Insurance Association of America, 1990. 10p. Free (single copies only).

> This pamphlet provides general information about long-term care insurance. The simple presentation belies the complexity of such policies, but it may provide a useful starting point for seniors trying to get an idea of what long-term care insurance might provide.

National Senior Citizens Law Center. *For Medicare Beneficiaries: Your Rights to Discharge Planning and Hospital Discharge Notices.* Washington, DC: National Senior Citizens Law Center, March 1989. 27p. Free.

> This publication explains patients' rights to discharge notices and planning, including advocacy tips, glossary terms, and sample documents. Although drafted for laypersons, seniors may find the descriptive text a bit dense, although the advocacy tips are helpful.

National Senior Citizens Law Center. *Medicare Part A—PRO Notice and Appeals.* Washington, DC: National Senior Citizens Law Center, 1988. 9p. Free.

> This "fact sheet" is actually a memorandum prepared by the staff of the National Senior Citizens Law Center outlining notice and appeals procedures under Medicare Part A for a senior or his or her doctor who dispute a Peer Review Organization (PRO) determination about a hospital discharge. It is intended for advocates, and the language may not be accessible to the general public.

Sabatino, Charles P. *Health Care Powers of Attorney.* Washington, DC: ABA Commission on Legal Problems of the Elderly, 1990. 16p. Free (single copies only).

> This pamphlet furnishes a brief overview of health care powers of attorney and an annotated sample form for assigning health care powers of attorney. Topics addressed include the definition of health care power of attorney, the advantages of assigning such power of attorney, differences between health care power of attorney and living wills, the legal validity of health care power of attorney in the 50 states, the content of a health care power of attorney, procedures for assigning and terminating a health care power of attorney, and organizational resources that can support anyone seeking to assign a health care power of attorney. The five-page sample form is annotated page by page, clarifying the meaning, parameters, and limits of each provision.

Articles

Bowe, John J. "Sale of a House in Trust for Medicaid Planning." *Taxation for Lawyers* 19 (March/April 1991): 276–279.

This article is one of a very few that address the complicated topic of Medicaid spend-down when the substantial asset of a family home exists. The transaction discussed is designed to enable the taxpayer to be eligible for Medicaid as well as capital gains tax benefits for the sale of the home.

Duggan, Patrice. "Power Shift." *Forbes* 147 (18 February 1991): 80.

Together with the following article by Janet Novak (pp. 85–88), this piece gives the reader an introduction to the forces driving employers and insurance companies to explore HMOs, PPOs, and managed care options as a way to control spiraling health costs.

Eakes, M. Garey, and Ron M. Landsman. "Medicaid, Money—and You." *Modern Maturity* 33 (February-March 1990): 85–90.

A good beginning point for middle- and lower-income seniors concerned about the cost of long-term care, and interested in some basic information about Medicaid's spousal impoverishment rules. The numbers are dated, but the concepts discussed still pertain.

Edelman, Toby S. "Nursing Home Discrimination against Medicaid Recipients: Discrimination in Admission: Rights and Remedies." *Clearinghouse Review* 20 (Summer 1986): 339.

This article provides a review of the all-too-common practice of discrimination against Medicaid recipients in nursing home admissions and services and litigation and legislative efforts to curb it. The article has been updated for developments in federal law by a National Senior Citizens Law Center memorandum dated 21 April 1988, available from the NSCLC or the National Clearinghouse for Legal Services (document no. 43,903).

"An Empty Promise to the Elderly?" *Consumer Reports* 56 (June 1991): 425–442.

The editors of *Consumer Reports* have outdone themselves on this update to their groundbreaking 1988 research into long-term care insurance. In addition to rating 94 different policies on factors such as overall quality, premium cost and inflation factors, and coverage, the article contains invaluable sections on dealing with insurance agents, and understanding Medicaid spend-down rules. Consumers Union, publisher of *Consumer Reports,* is a longtime and zealous advocate for national health insurance. The article argues forcefully for this cause. Reprints are available by writing to CU/Reports, 101 Truman Avenue, Yonkers, NY 10703-1057.

Fairbanks, Joan E. "Lifetime Care Contracts." *Probate and Property* (March/April 1990): 4–9.

> This article reviews life care or continuing care retirement communities, with a focus on admissions contracts. The author provides a checklist for analyzing such contracts. An excellent guide.

Paulson, Morton C. "Catching Up with Medigap." *Changing Times* 44 (November 1990): 81–84.

> The author summarizes the current state of affairs with Medigap insurance contracts and then makes some helpful suggestions about supplementing Medicare coverage, including investigating HMOs, individual conversion policies, and commercial Medigap coverages. The article lists sources for more information and gives helpful tips on securing and evaluating coverages.

"Update: The New Medigap Plans." *Consumer Reports* 56 (September 1991): 616–617.

> The ten standardized Medigap packages that were offered nationally by insurers beginning in 1992 are summarized here in text, along with a helpful table. Hints on shopping for a policy complete the article. Reprints are available by writing to CU/Reports, 101 Truman Avenue, Yonkers, NY 10703-1057.

Housing

Books

Gillespie, Ann E., and Katrinka Smith Sloan. *Housing Options and Services for Older Adults.* Choices and Challenges series. Santa Barbara, CA: ABC-CLIO, 1990. 279p. $39.50. ISBN 0-87436-144-3.

> A useful book for seniors considering a change in their living arrangements. The first section is divided into four chapters

addressing housing issues as wide-ranging as assistance programs, home health care, and maintenance concerns. The second section contains an annotated bibliography with citations to organizations and print and audiovisual references. A glossary and index conclude the book.

Gold, Margaret. *Guide to Housing Alternatives for Older Citizens*. Mt. Vernon, NY: Consumer's Union of the United States, 1985. 184p. $9.95. ISBN 0-89043-031-4.

> This book is designed to assist seniors in making informed decisions about their housing arrangements. It provides general information in a readable format with little legalistic detail. Each chapter treats a different housing alternative: staying put; moving to shared housing, life care, or retirement communities; or moving to a nursing facility, for example. At the end of each chapter citations to organizations and further reading are listed without annotations. Appendixes complete the work. Although some of the references cited might be outdated, the decision-making process remains the same, making this book useful to seniors.

Hare, Patrick H., and Jolene N. Ostler. *Creating an Accessory Apartment*. New York: McGraw-Hill, 1987. 240p. $16.95. ISBN 0-07-026087-7.

> One alternative open to senior homeowners intent on remaining in their homes is to take in tenants. For homes without finished apartments, that means renovation. This book covers each step of the process of creating an accessory apartment, from creating a new living space to evaluating zoning regulations and building codes to setting up the landlord-tenant relationship. Appendixes include various tax forms and sample documents.

U.S. Department of Housing and Urban Development (HUD). *Housing Special Populations*. Washington, DC: HUD, 1988. $3.

> This resource guide gives a brief overview of public housing and rental assistance programs available to seniors, the disabled, and the homeless. A review of books and studies on housing completes the publication.

Booklets and Pamphlets

AARP. *Understanding Senior Housing for the 1990s.* Washington, DC: AARP, 1990. 92p. Free.

> This booklet summarizes the AARP's 1989 survey of consumer housing preferences, concerns, and needs and compares findings with the 1986 survey. The booklet is primarily of interest to professionals and policymakers and encompasses current housing arrangements, community preferences, housing option preferences, household activities, costs, safety and security concerns, and planning for future housing needs.

ABA. Division of Communication. *Landlords and Tenants: Your Guide to the Law.* Washington, DC: ABA, 1982. 50p.

> This book includes useful information on topics such as leases, warranties of habitability, housing codes, privacy, repairs, payment and nonpayment of rent, and eviction (landlord and tenant rights). The appendixes address discrimination in renting, special local conditions (including rent control, condominium conversion, and public housing), additional sources of help (which may be out of date), and a glossary of relevant terms.

Fairbanks, Joan E. *Emerging Legal Issues in Housing Options for the Elderly: An Overview.* ABA. Commission on Legal Problems of the Elderly. Prepared for the ABA National Institute on Housing for the Elderly. Washington, DC: ABA, 25 March 1988. 24p. Free.

> This pamphlet summarizes the legal and ethical implications of public- and private-sector housing options available to seniors, focusing on the due process rights of the elderly in a variety of housing situations.

Goliath, Stephen M. *Is There Anything New Under the Sun? Housing Packages for Our Older Population.* Issues in Aging series, no. 3. Chicago: Center for Applied Gerontology, 1987. 38p. $XXX.

> This booklet briefly describes common housing packages available to seniors, reviews their track records, and includes a brief but somewhat dated bibliography. The booklet is academic in tone but includes some useful information on packaging of current housing options, nonprofit and private-sector housing

packages, substitutability of service options, groups served by current housing packages for seniors, and marketing and disseminating information about housing options.

Scholen, Ken. *Home-Made Money: Consumer's Guide to Home Equity Conversion.* Washington, DC: AARP, January 1990. 48p. Free.

> This helpful guide is authored by the director of the National Center for Home Equity Conversion. It reviews the basic types of home equity conversions, illustrating the income generated with tables covering sample periods. The author candidly evaluates the advantages and disadvantages of each option. Appendixes provide side-by-side comparisons of basic features of different conversion options and note the effect of home equity conversions on public benefits, most particularly SSI. A brief listing of organizations concludes the work.

Articles

"Communities for the Elderly." *Consumer Reports* 55 (February 1990): 123–131.

> This article provides a good overview of life care and continuing care retirement communities. After introducing the operating principles of such institutions, it gives sound advice about what to look for—and what to avoid. The article also includes a helpful discussion of the current state of affairs in publicly funded facilities for lower-income seniors. Reprints are available by writing to CU/Reports, 101 Truman Avenue, Yonkers, NY 10703-1057.

Fairbanks, Joan E. "Home Equity Conversion Programs: A Housing Option for the 'House-Rich, Cash-Poor' Elderly." *Clearinghouse Review* 23 (Summer 1989): 481–487.

> This article is one of the best discussions of home equity conversion programs. The "Legal Issues" section is particularly helpful. In addition, a table at the end of the article lists operating programs throughout the country as of 1989.

Sloan, Katrinka Smith. "Home Equity Conversion: A Promising Alternative." *The Southwestern Journal of Aging* 5 (Winter 1989): 31–36.

The article explores the development of home equity conversions, focusing on the involvement of state housing authorities.

Consumer Issues

Loose-Leaf Services

Consumer Credit Guide. Chicago: Commerce Clearing House.

Books

ABA. Public Education Division. *Your Legal Guide to Consumer Credit.* You and the Law Series. Chicago: ABA, 1988. 50p. $2. ISBN 0-89707-356-8.

> This book is designed to help lay readers understand how to acquire credit, use it, ensure that they do not exceed their credit-debt limits, and act wisely if they do exceed them. The book also offers information on federal rules, regulations, and laws on consumer installment credit. In addition, the book helps identify credit situations that may require professional legal advice.
>
> The book includes discussions on selection of a credit card and limits on finance rates and disclosure requirements. Application for credit is explained, including factors such as age discrimination, marital status changes, discrimination against women, and appeals of credit denials. The process of establishing a credit record, monitoring it for accuracy, and correcting mistakes is described. Credit limits, debt collection, and bankruptcy are among the other issues reviewed.
>
> Additional sections discuss relevant federal laws, filing a complaint, credit counseling, and related publications.

Elias, Stephen. *Make Your Own Contract.* Self-Help Law Series. Berkeley, CA: Nolo Books, 1990. 200p. $14.95. ISBN 0-87337-016-3.

> This constitutes a book of forms for laypersons. Each chapter addresses a different type of contract, including everything from promissory notes to leases to releases. After a general discussion of the legal implications of such documents and their uses, the author supplies a number of standard form documents to be

altered and used by the reader in given situations. Seniors dealing with merchants or service providers without form contracts of their own might find the forms in this book particularly helpful.

Gershen, Howard. *A Guide for Giving: 250 Charities and How They Use Your Money*. New York: Pantheon, 1990. 52p. $12.95. ISBN 0-679-73275-6.

A concise but thorough treatment of the way in which 250 nonprofit and charity organizations treat donations and manage their fiscal affairs.

Leonard, Robin. *Money Troubles: Legal Strategies To Cope with Your Debts*. Berkeley, CA: Nolo Press, 1991. 334p. $16.95. ISBN 0-87337-137-2.

Another extraordinarily user-friendly book by Nolo Press, *Money Troubles* is a comprehensive treatment of credit and credit-related issues. It provides the reader with a thorough, if basic, understanding of one's legal rights and obligations concerning debts of all kinds, and suggests strategies to resolve them. The book is part reference, part workbook, part resource. A useful glossary and appendixes detailing state laws and agencies finish the work.

Nader, Ralph, and Wesley Smith. *Winning the Insurance Game*. New York: Knightsbridge, 1990. 538p. $24.95. ISBN 1-877961-17-5.

This book offers a comprehensive discussion of all types of insurance—life, property, health, government, and the like. A chapter entitled "Senior Citizen Insurance" includes information concerning long-term care, Medigap, Social HMOs, and life insurance products specifically marketed to seniors, and is of particular interest. "Consumer Alert" boxes throughout the text highlight advice. Another chapter addresses resolution of claims disputes. Mr. Nader's coauthor is president of the National Insurance Consumer Organization.

Nelson, Thomas C. *It's Your Choice: The Practical Guide to Planning a Funeral*. Glenview, IL: Scott, Foresman, 1983. 124p. $4.95. ISBN 0-673-24804-6.

The potential for exploitation of consumers following the death of a loved one led the Federal Trade Commission (FTC) to promulgate regulations in the 1970s governing disclosure and marketing practices in the funeral industry. This book, written for the AARP Consumer Action Project by a former FTC staff member who participated in the agency's investigations, explores the ins and outs of funeral expenses and services. Appendixes include checklists for planning a funeral and facilitating comparison shopping. Sample costs have obviously increased since this book was written.

Rosmarin, Yvonne, and Jonathan Sheldon. *Sales of Goods and Services.* 2d ed. Consumer Credit and Sales Legal Practice Series. Boston: National Consumer Law Center, 1989. 790p. $60. ISBN 0-943116-67-8.

> Not for the casual reader, this book is a practice manual for attorneys and other professionals dealing with sales of goods and services. The first section consists of practice checklists keyed to certain types of consumer transactions, for example: used cars, home improvements, and key litigation strategies. The next four sections comprise a thorough discussion of the Uniform Commercial Code and its remedies. Part VI discusses other consumer laws and standards. Ten appendixes consisting of statutes, regulations, and practice aids complete the manual. Supplements are published at the end of each year and are available to subscribers for $33.

Rudy, Theresa Meehan, and HALT. *Small Claims Court: Making Your Way through the System: A Step-by-Step Guide.* New York: Random House, 1990. 160p. $8.95. ISBN 0-679-72950-X.

> This book explains the use of small claims court to resolve small financial disputes and also identifies alternative options that might be superior to full-fledged litigation. The book is easy to read and offers sound, step-by-step advice on lodging successful small claims, as well as defending oneself against such claims. Appendixes include a summary of each state's rules governing small claims, a list of alternative resources, a list of state consumer action agencies, a glossary, and a brief bibliography.

Sheldon, Jonathan. *Unfair and Deceptive Acts and Practices.* 2d ed. Consumer Credit and Sales Legal Practice Series. Boston: National Consumer Law Center, 1988. 446p. $60.

ISBN 0-943116-62-7. 1990 Cumulative Supplement, 219p. $33.
0-943116-86-4.

> This is a practice manual for attorneys and other professionals
> dealing with consumer fraud and related issues. The format is
> decidedly dry, but it includes helpful checklists and is extensively
> annotated. Appendixes include state-by-state analyses of unfair
> and deceptive act and practice statutes, Federal Trade Commis-
> sion rules, and practice aids for professionals. Annual supple-
> ments are published at the end of each year and are available to
> subscribers for $33.

Warner, Ralph. *Everybody's Guide to Small Claims Court.* 4th ed.
Self-Help Law Series. Berkeley, CA: Nolo Books, 1990. 370p. $14.95.
ISBN 0-87337-060-0.

> A very readable, step-by-step guide to small claims court in-
> cluding advice on how to prepare successfully before proceeding
> to court. The book is filled with helpful examples and sample
> forms. "Legalese" is confined to the footnotes, to be read only if
> the consumer wishes. An appendix summarizes important fea-
> tures of each state's law such as dollar limitations, causes of
> action, and statute citations.

Booklets and Pamphlets

AARP Consumer Affairs Section and Federal Trade Commission, Office
of Consumer and Business Education, Bureau of Consumer Protection.
How To Write a Wrong: Complain Effectively and Get Results.
Washington, DC: AARP and U.S. Government Printing Office, 1983.
17p. Free from AARP.

> This pamphlet briefly explains when a consumer should com-
> plain and the advisability and advantages of effective complaints
> for both consumers and businesses. The pamphlet specifically
> addresses door-to-door and mail order sales, addressing the
> buyer's rights and seller's obligations and procedures for lodging
> a complaint. The pamphlet also includes a brief directory of
> consumer resources.

Consumer Information Center, U.S. General Services Administration.
Consumer Information Catalog. Pueblo, CO: Consumer Information
Center. Quarterly. 15p. Free.

This pamphlet lists federal publications of interest to consumers and covers topics such as careers, education, federal benefits, food, health, housing, money management, and sources of assistance. Most of the publications listed are booklets that are free or available for a nominal charge. Order by writing: Handbook, Consumer Information Center, Pueblo, CO 81009.

U.S. Office of Consumer Affairs. *Consumer's Resource Handbook*. Washington, DC: U.S. Government Printing Office, 1990. 93p. Free (single copies).

Designed for the individual consumer and the consumer affairs professional, this handbook includes a brief section on how to be a smart consumer and a more extensive section that lists contacts that can help resolve consumer complaints. The first section describes preventive steps for avoiding consumer problems and techniques for consumers to handle their own complaints. The second section is a directory that lists contacts in each state and the District of Columbia, including corporate consumer affairs offices; Better Business Bureaus; trade associations and other dispute resolution programs; state, county, and city consumer protection offices; state agencies on aging, which coordinate services for seniors; state banking authorities; state insurance regulators; state utility commissions; state vocational and rehabilitation offices; federal information centers and selected federal agencies; and the federal Telecommunications Device for the Deaf (TDD) directory. Single copies are available for free by writing: Handbook, Consumer Information Center, Pueblo, Colorado 81009.

Articles

Galen, Michele. "If Personal Bankruptcy Is Your Only Out." *Business Week* 3196 (21 January 1991): 90–91.

A brief discussion of the pros and cons of personal bankruptcy. A helpful start for those thinking about filing, along with a list of resources for further inquiries.

Leonard, Robin. "When You Don't Want What You Bought." *Consumers' Research* 74 (May 1991): 28–30.

An excerpt from Ms. Leonard's book *Money Troubles: Legal Strategies To Cope with Your Debt* (see above), this article is a succinct review of consumers' rights in certain contracts and financial transactions. The sections dealing with sales by phone or mail are of particular relevance to seniors.

Martin, Elmer Dean, III. "In Bankruptcy Planning Consider Federal and State Law." *Taxation for Lawyers* 20 (July/August 1991): 23–25.

This article provides a concise explanation of the tax effect of bankruptcy proceedings.

Washington State Attorney General's Office. "Con Games That Target the Elderly." *Consumers' Research* 74 (September 1991): 30–32.

A brief piece that identifies some prevalent con schemes targeted at seniors. Sidebars contain tips on how to uncover the deception.

Family Law

Books

ABA. Public Education Division. *Your Legal Guide to Marriage and Other Relationships*. You and the Law Series. Chicago: ABA, 1989. 79p. $2. ISBN 0-89707-436-X.

This book uses a question-and-answer format to define marriage and address its financial as well as personal ramifications. In addition, the book includes information on (1) separation, annulment, and divorce (including a brief discussion of grandparents' rights) and (2) death of a spouse, including wills, laws, and inheritances. The book offers suggestions on obtaining additional help for various kinds of cohabitation, marriage, and divorce issues.

Leonard, Robin D., and Stephen R. Elias. *Family Law Dictionary: Marriage, Divorce, Children & Living Together*. Self-Help Law Series. Berkeley, CA: Nolo Press, 1988. 193p. $13.95. ISBN 0-87337-061-9.

Written in lay language, this book defines terms used in the family law field, such as marriage, separation and divorce, guardianship, living together, prenuptial contracts, court judgments and decrees, marital property. The dictionary defines relevant legal and non-legal terms contextually and provides extensive cross-references. Many entries include examples, tables summarizing laws by states, and charts to help the reader understand the term.

NOW Legal Defense and Education Fund and Renee Cherow-O'Leary. *The State-by-State Guide to Women's Legal Rights*. New York: McGraw-Hill, 1987. 523p. $12.95. ISBN 0-07-047778-7.

> This book is divided into two sections. The first section summarizes laws affecting women's rights in four areas—home and family, education, employment, and the community. The balance of the book is given over to a state-by-state synopsis of the laws affecting women. Specific issues addressed include the legal process, marriage and divorce, domestic violence and battered women, elderly women, age discrimination, handicapped workers, Social Security and pension laws, and housing and public accommodation.

Sack, Steven Mitchell. *The Complete Legal Guide to Marriage, Divorce, Custody & Living Together*. New York: McGraw-Hill, 1987. 305p. $19.95. ISBN 0-07-054404-3.

> After an introductory chapter on when, why, and how to secure the services of a good attorney, this book devotes itself to a discussion of family law issues from marriage to adoption to divorce. The author also addresses alternative dispute resolution mechanisms for disputing family members. The volume includes sample clauses and agreements dealing with separation and custody. Tables reveal differences among the state domestic relations laws, although the book may not be completely up-to-date at this point.

Segal, Ellen C., and Naomi Karp, eds. *Grandparent Visitation Disputes: A Legal Resource Manual*. Washington, DC: ABA Commission on Legal Problems of the Elderly, 1989. 129p. $19.95. ISBN 0-89707-430-0.

> The product of a one-year project funded by the Department of Health and Human Services, this resource manual is the only comprehensive publication on this topic. It furnishes practical and current information on statutory and case law; existing legal literature; guidance for attorneys representing parents, grandparents, or children in such cases and for judges hearing such cases; the role of mental health experts; and the use of mediation.
>
> The manual is geared primarily for legal professionals, mediators, and mental health practitioners. Nonetheless, interested laypersons will find that this is one of the few available resources

for assessing their rights and options. Of particular note is the chart on state laws in Chapter 2, though the laws may have changed since it was compiled. The discussion in Chapter 6 of mediation as an option for resolving visitation disputes is particularly important. An annotated bibliography completes the manual. Coauthor Naomi Karp is the assistant staff director of the ABA Commission on Legal Problems of the Elderly. Copies can be ordered from ABA Order Fulfillment, 750 N. Lake Shore Drive, Chicago, IL 60611.

Sitarz, Daniel. *Divorce and Dissolution of Marriage Laws of the United States.* Carbondale, IL: Nova, 1990. 195p. $21.95. ISBN 0-935755-05-5.

This is a comprehensive, state-by-state summary of the laws relating to divorce and dissolution of marriage. It clearly outlines the legal grounds for divorce, mediation or counseling requirements, property distribution rules, and custody and support laws in each state. It is a good beginning point for research, but the reader should bear in mind that even with such a recent publication date, changes in a state's law may have occurred.

Sitarz, Daniel. *Divorce Yourself: The National No-Fault No-Lawyer Divorce Handbook.* Carbondale, IL: Nova, 1990. 318p. $24.95. ISBN 0-935755-04-7.

For a couple who is willing to forgo counsel and able to deal with the divorce law's complexities, this book will offer assistance. Included are discussions of property division and alimony, among other topics. Legal guidelines, worksheets, and sample agreement clauses are also included. Even if one is not inclined to proceed alone, the background information and worksheets will prove helpful.

Articles

Edelstein, Stephanie. "Do Grandparents Have Rights?" *Modern Maturity* 33 (December 1990–January 1991): 40–42.

Submerged in a series of five articles about grandparenting, this is a brief summary and discussion of grandparents' visitation statutes in the several states.

Mathur, Anu R. "Indefinite Alimony: A Solution to the Financial Trauma of Divorce." *Probate Law Journal* 10 (1991): 303–329.

> Against the recent tide in the courts, the author argues for a return to alimony awards of indefinite duration on the basis of maintaining the pre-divorce standard of living. The concepts discussed are particularly important to seniors with long-term marriages who may have difficulty finding employment at older ages.

McCrimmon, Catherine A., and Robert J. Howell. "Grandparents' Legal Rights to Visitation in the Fifty States and the District of Columbia." *Bulletin of the American Academy of Psychiatry and the Law* 17 (1989): 355–366.

> Grandparent visitation statutes are viewed through the eyes of social scientists in this article. Although there have been some changes in statutory law, the discussion and the resources noted at the back of this article should prove helpful.

"Note: The Constitutional Constraints on Grandparents' Visitation Statutes." *Columbia Law Review* 86 (1985): 118–142.

> This is a copious review of the grandparents' visitation laws of the 50 states in the context of an academic evaluation of parents' rights to privacy under the U.S. constitution.

Estate Planning

Loose-Leaf Services

Federal Tax Coordinator. New York: Research Institute of America.

Federal Tax Reporter. Chicago: Commerce Clearing House.

Federal Taxes 2d. Englewood Cliffs, NJ: Maxwell Macmillan.

Books

Clifford, Denis. *Nolo's Simple Will Book*. Self-Help Law Series. Berkeley, CA: Nolo Books, 1989. 300p. $17.95. ISBN 0-87337-017-1. Purchase with audiotape, $19.95. ISBN 0-87337-056-2.

This book is a cookbook for those who wish to put together their own wills. The author's premise is that most people do not require the services of an attorney, though symbols in the margins throughout the book indicate where legal counsel is advisable (for example, gifts where there is a limited or shared interest in property). The balance of the book is given over to standardized clauses to be assembled by the reader into a final will document. The book may be easy to follow, but seniors may wish to have a lawyer review their handiwork to ensure it is correct. A glossary of estate terms is included at the back of the publication.

Commerce Clearing House Tax Law Editors. *Federal Estate & Gift Taxes Explained*. Chicago: Commerce Clearing House, 1990. 454p. $20.

This is the sort of handbook one finds on the shelf of many estate-planning professionals. Just the facts are given; no planning or strategy suggestions are included. The focus of this volume is on the federal taxes associated with various kinds of property, forms of ownership, and transactions. The law regarding estate, gift, and generation-skipping taxes is explained in a straightforward manner.

Estate, Financial, and Health-Care Planning Opportunities for Aging America. Philadelphia: ALI-ABA, 1990. 191p. $75.

This is a practical book destined for a professional audience, replete with sample forms and heavy footnoting. It consists of course materials prepared by attorneys Sanford J. Schlesinger and David P. Callahan for a 14 June 1990 video seminar on a broad range of planning issues for lawyers representing seniors. The bulk of the work is an extensive monograph by Schlesinger outlining estate-planning strategies, including Medicaid spend-down, advance directives and living wills, *inter vivos* trusts, and joint tenancies. Federal income tax benefits for seniors are also discussed. Audiocassettes of the program itself are available for an additional charge.

Kess, Sidney, and Bertil Westlin. *CCH Estate Planning Guide*. Chicago: Commerce Clearing House, 1989. 776p. $27.50. ISBN 0-317-30565-4.

Compiled from the multivolume *CCH Financial and Estate Planning* loose-leaf service, the *Estate Planning Guide* is a densely written road map to sophisticated estate-planning techniques. The text is heavily punctuated with citations from the Internal Revenue Code and regulations. This weighty tome is not for the faint of heart. The discussion includes treatment of the disposition of small business interests and federal tax planning.

Ostberg, Kay, and HALT. *Probate: Settling an Estate: A Step-by-Step Guide.* New York: Random House, 1990. 162p. $8.95. ISBN 0-679-72960-7.

> Written in lay language, this book is targeted for personal representatives (people named in a will or by a court to settle an estate). Its thesis is that anyone who can make lists, add and subtract, and ask questions can settle an estate. The book summarizes the steps to be taken, and discusses the personal representative's financial responsibilities in a commonsense way. The book details numerous topics, including wills, personal representatives, estate administration and inventory, creditor claims, real estate sales and property transfers, taxes, probate fees, options for closing the estate and distributing the assets, and the administration of small estates. Appendixes include a lengthy summary of probate and tax rules by state, a checklist for personal representatives, a glossary, and a brief bibliography.

Plotnick, Charles K., and Stephan R. Leimberg. *Keeping Your Money.* New York: Wiley & Sons, Inc., 1987. 333 p. $14.95. ISBN 0-471-85948-0.

> Written in a lively way, this book offers sound financial and estate-planning advice along with many examples, tables, and strategy tips. This is for a reader with financial assets to manage, minor or disabled dependents to provide for, or questions about options such as living trusts, life insurance, and guardianship. Some tables regarding taxes are a bit out of date due to changes in the law.

Soled, Alex J. *The Essential Guide to Wills, Estates, Trusts, and Death Taxes.* 2d ed. Glenview, IL: Scott, Foresman, 1987. $19.95. ISBN 0-673-24891-7.

> Although this book's treatment of death taxes has been superseded by changes in the law, its comprehensive and generally accessible discussion of basic concepts of wills and trusts makes it a valuable resource for the senior who wants some background

before meeting with an attorney. The text is structured in a question-and-answer format, asking not only "what is" but also "why." The author is a practicing lawyer and former chairman of the ABA Section on Taxation.

Booklets and Pamphlets

AARP, Consumer Affairs Section, Program Department. *A Consumer's Guide to Probate.* Washington, DC: AARP, December 1989. 10p. Free.

> This offers a good summary of the basic procedures, terminology, and phases of probate. It includes step-by-step instructions for personal representatives and includes helpful tips and a glossary of commonly used terms.

Austin, Louis. *End Probate Worries for Your Family—The Living Trust Alternative.* Kansas City, MO: Hudspeth, 1990. 58p. $7.95. ISBN 0-9625528-0-1.

> After dispensing with wills as a means to transfer property (the author is decidedly anti-probate), the booklet gets down to the business of explaining living trusts and focusing readers on their own situations and decisions. It is not a "do-it yourself" manual, however, as it urges readers to seek legal counsel when setting up a living trust. The information is good, practical advice, but seniors should be aware that the booklet is, at least in part, an attempt to garner business for the author's firm.

National Resource Center for Consumers of Legal Services. *About Joint Ownership.* Washington, DC: National Resource Center for Consumers of Legal Services. 10p. 75 cents.

> The booklet briefly describes facts about joint ownership, its impact on taxes, as well as the advantages and disadvantages of this form of ownership.

Articles

Fairbanks, Joan E. "Estate Planning and Small Estates Probate for the Elderly: A New Role for the Private Bar." *Clearinghouse Review* 23 (October 1989): 692–698.

This article identifies a growing need for probate and estate-planning services among lower-income seniors, and suggests a need for greater pro bono involvement by the private bar. It suggests resources for developing community-based education and assistance programs.

Geer, Carolyn T. "Shop before You Drop." *Forbes* 147 (24 June 1991): 208–209.

The author offers some clarification on the economics of shopping for term life insurance policies.

Gissel, L. Henry, and Karen R. Schiller. "Trusts Made Easy: A Simplified Overview of the Reasons for Creating, Modifying and Terminating Express Trusts." *Probate Law Journal* 10 (1991): 241–281.

Notwithstanding the title, the uninitiated may find some portions of this article less than "simplified." A lot of information is packed into relatively few pages, including the most recent changes in the federal income and estate tax treatment of trusts.

Jasen, Georgette. "Estate-Planning Can Mean More for Heirs." *The Wall Street Journal* (27 March 1990): B-1.

This article discusses the pitfalls of joint ownership of property for individuals with estates in excess of $600,000 and suggests some strategies to avoid federal estate taxes including the use of trusts.

Rogers, George H., III. "New Life Insurance Forms Enhance Its Use as an Effective Estate Planning Tool." *Taxation for Lawyers* 19 (July/August 1990): 44–47.

This article explores the use of life insurance as a mechanism for paying estate taxes, after discussing other alternatives such as liquidation of assets or borrowing.

Scroggin, John J. "Planning for the Elderly and Terminally Ill." *The Practical Lawyer* 36 (December 1990): 41–70.

This article is intended as a thorough outline for practitioners about the issues they should raise with their clients: wills, living wills and advance directives, forms of joint ownership, and taxes. Terms and concepts are clearly explained, and the text is uncluttered by the copious footnotes so common in most legal publications. It provides a good outline for laypersons as well as professionals.

Strauss, Peter J. "The Geri-Hat-Trick: Three Goals of Estate Planning for the Elderly." *Institute on Estate Planning* (1990): 13-1–13-43.

These materials were prepared for an annual symposium on estate planning. Strauss takes the broad view of the estate planner's responsibility for his client. His main topics are: Medicaid and estate-planning options including trusts and spend-downs, planning for incapacity, and planning techniques viewed from an elder law perspective.

Audiovisual Resources

From audiocassettes to videocassettes to slide/tape presentations, a number of nonprint materials address legal issues or topics with legal implications. The following is a list by organization of some of these materials.

AARP

The AARP Audiovisual Library contains dozens of educational programs on consumer issues, crime prevention, employment, health and long-term care, housing, lifelong learning, personal financial security, safety, volunteerism, and women's issues. AARP audiovisual materials may be purchased or borrowed for free for a short period. For additional information, contact AARP's Resource Center or the Program Resources Department and request the latest list of available audiovisual materials.

ABA Commission on Legal Problems of the Elderly

The ABA has developed numerous audiovisual materials, including:

In Your Hands: The Tools for Preserving Personal Autonomy
Type: Videotape
Length: 16.5 min.
Date: 1989
Cost: Purchase $48, rental $18

Source: Modern Talking Picture Service
           5000 Park Street, North
           St. Petersburg, FL 33709
           (813) 541-7571

           Helen Hayes narrates this. Aimed at public performances, the
           package includes a 31-page program guide and 50 copies of a
           12-page viewer's pamphlet.

You're in Control: Older Americans and the Law
Type: Videotape
Length: 19 min.
Date: 1985
Cost: Purchase $45, rental $20
Source: Modern Talking Picture Service
           5000 Park Street, North
           St. Petersburg, FL 33709
           (813) 541-7571

Bar Associations

Many state and local bar associations have produced videotapes
and other presentations on legal issues. Contact your local bar
association and ask about available materials.

Legal Counsel for the Elderly

LCE has a slide-tape presentation on the steps a person should
take after receiving a written notice about government benefits.
The presentation is loaned for free to legal and social services
agencies as an outreach and community education tool. LCE also
sends a program leader's guide and handouts for the audience.

National Council on the Aging

NCOA offers a four-module audiovisual program for community outreach on four topics: housing options, home services,
home safety, and home security. The program was developed by
NCOA in cooperation with the Public Service Electric and Gas
Company of Newark, New Jersey. The package includes a
leader's guide and overview, slides and slide narrative, and handouts. The set of four modules is $400, and four videotapes of the

program can be requested for an additional $60. Individual slide-tape modules are $150; the video versions are $165 each.

Databases

As a rule, research databases can be a valuable reference tool, but the time required to update them means that the databases may lag behind the literature by at least one to several months. Statistical databases are updated periodically, offering limited but useful numerical snapshots of seniors at different points in time.

AgeLine

AARP sponsors AgeLine, a computerized bibliographic database that is updated every two months and includes citations and abstracts for selected journal articles, books, government documents, reports, and research projects on middle age and aging. AgeLine contains 30,000 references, beginning in 1978 but including selected earlier works. Topics covered in the database include family relationships, social sciences, business, economics, population studies, consumer interests, and health care services. The database can be accessed in many libraries and is available commercially through DIALOG Information Services and BRS Information Technologies. For more information on DIALOG, call (800) 3-DIALOG or, in California, (415) 858-2700. For more information on BRS, call (800) 289-4277 or, in Virginia, (703) 442-0900. For additional information on Age-Line itself, contact the AgeLine Database Manager at AARP's National Gerontology Resource Center, (202) 728-4895.

LEXIS

LEXIS is a multidisciplinary online database produced by Mead Data Central that offers a wide variety of primary and secondary source materials in full-text format for legal research. Databases include federal and state statutes, legislative history, regulations, case law, administrative materials, and periodicals. Individual "libraries" are organized by subject and geographical region. Searches are conducted on the basis of key words. Database users are charged a fee per search transmitted plus online time charges. This database is commonly available in law schools and firms, and may be accessed through personal computers in other settings.

WestLaw

West Publishing Company, one of the foremost publishers of legal books in the United States, maintains the WestLaw online database of full-text primary and secondary legal resources. The breadth of materials online is generally the same as that under LEXIS. Materials are organized in much the same manner. Database users are charged based on online time only, regardless of the number of inquiries transmitted. Typically available in law schools and firms, WestLaw may also be accessed by personal computers in other settings.

Software

The application of software to legal issues is in its infancy. Still, a number of programs exist to help laypersons draft relatively simple legal documents such as wills and powers of attorney, bills of sale, and the like.

It is often said in legal circles that a lawyer who represents himself has a fool for a client. This may be no less true of the layperson who relies solely on the cold counsel of his or her personal computer and a software user's manual. It should not represent your sole source of legal information. Important documents should be reviewed by a lawyer.

Home Lawyer
Format: IBM, Macintosh
Source: MECA Ventures
            Fairfield, CT
Cost: $119.95

In effect, *Home Lawyer* is Hyatt Legal Services online. Hyatt, a national network of legal clinics, built its business on standardized documents. The software allows users to draft straightforward legal documents such as residential leases, powers of attorney, wills, promissory notes, as well as bills of sale, employment contracts, and other arguably commercial documents. The vendor claims that the documents are valid nationwide except in Louisiana. A glossary of legal terms is available online. A reference manual is included.

It's Legal
Format: IBM, Macintosh
Source: Parsons Technology
           Cedar Rapids, IA
Cost: $49

This software package assists the user in drafting a variety of personal legal documents: simple wills, living wills, certificates of guardianship, and leases. It is structured in a simple question-and-answer format. A 199-page manual outlining each document and including a glossary of legal terms completes the package.

Personal Law Firm
Format: IBM, Macintosh
Source: BLOC Publishing Corp.
           Miami, FL
Cost: $100

Personal Law Firm aids the user in drafting approximately 30 different legal documents for business and personal use. It includes forms for everything from simple contracts to trade secret protection as well as wills, living wills, powers of attorney, and pre- and postnuptial agreements. A 250-page user's guide accompanies the software.

Willmaker
Format: IBM, Macintosh, Commodore
Source: Nolo Press/Legisoft
           Berkeley, CA
Cost: $59.95 (IBM, Macintosh), $39.95 (Commodore)

This software features standardized clauses designed to be valid in multiple jurisdictions. The end result is an individualized will. *Willmaker* software comes with a 200-page manual that reviews probate avoidance and tax-planning techniques.

Glossary

Accrue   To earn pension credits for years of service under a defined benefit plan. In the case of a defined contribution plan, the process of accumulating funds in a participant's account.

Administrator   A person or corporation appointed by a court to settle the estate of a deceased person if no valid will can be found.

Advance directive   A document such as a living will or a durable power of attorney which provides instructions as to an individual's wishes in certain circumstances.

Agent   The person or organization designated in a power of attorney to act for the principal. This person is also referred to as an attorney-in-fact.

Alimony   Payments made to one former spouse by another pursuant to a court order for the financial support of the other former spouse. "Rehabilitative" alimony generally means alimony paid over a relatively brief period of time to allow the former spouse to move into employment.

Annuity   A contract with an insurance company that provides regular income over a specified period of time, often for life.

Annulment   A court proceeding by which a marriage is declared void. Legally speaking, the marriage is considered to never have existed.

Approved amount (also called "reasonable charge")   The maximum amount that Medicare considers for physician's services. Of this amount, Medicare pays 80 percent. The beneficiary is required to pay the remaining amount, including any charges in excess of the approved amount.

Assignment   Acceptance by a doctor of the approved fee set by Medicare for covered charges as full payment.

Beneficiary   An individual designated by a plan participant to receive pension or life insurance benefits in the event of the death of the participant.

Benefit period (also called "spell of illness")   For the purposes of determining benefits under Medicare Part A (hospital coverage), the period beginning on the first day a beneficiary is admitted to a hospital or a skilled nursing facility and ending 60 days after discharge from that facility.

Bequest   A gift of personal property pursuant to a will.

Child support   Payments made pursuant to a court order to financially provide for the care and maintenance of children.

COBRA continuation coverage   A right conferred by federal law to employees, their spouses, and dependents to continue participation in an employer-sponsored health care plan even after their coverage is terminated due to certain specified events such as death of the employee, or the divorce of the employee and his spouse.

Codicil   A document modifying the terms of a will in some respect regarding the transfer of property.

Coinsurance   The portion of covered health care charges that a beneficiary is required to pay. Under Medicare Part A, for the 60th through the 90th day in the hospital, a beneficiary is required to pay $157 a day, and $314 a day if he or she uses a lifetime reserve day. For services provided by a skilled nursing facility, the beneficiary is required to pay $78.50 per day. Under Part B, the beneficiary is required to pay 20 percent of Medicare's approved amount. The term is also used in the context of private group and individual insurance contracts.

Conservator   A court-appointed surrogate decision maker with the authority to make decisions about property only. In some jurisdictions the term is used synonymously with the term guardian.

Custodial care   Health and physical care that is unskilled and does not require the services of a doctor or registered nurse.

Custody   The decision of a court regarding the care and maintenance of dependents, generally in the context of the dissolution of a marriage. A court may award physical custody to one parent or another, while retaining joint custody in respect of important decisions concerning the child's welfare.

Decedent   The person who has died.

Deductible   The costs which a beneficiary is required to pay out-of-pocket before insurance coverage begins under private insurance contracts, and in Medicare. In Medicare, the deductible under Part A is $628 for each benefit period in 1991. The deductible under Part B is $100 in 1991. The deductible under a private insurance contract is determined by the contract itself.

Defendant   The party in a lawsuit against whom the plaintiff makes a legal claim.

Defined benefit plan   A pension plan which specifies the benefits to be provided to participants at retirement. In such a plan the employer makes contributions to fund the benefit defined by the plan.

Defined contribution plan   A pension plan under which the employer's contribution, but not the participant's ultimate retirement benefit, is determined by the plan. The participant bears the risk of investment performance of the assets allocated to the participant's account.

Divorce or Dissolution   The legal termination of a marriage pursuant to a state's family or matrimonial law.

Durable power of attorney   A written document authorizing another to act as an individual's agent or attorney-in-fact that survives the subsequent incapacity or disability of the individual. A medical durable power of attorney specifically allows an individual to make health care decisions on behalf of another.

Executor/executrix   A person or corporation appointed by the deceased person's will to administer the estate. Also called a personal representative.

Fiduciary   An individual or organization that exercises discretionary control or authority over the management of assets or funds for the benefit of another person or group of people. In the context of pension plans, for example, the trustee of the pension fund would be a fiduciary.

401(k) plan   Generally, an arrangement under which the participant may elect either to have the employer contribute an amount to the plan or to receive that amount in cash as salary or bonus payments.

Guardian   A court-appointed surrogate decision maker with the authority to make both personal and financial decisions. Some jurisdictions also use the term conservator.

Guardian ad litem   The term used to describe a court-appointed attorney who serves as an independent, neutral assembler of facts and arguments, guided by his or her perception of the best interests of a proposed ward in guardianship proceedings. The person does not represent the proposed ward.

HCFA   The Health Care Financing Administration, a federal government agency that is part of the U.S. Department of Health and Human Services, charged with responsibility for Medicare.

Health Maintenance Organization (HMO)   A public or private health care organization that is designed to provide comprehensive medical care to its members. Such organizations are licensed by the federal and state government. Members are required to use only health care professionals associated with the HMO, except in certain limited circumstances.

Incapacity   A term used to describe a person who lacks the ability to make a decision concerning health care, or more generally, personal matters. The incapacity may be physical (as in the case of a stroke) or mental.

Incompetent   A term meaning that the individual lacks the capacity to make his or her own decisions. It also describes a legal disability to perform a specific act or acts.

Inter vivos trust   A trust created during the lifetime of the trust creator (called the grantor), sometimes called a "living trust." With careful planning these trusts can be used to provide income to the grantor during his/her lifetime and bypass probate administration at his/her death to pass directly to the grantor's intended beneficiaries.

Intestate/intestacy   Dying without a valid will in place. Property of the deceased person then passes to his or her heirs according to provisions of state law.

Joint tenancy   A form of property ownership in which two or more individuals have equal rights to property. In an estate planning context, most references to joint tenancy or ownership also carry a right of survivorship, meaning that on the death of one joint owner, the other acquires full ownership of the property automatically.

Living will   A declaration that states an individual's view about artificial life support decisions.

Mediation   An alternative dispute resolution method whereby a third party (a mediator) assists disputing parties in settling the conflict between themselves.

Money purchase plan   A defined contribution plan under which contribution rates are fixed, most commonly as a percentage of participants' pay. A participant's benefits are determined by the amount contributed, plan expenses, and the investment returns on those funds.

Multiemployer plan   A pension plan, the terms of which are determined in collective bargaining between several employers and a union. A multiemployer plan is generally administered by a joint union-employer board.

Paralegal   A paraprofessional with special training in legal issues. Although a paralegal may perform many of the same tasks as lawyers (such as legal research, drafting of legal documents, and client counseling), they must do so under the supervision of an attorney.

Personal representative   (see executor/executrix)

Plaintiff   The party who files the lawsuit, as distinguished from the defendant who must answer the charges brought by the plaintiff.

Power of attorney   A written document in which a mentally competent adult (the principal) appoints another mentally competent adult or entity (the agent) to act on his or her behalf. The agent (or attorney-in-fact) may perform any legal function or task which the principal has a legal right to do and which has been delegated to him or her.

Preferred Provider Organization (PPO)   A preferred provider organization is an affiliation of health care providers constructed by an insurer or an employer to provide medical care to a subscribing group's members on a reduced fee basis. Usually such an arrangement is part of an employer's indemnity plan and provides incentives to employees to utilize PPO providers through enhanced reimbursements.

Prima facie case   Translated from the Latin, prima facie means "at first appearance." In a court it refers to the individual who has filed a lawsuit having set forth sufficient facts which, if not contradicted by the other party to the lawsuit, would establish his or her claim of injury.

Principal   The individual authorizing another to act in his or her place by way of a power of attorney.

Probate   The legal process by which the state government, through the court system, validates a deceased person's will and assists his or her personal representative in settling the estate under its terms.

Profit sharing plan   A defined contribution plan under which the employer may not be obliged to contribute any set amount on an annual basis. The employer may vary the amount of contributions annually, and may not make any contribution in a given year if it so chooses.

Res   The property underlying a trust.

Residue   The property left over after all specific bequests have been made and claims satisfied. Also called the residuary estate.

Separation agreement   An agreement between two spouses regarding a period of legal separation. Terms of the agreement address property and income division during the period of separation, as well as child custody, visitation, and other issues.

Summary plan description (or SPD)   A booklet containing a summary of the major terms of a pension plan. The booklet is required by law to be written in easily understandable language.

Testate   Dying with a valid will in place.

Trust   A legal relationship in which one party holds title (legal ownership) to property and manages it for the benefit of another. In the estate planning context, the most common types of trusts are inter vivos (also called "living" trusts) and testamentary trusts (a trust established by the terms of a will).

Vesting   Completion of years-of-service requirement by a plan participant, giving the participant a nonforfeitable right to benefits earned by the participant under the terms of the plan.

Visitation rights   An order by a court concerning the rights of family members and friends to visit with dependents in the custody of others. For example, a court may order a custodial parent to allow the noncustodial parent's mother to visit with her grandchildren on a prescribed schedule.

Ward   A person for whom a guardian (or conservator) has been appointed.

Will   A legal document which sets forth the manner in which an individual wishes his or her property to be disposed of once he or she dies.

Index